PENGUIN BOOKS

THE ACTOR'S BOOK
OF MONOLOGUES FOR WOMEN

STEFAN RUDNICKI was born in Krakow, Poland, and lived in Stockholm, Sweden, and Montreal, Canada, before arriving in the United States—where he was educated principally at Columbia University and the Yale School of Drama.

In addition to having directed over one hundred and thirty theatrical productions in New York, regional theatre, and abroad (more than a quarter of them classics and fifteen by Shakespeare), he is also an actor, producer, award-winning playwright, photographer, and film and video director.

He has taught at the University of Rochester, the Eastman School of Music, New York University, Dartmouth College, the State University of New York at Old Westbury, and Long Island University's C. W. Post Campus, where for six years he chaired the Department of Theatre and Film.

He has been artistic director of Skyboat Road Company since 1979, and with his wife, Judith, resides alternately in New York City and Los Angeles, teaching, coaching, developing new film and television projects, and continuing to evolve his Interactive Matrix Process for performers. He is the author of *The Actor's Book of Classical Monologues* and the forthcoming *Actor's Book of Classical Scenes*, both published by Penguin USA.

THE
ACTOR'S BOOK
OF
MONOLOGUES
FOR WOMEN
from Non-Dramatic Sources

COLLECTED AND INTRODUCED BY

Stefan Rudnicki

PENGUIN BOOKS

PENGUIN BOOKS

Published by the Penguin Group

Penguin Group (USA) Inc., 375 Hudson Street, New York, New York 10014, U.S.A.

Penguin Group (Canada), 10 Alcorn Avenue, Toronto,

Ontario, Canada M4V 3B2 (a division of Pearson Penguin Canada Inc.)

Penguin Books Ltd, 80 Strand, London WC2R 0RL, England

Penguin Ireland, 25 St Stephen's Green, Dublin 2, Ireland (a division of Penguin Books Ltd)

Penguin Group (Australia), 250 Camberwell Road, Camberwell,

Victoria 3124, Australia (a division of Pearson Australia Group Pty Ltd)

Penguin Books India Pvt Ltd, 11 Community Centre,

Panchsheel Park, New Delhi – 110 017, India

Penguin Group (NZ), cnr Airborne and Rosedale Roads,

Albany, Auckland, New Zealand (a division of Pearson New Zealand Ltd)

Penguin Books (South Africa) (Pty) Ltd, 24 Sturdee Avenue,

Rosebank, Johannesburg 2196, South Africa

Penguin Books Ltd, Registered Offices: 80 Strand, London WC2R 0RL, England

First published in Penguin Books 1991

20

LIBRARY OF CONGRESS CATALOGING IN PUBLICATION DATA
The Actor's book of monologues for women
collected and introduced by Stefan Rudnicki.

p.   cm.

ISBN 0 14 01.5787 5

1. Acting.   2. Monologues.   3. Women—Literary collections.
I. Rudnicki, Stefan, 1945–
PN2080.A285   1991
808.82'45'082—dc20   91–10091

Printed in the United States of America
Set in Caledonia
Designed by Robert Bull Design

ACKNOWLEDGMENTS

I am grateful to all those persons who, by suggesting sources and authors unfamiliar to me, pointed me down glorious paths of discovery. Most prominent among them are Sally B. Owen of Judith's Room Book Shop in New York City, Rachel Fletcher, Ann Harvey, Sally Cummings, and Lisa Juliano. For their help in bringing these monologues to life for me, I thank the dozens of students, particularly the members of Classical Matrix Laboratory, who spoke these speeches so earnestly and listened so attentively. For more material support I thank Edith Cummings, David Skolkin, Betty Binns, and Martin Lubin. I thank the parade of encouraging editors at Viking Penguin: Will Nixon, Laura Ross, Lisa Kaufman, Leslie Herzik, and Michael Millman. And I thank my wife, Judith Cummings, whose impeccable taste and fine eye for detail have contributed essential clarity and elegance.

I dedicate this book to my mother, Danuta Podworska Rudnicki, her mother, Maria Podworska, to all women in their ever blessed and infinite variety, and to the Goddess.

Stefan Rudnicki
Hollywood, 1991

CONTENTS

3. Journeys in History
INTRODUCTION   64

4. Witnesses to War
INTRODUCTION 92

PART II
Actor

5. Polemics
INTRODUCTION   123

6. Choices
INTRODUCTION   146

7. Friends, Lovers and Wives
INTRODUCTION   177

8. Daughters, Sisters and Mothers

INTRODUCTION 199

PART III
Dreamer

9. Intimate Visions
INTRODUCTION 225

10. Epics and Gothics
INTRODUCTION   254

11. Revelations and Transformations
INTRODUCTION   290

THE
ACTOR'S BOOK
OF
MONOLOGUES
FOR WOMEN

GENERAL INTRODUCTION

> *I know what madness is.*
> *It's not-knowing how another man feels.*
> *A madman has never been*
> *In another man's shoes.*
> —Maria Irene Fornés, *Promenade*

The purpose of this collection is simple: to bring a wide range of monologue material to women of as many ages, backgrounds, and sensibilities as possible. Non-dramatic sources include any written or spoken material that was not originally intended to be theatrically or cinematically performed, although a few of these selections have been adapted for the stage and screen. It is also my hope to bring to the attention of actors, speakers, students, and all those generally interested in women's studies, the resources available in the form of poetry, fiction, diaries and journals, and documents of public record, all crying out to be performed. Although I have included authors and specific works familiar to the general reader, I have given more attention to obscure writing and unlikely sources, even admitting several uniquely useful selections written by men.

DIVERSITY AND FASHION

Early in the preparation of this manuscript I began bringing monologues to whatever class I happened to be teaching and asking students to read aloud selections with which I thought they might feel a strong connection. The responses from the readers were usually very positive and were always useful to me editorially, but I did encounter surprising difficulty on another front, an occasional lack of tolerance for certain monologues from those who were involved as audience. Jane Carlyle's Victorian miniature *To a Swallow Building under Our Eaves*, for example, elicited a violent response from several women in one class, who stated that the piece was offensive to them and that any author capable of perpetrating this kind of writing was wholly reprehensible. Citing sentimentality, criminal self-effacement, and plain bad writing as their principal objections, they strongly counseled me against including the poem in this book. Curiously, they had no such problem with Carlyle's other selection, her *Letter to John Sterling*, a witty, canny piece of social satire. The woman who had read *To a Swallow* . . . aloud, however, felt a powerful kinship with the piece and decided to devote considerable time and effort to preparing it. Only in the face of her staunch preferment would the objectors acknowledge that the poem might have some worth.

This event sensitized me to the importance of diversity as a humanistic value, and I began to feel more strongly than ever the responsibility to present the broadest selection possible, culturally and aesthetically as well as dramatically, realizing that no particular agenda could serve everyone and that not everyone would be equally served or equally pleased with every item. Most of the many women's anthologies I have perused, for example, espouse a particular view of women or of the *experience* of being a woman and in this way limit their field of vision by omitting material that might be either politically, aesthetically, or socially out of keeping with the particular bias—or perhaps simply out of fashion. It is any deference to fashion that I have tried particularly to avoid; I have attempted instead to provide contrasting perspectives with an emphasis on minority viewpoints. It is by actually speaking the words of others, by sharing, however momentarily, another person's perspective, that real understanding, true collaboration, and genuine freedom are achieved. Freedom of speech itself has two sides: the license to express oneself and the opportunity to hear another side. In the long run, I believe the latter to be by far the more important.

CHOOSING A MONOLOGUE

I have intentionally avoided organizing this collection by stock type or age range since most of the selections can be comfortably presented by most women. Because so much of the material is narrative in form, often even supplying a situation to serve as a frame for the central monologue, it is a relatively simple matter for the actor to justify speaking as someone quite different from herself. In one extreme case, for example, Anaïs Nin records the story of a grounded aviator during World War II, and the selection is enriched by the contrasting textures of the aviator's male perspective and Nin's own reactions. Anyone may successfully perform this monologue, because the narrator is never physically identified. She is a kind of Everywoman, showing us something about a particular man's experience and then commenting on it.

The only way to know whether a piece is suitable for you is to experience it, so I recommend reading, out loud, as many selections as seem interesting. When the words of someone's story are spoken, an entire world is set in motion, with the actor at the center of it, assuming the author's place. Even a first rough reading will provide a good indication of whether it is a world you wish to inhabit for any length of time.

The monologues in Part I, *Witness*, tend to be more about observation than engagement. This does not mean that they are passive in mood, but rather that there tends to be a distance between the writer (and so, the speaker) and the subject, which is sometimes the critical remove of social commentary, sometimes the distance of time and place. Part II, *Actor*, is characterized by a more public dimension and includes many pieces that either address issues or examine the many roles that women assume both at home and in society. Part III, *Dreamer*, is the grandest in scale, exceeding the merely mundane, filled with samples of the most imaginative and compelling visions ever set down. These selections tell of the experience of transformation and the sources of creativity—personal, spiritual, and universal.

PREPARING THE MONOLOGUE

Despite the tremendous range of material in this book, it is possible to suggest certain guidelines in preparing a monologue for presentation.

First, commit to a little basic **research.** I am daily amazed at how many actors do not bother to look up unfamiliar words, or names, or places. It is extremely poor form to try to get by without knowing what you are talking about; you have only to mispronounce a crucial word and the game is up. Beyond this and more to the point, if the selection is autobiographical or in some other way expressive of a real person's thoughts and actions, the actor has a responsibility to the woman she is portraying to discover as much as possible about her.

Next, determine the **structure** of your chosen piece. Even when the selection is not strictly narrative, there is a story being told, and a story is best told with a beginning, a middle, and an end. So, wherever possible, begin organizing your piece in terms of a three-part structure. To determine an appropriate three-part structural division, look

for changes in subject matter, significant shifts in focus—
from one audience to another, for instance, and whatever
clues the author or editor may have provided by the use—
or absence—of verse stanzas, prose paragraphs, or punctuation. For example, Merle Woo in *Whenever You're Cornered, the Only Way Out Is to Fight* uses verse lines and
prose lines; long, short, and single-word lines; and italics,
quotations, and various degrees of indentation to control
the phrasing of her poem. Once the three larger divisions
are set, I suggest dividing each of these into its own beginning, middle, and end, and so on, until you have settled
on the smallest comfortable dramatic unit, or "beat." Try
also to discover what fundamental change occurs over the
course of the monologue as a whole; time has passed in the
reading, and something *must* be different. All too many
actors seem to treat monologues as if they were single,
complete statements, placing a premium on consistency at
the expense of the sort of variety that can really make a
speech interesting.

Another issue is **length.** I expect that these monologues
will be used for a variety of purposes, so I have not imposed
any severe limitations on the length of individual pieces,
which range from four lines to eighty or more. For actors
seeking audition pieces especially, ideal lengths can be anywhere from one to four minutes, and a certain degree of
cutting will be required for many of the selections. The
structuring process I have suggested will facilitate intelligent and intelligible editing.

When the initial structuring is completed, a more detailed study of the **language** is called for, and these guidelines I've developed for working with classical texts are just
as effective when working with modern material. Look for
the patterns and for the exceptions to those patterns. Look
for repetitions of sounds, words, and phrases (alliteration
or assonance). Does the punctuation suggest easy flow or

a stop-and-go rhythm? Is the language common or refined; is it grounded in the senses, in things you can touch, see, and hear, or is it adrift in a sea of images? I have generally kept the punctuation and spelling of each original text intact, believing from my work with Shakespeare's First Folio that excessive editing obscures clues which are essential to understanding and performance. For the classical—pre-1750—English-language verse selections I have adopted a consistent treatment indicating which syllables are spoken and which are not, as demonstrated by comparing two lines from Anne Bradstreet's *A Letter to Her Husband*. . . . In the first line,

Whom whilst I 'joy'd, nor storms, nor frosts I felt,

the two apostrophes indicate first a contraction ('joy for *en*joy) and, next, a syllable omitted that would otherwise be pronounced, (joy'd for joy*ed*). In the second line,

My chilled limbs now nummed lye forlorn,

the syllable "ed" is pronounced both times, "chill*ed*" and "numm*ed*."

Power, focus, and **scale** are next. Simply put, you must make some decisions about what surrounds you and about the size of the world you inhabit. In order to create a complete environment, you must determine a past and a future as well as a present. The past, always implied if not actually spoken of, is behind you. It is the place you have come from, your history, your reason for coming to *this* place, your motivation, if you will. Consequently it serves as your source of **power.**

The future is, of course, ahead of you—literally, in front of you. It is the world you hope to affect with your actions. Your goal is out there, your objective, your audience. Between the two is *this moment*, the plane of the present, clearly defined. On either side of you, in this present plane, are your helpers—other actors, perhaps, and the props, real or imaginary—that you require to fill this moment. Borrowing a term common to architecture, computer science, and other contemporary disciplines, I call this entire field, which is made up of past, present, and future, a "matrix," or grid, the "present" plane of which can now be populated with those persons and objects that are necessary to the world of the particular monologue you are working on. These persons and objects, placed in the matrix, become your **focus** points and give that world its unique character and tone.

Scale derives from the size of the world you must create given the future—your goal, your audience—and the past, your power source.

To whom are you speaking? How large is your audience? Are there separate factions? This audience need not be physically present; it may be created instead by the importance or ultimate impact of the material spoken. A declaration of war made in front of a microphone in a broadcast studio may be a matter of life and death to millions, and this importance is never lost on the speaker, no matter how quietly he speaks, so the words gain weight and come more slowly, very much as if he were addressing a present multitude.

For whom are you speaking? I am convinced that in theatre there is no such thing as a privately motivated action. Somewhere outside the physical person of the actor lies the source of each action. Is that power source a single incident or person in the past? Rarely. The scale of a great deal of women's material especially derives precisely from the accumulated weight, and so the power, of both natural and historical cycles, of generations on generations past, of *all* women.

Part I

WITNESS

1
MIRRORS TO NATURE

Introduction

We have here a group of selections that define special relationships between women and the natural world, women who find in that world a reflection of their own lives as well as access to much wider spiritual contexts.

I open this section and the collection with Linda Hogan's *Walking*, a contemporary piece that finds in that most simple of activities a connection to all history and time. Because the words move and the images travel, I recommend stillness in the presentation, allowing a clear flow of focus to be traced, leading the audience from landmark to landmark.

As wildly extravagant as Aphra Behn's picaresque travelogue may seem, it is at least in part autobiographical, she herself having been marooned around 1663 on a plantation in Surinam (four years later, Dutch Guiana) after the death of her father, the Lieutenant-General-*designate*, on board ship. There is consequently a freshness of color and image in *Oroonoko* that would be the natural expression of a young European woman's delight in this brave new world of tropical abundance. "Caesar" is her Indian guide and teacher.

The next four selections are special examples of a kind of nature poem popular among eighteenth- and nineteenth-century women writers, each with a special twist of its own. Mary Howitt's *The Sea Fowler* depends on the energy of the rhymed couplets that drive it with the sort of inexorability we might associate with waves and breakers on a wild seacoast. Frances Brooke's *To the Chase* . . . also begins with a highly masculine cadence, suggesting the barely controlled violence of a hunting song, but then softens in the third stanza to a gentle plea for mercy. Emily Pfeiffer's

13

Moth is, by contrast, a perfect miniature, with a special warmth provided by the poet's very active presence. She is in genuine dialogue with the creature, speaking to it while taking in the message of its life from its activities. As she moves from moth to swallow, and then to Nature at large, the scale of the poem shifts and expands, to end with an indictment of mankind's relative rigidity. And Jane Carlyle, very much in dialogue with her subject as well, sees in her *Swallow* a contrast to her own limitations, but only after exhaustive speculation on the bird's history and motives which draws one completely into that other's life. To represent Emily Dickinson, a significant number of whose nearly 1,800 poems involve her garden, I've chosen *Dear March—Come in* because it also has the properties of a dialogue, with March, April, and their harbingers intensely present to the speaker. The poem deliciously contrasts the immensity of Nature with the domesticity of backyard conversation. Clarissa Scott Delany, a young Black poet of the first quarter of this century, chooses to find *Solace* in the full year's cycle, "the shifting pageant of the seasons." Her images are simple, even occasionally trite, but when read aloud their familiarity seems actually to add impact, much the way song lyrics may appear overworn and hackneyed on the page, but become intensely moving when sung.

A White Heron places Sylvia, our young heroine, amidst the enormity of all outdoors, as if seen through a telescope, from a great distance. The narrative is fairly straightforward until the end, when the speaker addresses the girl directly. The "wait! wait!" is a completely arresting moment, suddenly bringing the narrator into the story. The author, Sarah Orne Jewett, has been praised for her attention to detail and her ability to turn the familiar into the exceptional. She wrote of her work, "The thing that teases the mind over and over for years and at last gets itself put down rightly on paper, whether little or great it belongs to literature," a thought that could well be applied to most of the material in this section.

Soge Track's young girl in *The Clearing in the Valley* is herself the storyteller, and this more simply structured first person narrative becomes remarkable for its present-tense immediacy, the wealth of personal detail, and the degree to which it communicates the special and constant presence of Nature in Native American life.

Linda Hogan
from *Walking*

Tonight I walk. I am watching the sky. I think of the people who came before me and how they knew the placement of stars in the sky, watched the moving sun long and hard enough to witness how a certain angle of light touched a stone only once a year. Without written records, they knew the gods of every night, the small, fine details of the world around them and of immensity above them.

Walking, I can almost hear the redwoods beating. And the oceans are above me here, rolling clouds, heavy and dark, considering snow. On the dry, red road, I pass the place of the sunflower, that dark and secret location where creation took place. I wonder if it will return this summer, if it will multiply and move up to the other stand of flowers in a territorial struggle.

It's winter and there is smoke from the fires. The square, lighted windows of houses are fogging over. It is a world of elemental attention, of all things working together, listening to what speaks in the blood. Whichever road I follow, I walk in the land of many gods, and they love and eat one another.

Walking, I am listening to a deeper way. Suddenly all my ancestors are behind me. Be still, they say. Watch and listen. You are the result of the love of thousands.

Aphra Behn
from *Oroonoko*

My stay was to be short in that country; because my father dy'd at sea, and never arriv'd to possess the honour design'd him (which was Lieutenant-General of six and thirty islands, besides the continent of Surinam), nor the advantages he hop'd to reap by them: so that though we were oblig'd to continue on our voyage, we did not intend to stay upon the place. Though, in a word, I must say thus much of it; that certainly had His late Majesty, of sacred memory, but seen and known what a vast and charming world he had been master of in that continent, he would never have parted so easily with it to the Dutch. 'Tis a continent whose vast extent was never yet known, and may contain more noble earth than all the universe beside; for, they say, it reaches from east to west one way as far as China, and another to Peru: it affords all things both for beauty and use; 'tis there eternal spring, always the very months of April, May, and June; the shades are perpetual, the trees bearing at once all degrees of leaves and fruit, from blooming buds to ripe autumn: groves of oranges, lemons, citrons, figs, nutmegs, and noble aromaticks, continually bearing their fragrancies. The trees appearing all like nosegays adorn'd with flowers of different kinds, some are all white, some purple, some scarlet, some blue, some yellow; bearing at the same time ripe fruit, and blooming young, or producing every day new. The very wood of all these trees has an intrinsic value above common timber; for they are, when cut, of different colours, glorious to behold, and bear a price considerable, to inlay withal. Besides this, they yield rich balm, and gums; so that we make our candles of such an aromatick substance, as does not only give a sufficient light, but, as they burn, they cast their perfumes all about. Cedar is the common firing, and all the houses are built with it. The very meat we eat, when set on the table, if it be native, I mean of the country, perfumes the whole room; especially a little beast call'd an armadilly, a thing which I can liken to nothing so well as a rhinoceros; 'tis all in white armour, so jointed, that it moves as well in it, as if it had nothing on: this beast is about the bigness of a pig of six weeks old. But it were endless to give an account of all the divers wonderful and strange things that country affords, and which we took a very great delight to go in search of; tho those adventures are oftentimes fatal, and at least dangerous: but while we had Caesar in our company on these designs, we fear'd no harm, nor suffer'd any.

Mary Botham Howitt
The Sea Fowler

The baron hath the landward park, the fisher hath the sea;
But the rocky haunts of the sea-fowl belong alone to me.

The baron hunts the running deer, the fisher nets the brine;
But every bird that builds a nest on ocean-cliffs is mine.

Come on then, Jack and Alick, let's to the sea-rocks bold:
I was train'd to take the sea-fowl ere I was five years old.

The wild sea roars, and lashes the granite crags below,
And round the misty islets the loud, strong tempests blow.

And let them blow! Roar wind and wave, they shall not me
    dismay;
I've faced the eagle in her nest and snatch'd her young
    away.

The eagle shall not build her nest, proud bird although she
    be,
Nor yet the strong-wing'd cormorant, without the leave of
    me.

The eider-duck has laid her eggs, the tern doth hatch her
    young,
And the merry gull screams o'er her brood; but all to me
    belong.

Away, then, in the daylight, and back again ere eve;
The eagle could not rear her young, unless I gave her leave.

The baron hath the landward park, the fisher hath the sea;
But the rocky haunts of the sea-fowl belong alone to me.

Frances Moore Brooke
To the Chase, to the Chase!

To the chase, to the chase! on the brow of the hill
   Let the hounds meet the sweet-breathing morn;
Whilst full to the welkin, their notes clear and shrill,
   Join the sound of the heart-cheering horn.
What music celestial! when urging the race
Sweet Echo repeats—"To the chase, to the chase!"

Our pleasure transports us, how gay flies the hour!
   Sweet health and quick spirits attend;
Not sweeter when evening convenes to the bower,
   And we meet the loved smile of a friend.
See the stag just before us! He starts at the cry:—
He stops—his strength fails—speak, my friends—must he
die?

His innocent aspect while standing at bay,
   His expression of anguish and pain,
All plead for compassion,—your looks seem to say
   Let him bound o'er his forests again.
Quick, release him to dart o'er the neighboring plain,
Let him live, let him bound o'er his forests again!

Emily Pfeiffer
To a Moth that Drinketh of the Ripe October

I

A Moth belated, sun and zephyr-kist,
Trembling about a pale arbutus bell,
Probing to wildering depths its honey'd cell,—
A noonday thief, a downy sensualist!
Not vainly, sprite, thou drawest careless breath,
Strikest ambrosia from the cool-cupp'd flowers,
And flutterest through the soft, uncounted hours,
To drop at last in unawaited death;
'Tis something to be glad! and those fine thrills,
Which move thee, to my lip have drawn the smile
Wherewith we look on joy. Drink! drown thine ills,
If ill have any part in thee; erewhile
May the pent force—thy bounded life, set free,
Fill larger sphere with equal ecstasy.

II

With what fine organs art thou dower'd, frail elf!
Thy harp is pitch'd too high for dull annoy,
Thy life a love-feast, and a silent joy,
As mute and rapt as Passion's silent self.
I turn from thee, and see the swallow sweep
Like a wing'd will, and the keen-scented hound
That snuffs with rapture at the tainted ground,—
All things that freely course, that swim or leap,—
Then, hearing glad-voic'd creatures men call dumb,
I feel my heart, oft sinking 'neath the weight
Of Nature's sorrow, lighten at the sum
Of Nature's joy; its half-unfolded fate
Breathes hope—for all but those beneath the ban
Of the inquisitor and tyrant, man.

Jane Welsh Carlyle
To a Swallow Building under Our Eaves

Thou too hast travell'd, little fluttering thing—
Hast seen the world, and now thy weary wing
    Thou too must rest.
But much, my little bird, couldst thou but tell,
I'd give to know why here thou lik'st so well
    To build thy nest.

For thou hast pass'd fair places in thy flight;
A world lay all beneath thee where to light;
    And, strange thy taste,
Of all the varied scenes that met thine eye,
Of all the spots for building 'neath the sky,
    To choose this waste.

Did fortune try thee? was thy little purse
Perchance run low, and thou, afraid of worse,
    Felt here secure?
Ah, no! thou need'st not gold, thou happy one!
Thou know'st it not. Of all God's creatures, man
    Alone is poor.

What was it, then? some mystic turn of thought
Caught under German eaves, and hither brought,
    Marring thine eye
For the world's loveliness, till thou art grown
A sober thing that dost but mope and moan,
    Not knowing why?

Nay, if thy mind be sound, I need not ask,
Since here I see thee working at thy task
    With wing and beak.

A well-laid scheme doth that small head contain,
At which thou work'st, brave bird, with might and main,
      Nor more need'st seek.

In truth, I rather take it thou hast got
By instinct wise much sense about thy lot,
      And hast small care
Whether an Eden or a desert be
Thy home, so thou remainst alive, and free
      To skim the air.

God speed thee, pretty bird; may thy small nest
With little ones all in good time be blest.
      I love thee much;
For well thou managest that life of thine,
While I! Oh, ask not what I do with mine!
      Would I were such!

Emily Dickinson
Dear March—Come in

Dear March—Come in—
How glad I am—
I hoped for you before—
Put down your Hat—
You must have walked—
How out of Breath you are—
Dear March, how are you, and the Rest—
Did you leave Nature well—
Oh March, Come right up stairs with me—
I have so much to tell—

I got your Letter, and the Birds—
The Maples never knew that you were coming—till I called
I declare—how Red their Faces grew—
But March, forgive me—and
All those Hills you left for me to Hue—
There was no Purple suitable—
You took it all with you—

Who knocks? That April.
Lock the Door—
I will not be pursued—
He stayed away a Year to call
When I am occupied—
But trifles look so trivial
As soon as you have come

That Blame is just as dear as Praise
And Praise as mere as Blame—

Clarissa Scott Delany
Solace

My window opens out into the trees
And in that small space
Of branches and of sky
I see the seasons pass
Behold the tender green
Give way to darker heavier leaves.
The glory of the autumn comes
When steeped in mellow sunlight
The fragile, golden leaves
Against a clear blue sky

Linger in the magic of the afternoon
And then reluctantly break off
And filter down to pave
A street with gold.
Then bare, gray branches
Lift themselves against the
Cold December sky
Sometimes weaving a web
Across the rose and dusk of late sunset
Sometimes against a frail new moon
And one bright star riding
A sky of that dark, living blue
Which comes before the heaviness
Of night descends, or the stars
Have powdered the heavens.
Winds beat against these trees;
The cold, but gentle rain of spring
Touches them lightly
The summer torrents strive
To lash them into a fury
And seek to break them—
But they stand.
My life is fevered
And a restlessness at times
An agony—again a vague
And baffling discontent
Possesses me.
I am thankful for my bit of sky
And trees, and for the shifting
Pageant of the seasons.
Such beauty lays upon the heart
A quiet.
Such eternal change and permanence
Take meaning from all turmoil

And leave serenity
Which knows no pain.

Sarah Orne Jewett
from *A White Heron*

Sylvia's face was like a pale star, if one had seen it from
the ground, when the last thorny bough was past, and she
stood trembling and tired but wholly triumphant, high in
the treetop. Yes, there was the sea with the dawning sun
making a golden dazzle over it, and toward that glorious
east flew two hawks with slow-moving pinions. How low
they looked in the air from that height when one had only
seen them before far up, and dark against the blue sky.
Their gray feathers were as soft as moths; they seemed only
a little way from the tree, and Sylvia felt as if she too could
go flying away among the clouds. Westward, the woodlands
and farms reached miles and miles into the distance; here
and there were church steeples, and white villages, truly
it was a vast and awesome world!

The birds sang louder and louder. At last the sun came
up bewilderingly bright. Sylvia could see the white sails of
ships out at sea, and the clouds that were purple and rose-
colored and yellow at first began to fade away. Where was
the white heron's nest in the sea of green branches, and
was this wonderful sight and pageant of the world the only
reward for having climbed to such a giddy height? Now
look down again, Sylvia, where the green marsh is set
among the shining birches and dark hemlocks; there where
you saw the white heron once you will see him again; look,
look! a white spot of him like a single floating feather comes

up from the dead hemlock and grows larger, and rises, and comes close at last, and goes by the landmark pine with steady sweep of wing and outstretched slender neck and crested head. And wait! wait! do not move a foot or a finger, little girl, do not send an arrow of light and consciousness from your two eager eyes, for the heron has perched on a pine bough not far beyond yours, and cries back to his mate on the nest and plumes his feathers for the new day!

Soge Track
from *The Clearing in the Valley*

It is no longer summer at the Pueblo. My favorite tree which stands in back of North Pueblo, the side where I live, is naked. It has been stripped of its clothes, yet it is not embarrassed. A few dull, straw-colored leaves still hold onto dry gray twigs that stick out like crooked fingers, trying their best to claw down the heavens. I know not what kind of tree it is, but it has been there for as long as I can remember. It is so huge, taller than the Pueblo, because when I go after water from the creek I can see my tree, extending its branches to the sky.

The two five-story Pueblos stand dark brown against a slowly clearing blue-gray sky. It is in the dawn as the sun, Our Father, is not yet over our mountain. From where I lie I can hear faint noises of the Pueblo people getting up, and Pueblo creek rippling peacefully through the center of the plaza. This is the beginning of a new day for us. Oh, but so early it starts! It's so dark yet! But that is our way— be up before the sun so that we may pray as soon as he appears.

I decide to get up. I quickly slip into my one blue-flower

printed dress and up the ladder I go. You see, we live on the second story and our way of entering our abode is by way of a trapdoor through the roof. When I reach the top I look around, up, and below me. Oh, such beauty!

Many times I have seen this, but I still get such a feeling that I stand and turn round and round, trying to get my eyes full of this beauty. With my arms stretched out, I yawn.

I stand for a while with my head bent down, my long tangled hair over my face. Suddenly every bit of my body feels warm. With my eyes closed I turn my face toward the east and look. I can see that the heavens have opened a path for our sun. Still looking with eyes half-closed, I pull back my hair from my face, stretch my arms to the sun and take his light into my body.

I say, "My Father, it is the start of another day. For this day, I ask for good thoughts."

2
COMMENTARIES AND CHARACTER STUDIES

Introduction

Social commentary, both in England and America, has long been the province of highly educated women with sufficient time on their hands to witness and to remark. Most of these pieces are certainly meant to be funny, but their humor is delicate, requiring either totally serious delivery or, at most, an enigmatic smile. The verses that comprise the first half of this section stand out particularly for their keen verbal wit and their sense of distance, of observation from afar.

Anne Finch's *The Atheist and the Acorn* is a fable that pits mankind's arrogance against Nature's logic, allowing the commentator the opportunity to lampoon a broad character and then pull away for the coolly stated moral. Mrs. Leicester and Elizabeth Trefusis concentrate their spyglasses on the antics of young boys, but to different ends. Where *The Mock Hero* suggests an ironic parallel between childish warplay and adult self-pity, *The Boy and Butterfly* draws a bittersweet if cliché moral concerning man's inconstancy. Both poems begin actively, echoing the boys' frenetic energy, and then shift to more reflective moods.

More strictly literary, Carolyn Wells's *To a Milkmaid* derives its charm from hyperbole and tongue-twisting word combinations as well as an almost wistful admiration for the improbable creature she hails. Effective presentation requires sharp verbal skills. Phoebe Cary's brief *When Lovely Woman* is perhaps an early stand-up (or salon) comedy routine, complete with a punchline. A slight pause before the last phrase will provide a light edge of suspense.

Josephine Bacon's *The Woman Who Used Her Theory* is a fable, also with a punchline attached. Since much of it is dialogue, the piece sets up three clear personas: the benighted heroine, her discriminating suitor, and the all-knowing narrator, each of whom must be kept separate and distinct.

Although the two Jane Austen excerpts are character studies of a sort, they require no extra effort, as everything needed to suggest the oddity of the person speaking is already in the language. In the first, Sir Edward describes his reading preference in terms so magniloquent as to become incomprehensible. His speech may, of course, be used by itself, but I prefer it placed in the context of his encounter with Charlotte. The actor need not then become Sir Edward, but is instead Jane Austen or some other appropriate narrator telling the story. I have added the parenthetical expressions, "said he" and "she replied," for narrative convenience. Mrs. Johnson's letter to Lady Susan also requires restraint because of its epistolary understatement, a kind of shorthand style. Both monologues do depend on momentum for their effectiveness, by which I do not mean speed, necessarily, but rather that pauses should be kept to a minimum.

Dorcasina Sheldon's letter from *Female Quixotism* will likewise benefit from restraint, and Mrs. Tenney provides a narrator's context as well, distancing the content of the letter from the speaker, a device which allows for both comment and involvement alternately.

Character is not something to be invented randomly as the spirit moves us; it must emerge as a function of relationship. The monologues that follow are very much character studies because each supplies a complete and very specific environment, suggesting relationships to: persons present or absent (Adam and other husbands); the implied or actual audience (Aunt Hetty's sewing circle); the place either of the events told or of the telling itself (Eden, Widow Bedott's fireside); and, of course, the words themselves. Each of these women, unlike some of the British characters in other sections of this book who strive for a certain social uniformity, is characterisitically American by virtue of her unique turn of phrase, word choice, and accent. These are truly comic pieces, rendered funnier still by each speaker's complete seriousness.

Eve's charm lies in her ingenuous directness, and depends on a one-on-one sense of audience. Since the piece is in diary form, I suggest that the auditor be identified as the diary itself, a kind of personalized, friendly diary, perhaps some animal—the snake?—in the garden to whom Eve is particularly attached.

Sara Parton's Hetty is placed in a public stituation that is very specific and needs little invention. It is very important, however, that the girls she is addressing be as present as possible for the speaker. Unless she allows time to observe reactions, to see the effects of her diatribe on the audience, the closing paragraph will make no sense. Frances Whitcher's selection is more intimate in tone and suggests an audience of one, or at most, a small tea group. The setting becomes essential here, a parlor or kitchen, with perhaps the same fireplace that is mentioned in the story; as always, the more specific the better. Both monologues are long, but any editing should retain the sense of the speaker's rambling on and on, because part of the fun is never quite knowing where she is going to end up. There is also a mature feistiness to these women that is quite rare in modern dramatic writing.

Nineteenth-century music hall and vaudeville shows alternated musical numbers with recitations that were sometimes serious monologues related to current events or issues like temperance or war, meant to inspire pathos (a sort of six-o'clock news). At other times the recitations were comic character pieces of a sort comparable to some of the *Saturday Night Live* Father Guido Sarducci or Roseanne Roseannadanna sketches. Kate Ellis's *Platform Monologues* are a domesticized version of this sort of entertainment, probably written to be performed at civic events and club meetings. Everything is here: other characters, a fully realized environment, interesting clues about the character's motivation, a complete story. There is even a subtle sense of public arena about these little skits that makes it easy to acknowledge the presence of an audience without sacrificing the directness of the principal dramatic confrontation.

Although certainly not originally meant to be performed, Emily Post's *Etiquette* does suggest a public dimension born perhaps of its Olympian authority. She speaks for entire generations, from a sense of tradition, innate propriety, and common sense. Although first published in 1922, and so of a more recent vintage than the previous selections, *Etiquette* has a charming archness which makes these selections seem like relics of a much simpler time.

Modernity is as easy to recognize as it is difficult to define, and the remaining selections in this chapter demonstrate a distinct difference in style, tone, and consciousness from those preceding. Whereas the women already discussed seem to be in control of their lives, and indeed their environments, modern women (perhaps men as well) play a victim's part, very much at the mercy of others, the world at large, and their own inner life. The compulsive behavior in Eve Merriam's *Tryst* would obviously be alien to a nineteenth-century woman. Although the verse form here is very free, I call attention to the inconsistent punctuation and the way in which the lines tend to get shorter toward the end of the poem, exaggerating even further the jagged, uneven rhythms of the piece, suggesting perhaps a growing shortness of breath symptomatic of paranoia.

Maura Stanton's persona, together with her classmate,

is victim to another's obsession, the spectre of the dancer Nijinsky that haunts the music teacher, Sister Ursula. The story should probably be whispered for the appropriate sense of bewilderment and hushed schoolroom anxiety.

Rhoda Lerman's women share a helplessness that is curiously endearing. As the girl that Richard wants to marry, Stephanie is caught in a trap of her own making and is suddenly aware of it, appalled at all the little things about him she can't abide. "Cement mixer" refers to a joke that Richard cracks a little earlier in the chapter, when he says to Stephanie, "Who wants to get into your head? . . . Getting into your head would be like falling into a cement mixer." Of an apparently more independent turn of mind, Lillywhite Stevie of *God's Ear* falls victim to a Niagara of her own words, as all the psychological baggage created by her father's death finds a sudden outlet. Although written as a telephone conversation, the speech is most effective if the listener is placed in the room and the delivery is narrowly and precisely focused to prevent the energy of the assault from becoming scattered.

I suppose that Alice Kahn's depiction of a yuppie funeral qualifies best as a character*less* study, her object being at least in part to expose the emptiness of yuppiedom. The selection provides a great opportunity, however, for taking on, in brief capsule form, a multitude of characters to populate the event, and Joe's eulogy is a tour-de-force that can also be played out of context.

Anne Finch, Countess of Winchelsea
The Atheist and the Acorn

Methinks the world is oddly made,
    And every thing's amiss,
A dull, presuming Atheist said,
As stretch'd he lay beneath a shade,
    And instanc'd it in this:

Behold, quoth he, that mighty thing,
    A pumpkin large and round,
Is held but by a little string,
Which upwards cannot make it spring,
    Or bear it from the ground.

While on this oak an acorn small,
    So disproportion'd grows;
That who with sense surveys this all,
This universal casual ball,
    Its ill contrivance knows.

My better judgment would have hung
    The pumpkin on the tree,
And left the acorn, lightly strung,
'Mongst things which on the surface sprung,
    And small and feeble be.

No more the caviller could say,
    Nor farther faults descry;
For as he upwards gazing lay,
An acorn, loosen'd from its stay,
    Fell down upon his eye.

The wounded part with tears ran o'er,
  As punish'd for the sin;
Fool! had that bough a pumpkin bore,
Thy whimsies would have work'd no more,
  Nor skull have kept them in.

Mrs. Leicester
The Mock Hero

Horatio, of idle courage vain,
Was flourishing in air his father's cane:
And as the fumes of valour swell'd his pate,
Now thought himself this hero, and now that:
"And now," he cried, "I will Achilles be;
My sword I'll brandish;—mark! the Trojans flee!
Now I'll be Hector, when his angry blade
A lane through heaps of slaughter'd Grecians made!
And now my deeds still braver, I'll evince,
I am no less than—Edward the Black Prince!
Give way, ye coward French!———
                              As thus he spoke
And aim'd in fancy a sufficient stroke
To fix the fate of Cressy or Poictiers,
Heroically spurning trivial fears,
His milk-white hand he strikes against a nail,
Sees his own blood, and feels his courage fail;
Ah, where is now that boasted valour flown,
That in the tented field so late was shown?
Achilles weeps, great Hector hangs his head,
And the Black Prince goes whimpering to bed!

Elizabeth Trefusis
The Boy and Butterfly

Proud of its little day, enjoying
  The lavish sweets kind nature yields,
In harmless sports each hour employing,
  Ranging the gardens, woods, and fields,
A lovely butterfly extending
  Its grateful wing to Sol's warm beams,
No dreaded danger saw impending,
  But basked secure in peaceful dreams.

A wandering urchin view'd this treasure
  Of gaudy colours fine and gay;
Thoughtless, consulting but his pleasure,
  He chas'd it through the livelong day.
At last the young but sly dissembler
  Appear'd to follow other flies,
Then turning, seiz'd the little trembler,
  Who, crush'd beneath his finger, dies!

Surpris'd, he sees the hasty ruin
  His reckless cruelty had wrought;
The victim (which, so long pursuing,
  Scarce raised a wish or claimed a thought,)
Now bids the tears of genuine sorrow
  O'er his repentant bosom flow!
Yet—he'll forget it ere the morrow,
  And deal to others equal woe!—

Thus the vain man, with subtle feigning,
  Pursues, o'ertakes poor woman's heart;
But soon his hapless prize disdaining,
  She dies!—the victim of his art.

Carolyn Wells
To a Milkmaid

I hail thee, O milkmaid!
Goddess of the gaudy morn, hail!
Across the mead tripping,
Invariably across the mead tripping,
The merry mead with cowslips blooming,
With daisies blooming,
The milkmaid also more or less blooming!
I hail thee, O milkmaid!
I recognise the value of thy pail in literature and art.
What were a pastoral poet without thee?
Oh, I know thee, milkmaid!
I hail thy jaunty juvenescence.
I know thy eighteen summers and thy eternal springs.
Ay, I know thy trials!
I know how thou art outspread over pastoral poetry.
Rampant, ubiquitous, inevitable, thy riotings in pastoral
 poetry,
And in masterpieces of pastoral art!
How oft have I seen thee sitting;
On a tri-legged stool sitting;
On the wrong side of the cow sitting;
Garbed in all thy preposterous paraphernalia.
I know thy paraphernalia—
Yea, even thy impossible milkpail and thy improbable
 bodice.
Short-skirted siren!
Big-hatted beauty!
What were the gentle spring without thee!
I hail thee!
I hail thy vernality, and I rejoice in thy hackneyed
 ubiquitousness.

I hail the superiority of thy inferiorness, and
I lay at thy feet this garland of gratuitous
Hails!

Phoebe Cary
When Lovely Woman

When lovely woman wants a favor,
    And finds, too late, that man wont bend,
What earthly circumstance can save her
    From disappointment in the end?

The only way to bring him over,
    The last experiment to try,
Whether a husband or a lover,
    If he have feeling, is, to cry!

Josephine Dodge Daskam Bacon
The Woman Who Used Her Theory

There was once a Woman who had a Theory that Men did Not Care for Too Much Intellectuality in her Sex. After this Theory she shaped her Actions, which Shows her to have been a Remarkable Woman. One day a Man asked her if she Belonged to her Sister's Ibsen Club.

"Oh, no," she answered, "I Cannot understand Ibsen at all."

The Next Time he called he brought her a Bunch of Violets and asked her if she read Maeterlinck.

"No; I think it is Very Silly," she replied.

Then the Man brought her a Box of Chocolates, remarking, " 'Sweets to the Sweet'—do you not think Shakespeare was Right?"

The Woman saw that she was Making Progress. Now was her Time to Stop, but this she Did Not Perceive.

"Shakespeare?" said she. "Oh, yes, I have read a Little of His Works, but I do not see Much Sense in them, to tell the Truth."

"Nay, Nay," said the Man, "this is Too Much. Not to Understand Ibsen shows that you are a Good Woman; to think Maeterlinck Silly augurs Well for your Intelligence; but not to see Much Sense in Shakespeare implies that you are Uneducated."

And he did not Call Again.

This teaches us that it is Possible to Get Too Much of a Good Thing.

Jane Austen
from *Sanditon*

"You understand me I am sure?" [said he.]

"I am not quite certain that I do, [she replied.]—But if you will describe the sort of novels which you *do* approve, I dare say it will give me a clearer idea."

"Most willingly, fair questioner.—The novels which I approve are such as display human nature with grandeur— such as show her in the sublimities of intense feeling— such as exhibit the progress of strong passion from the first germ of incipient susceptibility to the utmost energies of reason half-dethroned,—where we see the strong spark of woman's captivation elicit such fire in the soul of man as leads him—(though at the risk of some aberration from the strict line of primitive obligations)—to hazard all, dare all, achieve all, to obtain her.—Such are the words which I peruse with delight, and I hope I may say, with amelioration. They hold forth the most splendid portraitures of high conceptions, unbounded views, illimitable ardour, indomitable decision—and even when the event is plainly anti-prosperous to the high-toned machinations of the prime character, the potent, pervading hero of the story, it leaves us full of generous emotions for him;—our hearts are paralyzed—. T'were pseudo-philosophy to assert that we do not feel more enwrapped by the brilliancy of his career, than by the tranquil and morbid virtues of any opposing character. Our approbation of the latter is but eleemosynary.—These are the novels which enlarge the primitive capabilities of the heart, and which it cannot impugn the sense or be any dereliction of the character, of the most anti-puerile man, to be conversant with."

"If I understand you aright"—said Charlotte—"our taste in novels is not at all the same."

Mrs. Johnson to Lady Susan

Edward St.

My dearest friend,

I congratulate you on Mr. De Courcy's arrival, and advise you by all means to marry him; his father's estate is we know considerable, and I believe certainly entailed. Sir Reginald is very infirm, and not likely to stand in your way long. I hear the young man well spoken of, and though no one can really deserve you my dearest Susan, Mr. De Courcy may be worth having. Manwaring will storm of course, but you may easily pacify him. Besides, the most scrupulous point of honour could not require you to wait for *his* emancipation. I have seen Sir James,—he came to town for a few days last week, and called several times in Edward Street. I talked to him about you and your daughter, and he is so far from having forgotten you, that I am sure he would marry either of you with pleasure. I gave him hopes of Frederica's relenting, and told him a great deal of her improvements. I scolded him for making love to Maria Manwaring; he protested that he had been only in joke, and we both laughed heartily at her disappointment, and in short were very agreeable. He is as silly as ever.—

Yours faithfully
Alicia

Tabitha Gilman Tenney
from *Female Quixotism, Exhibited in the Romantic Opinions and Extravagant Adventures of Dorcasina Sheldon*

Upon the perusal of this [Lysander's] letter, Dorcasina experienced but one sentiment, and that was mortification. She read it over and over again; and was, to the last degree, chagrined at his coldness. She compared it with various letters in her favorite authors, and found it so widely different in style and sentiment, that she abhorred the idea of a connexion with a person who could be the author of it. What added greatly to her disgust was that he said not a word of her personal charms, upon which she so much valued herself. Not even the slightest compliment to her person; nothing of angel or goddess, raptures or flames, in the whole letter. She determined, therefore, without much deliberation, to answer it in plain terms, and to give him a flat refusal; and accordingly wrote as follows:

"Sir—I received your letter safe by post, and will answer you with the same sincerity by which it appears to have been dictated. I know not the man who possesses a larger share of my esteem. I have noticed your good qualities, and acknowledge your merit; and your friendship I should think it an honor to deserve. But my heart is untouched; and I experienced not that violent emotion, at first sight of you, which always accompanies genuine love; nor do I think the passion with which I have inspired you, sufficiently ardent to insure my happiness; as your letter was such as I suppose your grandfather might write, were he, at the age of eighty, to take it into his head to marry. I hope you will not take amiss the freedom with which I speak my sentiments, or suppose it the effect of levity; but be assured

that it is from a firm conviction, that we are not destined
by Heaven to make each other happy.

    With sentiments of the highest esteem,

    I wish to remain your friend,

Dorcasina Sheldon."

Mark Twain
from *Eve's Diary*

Wednesday.—We are getting along very well indeed, now,
and getting better and better acquainted. He does not try
to avoid me any more, which is a good sign, and shows that
he likes to have me with him. That pleases me, and I study
to be useful to him in every way I can, so as to increase
his regard. During the last day or two I have taken all the
work of naming things off his hands, and this has been a
great relief to him, for he has no gift in that line, and is
evidently very grateful. He can't think of a rational name
to save him, but I do not let him see that I am aware of
his defect. Whenever a new creature comes along I name
it before he has time to expose himself by an awkward
silence. In this way I have saved him many embarrass-
ments. I have no defect like his. The minute I set eyes on
an animal I know what it is. I don't have to reflect a moment;
the right name comes out instantly, just as if it were an
inspiration, as no doubt it is, for I am sure it wasn't in me
half a minute before. I seem to know just by the shape of
the creature and the way it acts what animal it is.

    When the dodo came along he thought it was a wildcat—
I saw it in his eye. But I saved him. And I was careful not
to do it in a way that could hurt his pride. I just spoke up
in a quite natural way of pleased surprise, and not as if I

was dreaming of conveying information, and said, "Well, I do declare if there isn't the dodo!" I explained—without seeming to be explaining—how I knew it for a dodo, and although I thought maybe he was a little piqued that I knew the creature when he didn't, it was quite evident that he admired me. That was very agreeable, and I thought of it more than once with gratification before I slept. How little a thing can make us happy when we feel that we have earned it.

Fanny Fern (Sara Willis Parton)
Aunt Hetty on Matrimony

"Now girls," said Aunt Hetty, "put down your embroidery and worsted work; do something sensible, and stop building air-castles, and talking of lovers and honey-moons. It makes me sick; it is perfectly antimonial. Love is a farce; matrimony is a humbug; husbands are domestic Napoleons, Neroes, Alexanders,—sighing for other hearts to conquer, after they are sure of yours. The honey-moon is as short-lived as a lucifer-match; after that you may wear your wedding-dress at breakfast, and your night-cap to meeting, and your husband wouldn't know it. You may pick up your own pocket-handkerchief, help yourself to a chair, and split your gown across the back reaching over the table to get a piece of butter, while he is laying in his breakfast as if it was the last meal he should eat in this world. When he gets through he will aid your digestion,—while you are sipping your first cup of coffee,—by inquiring what you'll have for dinner; whether the cold lamb was all ate yesterday; if the charcoal is all out, and what you gave for the last green tea you bought. Then he gets up from the table, lights his cigar

with the last evening's paper, that you have not had a
chance to read; gives two or three whiffs of smoke,—which
are sure to give you a headache for the afternoon,—and,
just as his coattail is vanishing through the door, apologizes
for not doing 'that errand' for you yesterday,—thinks it
doubtful if he can to-day,—'so pressed with business.' Hear
of him at eleven o'clock, taking an ice-cream with some
ladies at a confectioner's, while you are at home new-lining
his coat-sleeves. Children by the ears all day; can't get out
to take the air; feel as crazy as a fly in a drum. Husband
comes home at night; nods a 'How d'ye do, Fan?' boxes
Charley's ears; stands little Fanny in the corner; sits down
in the easiest chair in the warmest nook; puts his feet up
over the grate, shutting out all the fire, while the baby's
little pug nose grows blue with the cold; reads the news-
paper all to himself; solaces his inner man with a cup of
tea, and, just as you are laboring under the hallucination
that he will ask you to take a mouthful of fresh air with
him, he puts on his dressing-gown and slippers, and begins
to reckon up the family expenses; after which he lies down
on the sofa, and you keep time with your needle, while he
sleeps till nine o'clock. Next morning, ask him to leave you
a 'little money,' he looks at you as if to be sure that you
are in your right mind, draws a sigh long enough and strong
enough to inflate a pair of bellows, and asks you 'what you
want with it, and if a half-a-dollar won't do?' Gracious king!
as if those little shoes, and stockings, and petticoats could
be had for half-a-dollar! O, girls! set your affections on cats,
poodles, parrots or lap-dogs; but let matrimony alone. It's
the hardest way on earth of getting a living. You never
know when your work is done. Think of carrying eight or
nine children through the measles, chicken-pox, rash,
mumps, and scarlet fever,—some of them twice over. It
makes my head ache to think of it. O, you may scrimp and
save, and twist and turn, and dig and delve, and economize

and die; and your husband will marry again, and take what you have saved to dress his second wife with; and she'll take your portrait for a fire-board!

"But, what's the use of talking? I'll warrant every one of you'll try it the first chance you get; for, somehow, there's a sort of bewitchment about it. I wish one half the world were not fools, and the other half idiots."

Frances Miriam Berry Whitcher
Hezekiah Bedott

He was a wonderful hand to moralize, husband was, 'specially after he begun to enjoy poor health. He made an observation once when he was in one of his poor turns, that I never shall forget the longest day I live. He says to me one winter evenin' as we was a settin' by the fire, I was a knittin' (I was always a wonderful great knitter) and he was a smokin' (he was a master hand to smoke, though the doctor used to tell him he'd be better off to let tobacker alone; when he was well, used to take his pipe and smoke a spell after he'd got the chores done up, and when he wa'n't well, used to smoke the biggest part o' the time). Well, he took his pipe out of his mouth and turned toward me, and I knowed somethig was comin', for he had a pertikkeler way of lookin' round when he was gwine to say any thing oncommon. Well, he says to me, says he, "Silly," (my name was Prissilly naterally, but he ginerally called me "Silly," cause 'twas handier, you know). Well, he says to me, says he, "Silly," and he looked pretty sollem, I tell you, he had a sollem countenance naterally—and after he got to be deacon 'twas more so, but since he'd lost his health he looked sollemer than ever, and certingly you wouldent wonder at it if you knowed how much he underwent. He was troubled with a wonderful pain in his chest, and amazin' weakness in the spine of his back, besides the pleurissy in the side, and having the ager a considerable part of the time, and bein' broke of his rest o' nights 'cause he was so put to 't for breath when he laid down. Why its an onaccountable fact that when that man died he hadent seen a well day in fifteen year, though when he was married and for five or six year after I shouldent desire to see a ruggeder man than what he was. But the time I'm speakin' of he'd been out o' health nigh upon ten year . . . But I was going to tell what husband said. He says to me, says he, "Silly," I says, say I, "What?" If I dident say "what" when he said "Silly," he'd a kept on saying "Silly," from time to eternity. He always did, because, you know, he wanted me to pay pertikkeler attention, and I ginerally did; no woman was ever more attentive to her husband than what I was. Well, he says to me, says he, "Silly." Says I, "What?" though I'd no idee what he was gwine to say, dident know but what 'twas something about his sufferings, though he wa'n't apt to complain, but he frequently used to remark that he wouldent wish his worst enemy to suffer one minnit as he did all the time, but that can't be called grumblin'—think it can?

Why, I've seen him in sitivations when you'd a thought no mortal could a helped grumblin', but *he* dident. He and me went once in the dead o' winter in a one hoss slay out to Boonville to see a sister o' hisen. You know the snow is amazin' deep in that section o' the kentry. Well, the hoss got stuck in one o' them are flambergasted snow-banks, and there we sot, onable to stir, and to cap all, while we was a sittin' there, husband was took with a dretful crick in his back. Now *that* was what I call a *perdickerment*, don't you? Most men would a swore, but husband dident. He only said, says he, "Consarn it." How did we get out, did you ask? Why we might a been sittin' there to this day fur as *I* know, if there hadent a happened to come along a mess o' men in a double team and they hysted us out. But I was gwine to tell you that observation o' hisen. Says he to me, says he, "Silly," (I could see by the light o' the fire, there dident happen to be no candle burnin', if I don't disremember, though my memory is sometimes ruther forgitful, but I know we wa'n't apt to burn candles exceptin' when we had company) I could see by the light of the fire that his mind was oncommon solemnized. Says he to me, says he, "Silly." I says to him says I, "What?" He says to me, says he, *"We're all poor critters!"*

Kate F. Ellis
A Sunday Morning Interview

Here I am almost ready for church, and you haven't made the first move toward getting ready. You must hurry or we shall be late, and you know how awkward it is to go in after every one is seated. And it is more noticeable, too, when you haven't been for the past three months. No, I said nothing of the kind. It isn't likely I was so foolish as to say that if you would go with me once that you needn't go again for three months. Oh, you thought so, *did* you? Most likely you've forgotten, and perhaps you've forgotten another thing, too; that when you married me you said—. Oh, you've heard that story before, *have* you? You know perfectly well that I gave up my church to please you and I thought you meant what you said, that you would go every Sunday with me to your church. What's that? You did mean it then, but circumstances have altered and you didn't know you were going to be so tired Sunday morning? Yes, I know

you're tired, and anybody could understand that after your
late hours Saturday night you wouldn't feel equal to much
exertion the next morning. But you recover quickly, don't
you? I have noticed that just about noon you begin to feel
better and are all right for the rest of the day. Yes, I *have*
noticed it. No, indeed, I don't go to show my clothes. If
that were my object I should have to dress better than I
am able to on the small allowance you give me. Not that I
mean to twit on facts, but—Phyllis, come here and let me
tie your sash. No, your father is not going with us to-day;
poor papa is tired because he had to work so late last night
and we must go without him. What? You want him to take
some of your medicine so he'll feel better? I don't think he
wants it, Phyllis; I'm giving him all the medicine he is able
to take at present. There, run along and help little brother
button up his boots; mamma will come in a minute and
we'll—

(Turning to husband) Now, what do you mean by that
smile on your face?

On the Servant Girl Question

Yes, yes, this is the place, come in. Sorry I can't ask you
to sit down, but you see for yourself that every chair is full.
No, no, don't take that chair, please, for there's the bread
that the girl left rising when she walked out of the house
last night. You don't mind standing? Well, I'm glad you
don't, but you are probably not as tired as I am. Hard for
me? I should say it was; you are the fifth one I have inter-
viewed since I began to wash these dishes and not one
hired yet. Yes, the advertisement said that I wanted a girl
for general housework. How many in the family? Really,

I'm sorry I can't tell you, but that is something I never know myself.

Have I a husband? *(Thoughtfully)* Yes, no, oh, yes I have; upon my word it is impossible to tell, as some of the time I have and then again I haven't; he travels most of the time and is home very little, so we never count him when speaking of the number in the family. Children? Yes, I have plenty of my own and generally some of my neighbors'. No, no, *plenty* of my own, not twenty. How many? Four or five, according to the way you count the twins, whether as one or two.

Are you through with your questions? Then it's my turn. How much can you cook? Oh, yes, they can *all* do "plain cooking." Can you make good bread? They preferred to buy bakers' bread at your last place, *did they?* One point is settled, then; you can't make bread. But how are you on pastry, pies, cake, etc.? You have never made any because the people in your last place didn't care for sweet things? Another point settled. Can you get up a meal? From the way you act, I judge you'd be longer getting it up than we should be getting it down, but tell me what you can do, — what can you cook? Of course you can boil potatoes and corn-beef, but how about the other things I want made? You expect to be taught, do you? And are willing to learn, are you? Excuse me, but I said nothing in the advertisement about this being a cooking-school. All ladies expect to teach girls, do they? Well, I am not at the head of a cooking-school yet, but suppose I should take you, would you pay me the five dollars a week or should you expect me to pay it to you? So you expect me to pay it; I thought so, but when I start my cooking-school I shall have more than one pupil. Take you? No, you won't do for me, but I would like to know how you happened to come around to the kitchen door instead of going to the front door like the other girls. Thought I'd be in the kitchen, did you? Right you are; I have taken up residence here for the morning, and if no one comes to my relief I shall hold the fort for a week.

Yes, you may go right out that door, and if you meet any one on the walk headed for this house, please hold her in conversation for a few minutes until I have a chance to get these dishes out of the way. You are sorry? So am I, but such is life and such is the servant girl question.

The Last Breakfast at the Mountains

Now, my husband is one of the men who are not happy to be away from their wives. Haven't you noticed that sad expression in his eyes when he leaves me each time? You haven't? Well, it's very noticeable to a keen observer, but I'm proud to say he's a man who can rise above his feelings on account of the health of his wife and boy. I'm sure nothing would induce me to leave the city and stay away two long months were it not for the boy? You thought *I* enjoyed it, did you? No, I've simply been making the best of an enforced absence. I'm very fond of my home, but circumstances do not permit me to remain in it as much as I would like to. Why not? Well, perhaps I'll have a month at home now, and then it's time to talk of going south and we have to remain there until April. Oh, yes, we have to go south on account of my health. You hadn't noticed that I was delicate? How glad I am to hear that, for many times my feelings have been injured by people commenting on my delicate appearance. Yes, we come home as early in the spring as I think it safe, and then I do long to remain in my own house until it's time to come up here, but invariably I run down and am forced to go to Lakewood or Atlantic City. Yes, indeed, it is a hardship to be on the go all the time, especially when one is fond of her own home and loves to lead a domestic life. But there are compensations in making so many friends and acquaintances. Of course, Mrs. White, I consider you in the former class,—a friend. Write you? Of course, I shall, and when you return to the city I shall come at once to see you. Yes, thank you, I have your card which you gave me last night.

No, I don't care about keeping up the acquaintance of the Greens or the Blacks. Yes, I've appeared to be friendly with them here, but in the city it's another thing, you know. They have never been in our set, and, confidentially, Mrs. White, they can never get there. Yes, I heard so, perhaps it was true, but in the country one can't take such rumors into account. Yes, indeed, it is different in the city. Yes, I did exchange cards with Mrs. Green and her daughter and ask them to call, but that amounts to nothing; such matters are very easily adjusted when once on our own ground.

What is it, John? Most time to start and the trunks are being brought down? I declare it is almost nine o'clock and I have spent more time talking with you than I meant to, but I have really enjoyed every minute of this last breakfast.

No, don't get up, Mrs. White, just let me say good-bye to you here at the table. Save yourself all you can and accept this informal farewell right here by ourselves. How very kind of you. Yes, indeed, you may think of me reaching home about six o'clock this afternoon, and having a real *home* evening with my husband, for I mean he shall not be lonely tonight. Yes, John, I am coming. Good-bye, Mrs. White.

Emily Post
Fad Followers

Fashion has the power to make any style seem acceptable, even though it has few elements of flattery or beauty. If you doubt it, look at old fashion plates. Even a woman with excellent taste succumbs occasionally to the epidemics of fashion, but she is more immune than most. All women who have any clothes sense whatever know more or less the types of things that are their style—unless they have such a temporary attack of "fashionitis" that they are completely irresponsible.

There is one unchanging principle which must be followed by everyone who would be well dressed—*suitability*. A great number of women do dress with this in mind, but there are many others who, like sheep, follow every turn of style, without the slightest sense of whether it is a good one or absurd, or even if it is in the least becoming to them. As each new season's fashion is defined, they all run and dress themselves one in a replica of the other; their own types and personalities have nothing to do with the case. Fashion says, "Wear your skirts six inches above the knee," and daughter, mother, and grandmother wear the same length. Utility, becomingness, suitability, and beauty are of no importance. Fashion is followed to the letter—therefore they fancy, poor sheep, that they are the last word in smartness.

Gloves

Gloves are worn on city streets, to luncheons, dinner parties, and other social gatherings, to churches, restaurants, theaters, and all other public places of entertainment. At a restaurant, theater, or the like, they may be removed on arrival, but they are generally left on in church except during communion or when it is very warm.

A lady never takes off her gloves to shake hands, no matter when or where, and *never* apologizes for not doing so. But she *always* removes them for dining. On formal occasions the hostess should wear gloves to shake hands with her guests—and keep them on until food is served. Gloves are *always* worn when standing in a receiving line. When long gloves are an intrinsic part of your costume at a ball, they may be left on for dancing—otherwise they are taken off. A bracelet may be worn outside a long glove, but never a ring. Gloves which come above the elbow are worn only with sleeveless or strapless evening dresses. Wrist-length or three-quarter length gloves are correct with less formal gowns. At informal dances it is not necessary to wear gloves at all if you prefer not to do so.

Smoking Don'ts

First of all, it is unforgivable to lay a cigarette (or cigar) on the edge of a table or other piece of furniture—ever! Forgetting it and letting it burn a charred groove on a table edge or a brown scar on a marble mantel is the inevitable result of putting it down on the wrong place to begin with. Find an ash tray to lay it on—or ask for one.

Striking a match directly toward someone is dangerous—the head may fly off and cause a painful burn.

Never press a cigarette out without being sure that the object pressed on is intended for that purpose. Cigarettes put out against lamp bases, ornaments, and the like may mar or destroy objects of value. And potted plants do not thrive on ashes or unburned tobacco!

Lighted cigarettes should not be thrown into fireplaces. If the fire is laid, a roaring blaze started on a hot July day may be the reward of such carelessness, and if it is not, remains of cigarettes or unburned filter tips look dreadfully messy in a freshly swept fireplace. Never toss a cigarette out the window—it may land on an awning or the top of someone's new convertible parked outside.

Other don'ts include such untidiness as spilling ashes on the floor or upholstery, or throwing filter-tipped cigarettes on a lawn or terrace where the fireproof, rainproof tip will remain until someone rakes or sweeps it away. And worst of all is the smoker who leaves his lighted cigarette in the ash tray to burn itself out, making even the other smokers present ill from the smell.

Eve Merriam
Tryst

When we were married eight years,
we saved up enough money
for my husband to buy me
an engagement ring.
I wear it to the office
to take dictation from the boss,
but then when I go to type
I take it off and
hide it in my cosmetic bag,
you never know with the
messengers or temporaries
the agencies send around.
Then when I finish up
at the end of the day,
I go to the ladies' room and
hang it on a chain
around my neck,
that way I don't have to
worry in the subway.
Cooking or doing the dishes,
I hide it in the candy jar
mixed in with the mints,
nobody would ever look there
and sometimes I find new places
like in the plaid stamp books,
it's hard even for me
to know all the nooks where
I put it.
Sometimes I think
when I take off my nightgown
for us to make love

I ought to
put it on
it's really beautiful,
but there's enough
to worry about then
on my mind,
I don't want
more responsibility.

Maura Stanton
from *Nijinsky*

The girl beside me, who had long, straight hair that she must have ironed carefully every morning, raised her pale eyebrows discreetly and shook her head in the direction of the podium. I felt immediately comforted. I reached up to wipe the sweat off my forehead, but the same girl leaned toward me warningly.

"Don't touch your face," she hissed.

"What?"

She was unable to answer, for the sister at the podium was staring in our direction. I dropped my hands to my lap.

"Now I want you girls to listen to this music with pure souls," the tall sister said, her voice lower and calmer. At first I thought her white face was fuzzy, but looking at her more closely, I realized that her skin was only heavily wrinkled—her face, in the frame of her pleated wimple, looked like a drawing by Picasso. She extended her arms on either side of her body. "I don't want you to have any erotic thoughts when you listen to this music. It's beautiful music. Nijinsky was sorry afterwards for the evil way he danced.

He was a pure man, a good man, but sometimes he was tormented. He always asked for forgiveness. We were close friends. Perhaps I'll tell you more about him sometime. But now I want you to listen to this beautiful music by Debussy."

She turned to a record player with fold-out speakers on the edge of the stage behind her, and touched the switch very quickly, as if she were afraid of it. A record dropped to the turntable and in a minute the haunting notes filled the Little Theater. The sister kept her back to us, and watched the record spin around as attentively as if it were a whole orchestra of musicians.

I took advantage of the music: "Are we going to be tested on this?"

The girl next to me shrugged. She shifted in her chair so that her mouth was close to my ear. "Her name's Sister Ursula. She says if you touch your face, you'll touch anything."

"What do you mean, touch your face?"

"Sex." The girl stifled a giggle. "She means sex."

Rhoda Lerman
from *The Girl That He Marries*

Richard dried himself happily and conscientiously with his warmed towel, whistling his overture of the tunes he'd already presented me with, then dragged the clear Lucite wastebasket over to the side of the tub, unzipped his new Gucci dop kit from Blossom, sat on the edge of the tub with his nail scissors and clipped his fingernails into the wastebasket between his legs.

My anger and pain had focused within me. I knew what it meant. I no longer had to scream. Sanity and quietude washed over me and I could speak softly. "I don't think I can marry a man like you, Richard."

"Well." One hadn't been cut deeply enough. He measured and snipped. "Listen, like everything else, it's a challenge. But we can meet it. Together. Just like doubles. You have to get rid of that old ego if you're going to play a good game. Hey, turn off the towel heater like a good girl, will you? I think it gets too hot. Maybe you ought to call the store."

"Richard, you don't seem to understand me. I don't want to marry you."

"You're afraid of the challenge. That's all. Perfectly normal." He found his cuticle scissors in his new Gucci dop kit and concentrated with absolute worshipful intensity on his cuticles. I watched the cuticles drift in on top of the fingernails. They fell exactly. None misbehaved. Richard must have felt good about his clear Lucite wastebasket, his new Gucci dop kit, his richly warmed bath towel, his good aim, and his new grip.

"The only challenge in marriage, Richard, is how not to make a man feel inadequate. The rest is easy."

He looked up. I think I had communicated because a

cuticle fell unobserved beyond the confines of the waste-basket. "Are you serious?"

"Yes. I don't want to marry you."

And then he examined the spaces between all of his toes for athlete's foot, found his toenail clippers in his new Gucci dop kit and proceeded to manicure his toes. "I do this once a week. It's a good habit. Do you do it often?"

"No, I rip them out with my teeth. Richard, you aren't listening to me. I'm telling you I don't want to marry you."

I watched Richard clip his toenails. I watched the toenails drop neatly into his clear Lucite wastebasket on top of the fingernails and the cuticles. When he had ten even clip-pings of toenails in a pile in his clear Lucite wastebasket and he had washed the scissors with hot soapy water, dried them, and put them back into his new Gucci dop kit, zipped up his new Gucci dop kit, rubbed Keri lotion on his cuticles, held them a few inches before my eyes for inspection, slipped into his new monogrammed fleecy LeRon robe, let me follow him to the sofa, tried a few more backhands, forehands, and short net serves with his Yamaha and laid it gently on the sofa, when he had done all that, he turned to me, with a look of true helplessness, and said to me what I realized, looking back, was probably what I would have said to him: "The invitations are out already. It's too late."

What still surprises me is that I never cried.

Much later, I heard him laughing out loud from the bedroom. "What's so fucking funny, Richard?" I yelled at him from the sofa.

"Cement mixer."

"Richard, do you know what the elephant said to the alligator after the alligator bit off his trunk?"

"No, what?" he called.

I held my nose. "Very funny. *Very* funny."

"Good night, Stephanie."

"Good night, Richard."

from *God's Ear*

You look like someone I once knew . . . You rented a room in Cambridge. We had to share a bathroom. You were Orthodox, forty. You weren't a Hasid, but you wore a yarmulke. You were studying something at Harvard with permission from your Rabbi. That's what the landlady told me. My father had just died. We weren't speaking. I'd walked out on him and everything Jewish. You probably didn't even think I was Jewish. You were right. I'm not. I wanted to tell you about my father, how he was a religious man, how he brought me up to be religious, how he sold pesticides that caused abortions in Third World countries, how I called him a murderer, how he had a stroke, how he died. I wanted to talk to you. I wanted to tell you that I never said goodbye to him, or I love you, or I'm sorry. Or anything. I just pulled the plug. And there you were, a religious man, with answers, in the room next to mine. You never came out of your room except to go someplace to pray, use the bathroom, get the mail. I wanted to ask you about pulling the plug. I wanted to ask you if I killed him. Once you came into the kitchen and saw me cooking sausage. "What's that?" you asked. You looked at me as if I'd shit on the floor and was frying my stool. "Sausage," I said. "Pig." From then on you ate cornflakes with grape juice in your room three times a day and raw vegetables and never came near the kitchen. I heard you in your room next to mine, singing, praying. You washed your clothes out every night and hung them in our bathroom. I wanted to talk to you. I needed to talk to you. I wanted to go with you to synagogue, to ask you if I should have pulled the plug, to ask you where souls go, to ask you why things happen. You looked like you knew. Once when you went for the mail, I looked in your room. It was filthy. It smelled of old socks. I saw the broccoli and the paper bowls of soggy cornflakes purpled in grape juice. One morning I followed you to a synagogue to pray for my father. It was a big mistake. I was climbing the steps to the women's section. They were concrete steps. I had to pass a dozen dry old men in the men's section. One pulled up his pants leg and showed me that his flesh was still firm on his ankle. You know how old men smell in the morning? I fell on the concrete steps, on my face, right next to the old men. Not one saw me. Not one helped me up. I had blood all over my face. Not one stopped to help me. I didn't exist. One day you knocked on my door. I thought the moment had come, you'd heard me, you knew. "At night," you said, "when you use the toilet," you said, eyes on the radiator behind me, "could you please put the seat up so when I go to use it in the morning, I don't have to touch it before I pray?" I took your boots and burned them in the incinerator. Remember your boots were missing and no one knew where they were and you kept accusing everybody? You were right. You refused to pay your rent until you got your boots back. Finally the landlady kicked you out.

Alice Kahn
The Brie Generation

Imagine, if you will, a funeral you could die for. The caskets
are made of natural redwood and lined with sheets of pearl
grey and pale blue—Coastal Fog by Ralph Lauren. The
chapel is done in earth tones. In one corner, a string quartet
plays wistful renditions of Beatles' "white album" music.
The guests are standing around eating tiny vegetables and
Tex-Mex spareribs. Some drink the Bordeaux; others don't.
The press is positively drooling over the occasion, of course,
swigging down fingers of single-malt Scotch and goniffing
fistfuls of baguette and cheese. They will spend the service
clinging to the Father, Son, and no-Host bar.

Finally, Joe, the Universal Humanist minister, gets up
to speak. The guests stop telling horrible jokes and dis-
cussing their friends' eating disorders and begin listening
attentively. "We gather here today not to praise these yuppies but to bury them," Joe might say. "And not a moment
too soon. They've been nothing but an embarrassment to
our once morally superior generation. Who amongst us has
not had his parents walk into his tastefully furnished yup-
pitorium and heard them say, 'Ha. Ha. Ha. Whatever happened to "there's more to life than work and possessions?" '
No, we weep not for these rats trapped within the maze of
striving and acquiring. Their souls fly not to heaven because
they had no souls and none of us believe in any of that stuff
anyway.

"Some will ask: What killed Dirk and Bree—that plu-
perfect young, professional couple? More significantly,
some will walk over to the caskets and look in at the neatly
folded suits and ties and say, 'Where are the bodies?' But
we speak not of bodily death here, for bodily death is a
painful concept none amongst us can bear to consider. Our

lives have not prepared us for suffering. We speak here of the only death we with no memory of world war or Depression hunger or low-tech labor can understand—we speak here of trend death. We're talking about our generation. Trend death. The end of an era. The end of the opportunity to relive one's childhood with a credit card and an expense account. Only one question remains. If it is true that yuppies are dead, that the tide is turning away from materialism and towards a New Synthesis, how then, we must always ask ourselves—how then can we profit from this knowledge?"

3
JOURNEYS IN HISTORY

Introduction

The witnesses to history represented in this section were somehow in touch with the pulse of their time—through travel, or by their nearness to those who make history, or by their own greatness.

Between 1786 and 1791, Fanny Burney occupied a subordinate position at the court of England's George III, after he had lost the American colonies and at the very time when he was falling prey to a violent form of insanity. A noted novelist and shrewd storyteller comfortable in dramatic circles, Miss Burney's *Letter* has all the breathlessness of a romantic adventure, with herself as the startled, fawnlike heroine.

As a familiar of the court, and later a close confidante of Queen Victoria, Lady Augusta Stanley provides unparalleled intimate glimpses of the British Empire at its most opulent. The stately pageantry of the Duke of Wellington's funeral is rendered human by personal comments referring to creature comforts or to close friends. And the Queen's condition after the death of the Prince Consort becomes an occasion for private forebodings and a meditation on alienation and love. If told simply, uncluttered by extra "behavior," each of these selections can be very moving.

Contrasts and clashes of cultures are the substance of the next four monologues, beginning with Lady Montagu's *Verses*, a curious mixture of spying, introspection, and social criticism. One of the earliest in the tradition of British women travelers, she looks out from what is apparently a hidden perch onto the full pomp of eighteenth-century Constantinople, drawing associations to classical antiquity and the "vicious age" at home. A hundred or so years later, home doesn't fare well in Ellen Terry's eyes either, as she compares her bright, hopeful vision of New York with tame, dejected London, in an infatuated paean to America. Elizabeth Barrett Browning finds home, heritage, and paternal presence in Italy, tracing the landmarks of an actual sea voyage, yearning to recapture a part of herself. As different as these pieces are, they have in common a mature kind of sadness, as each traveler reflects on the larger implications of time and place. Not so for Susan Hale's brash, American superiority, traveling in Germany and trashing any accommodations that don't hold up to the comforts and privacies of home. She would probably be insufferable were it not for her uncanny ability to win over reader or listener to her perspective by never for a moment considering the possibility that she could be wrong. In the original letter, her description of the odious feather bed is accompanied by a drawing. Without benefit of pen and paper, the diagrammatic "*a, b, c,* and *d*" offers wonderful opportunities for a physical demonstration of the bed's discomforts.

Sylvia Ashton-Warner's reminiscences elevate the *idea* of travel, arrivals and departures, really, as seen from the point of view of an eleven-year-old girl. The Hastings railway station acquires a kind of mystic presence—thrilling, contagious, even musical—a "miracle of reality" that can even reunite the living with those passed on. Although perceived across a great gap of years, these recollections must have immediacy to be effective, the speaker needing to surround herself as much as possible with the bustling sights and sounds of the past.

Not so much traveling as living abroad, Isadora Duncan lays a plot to foil her continental suitor, D'Annunzio. Even writing about the event years later, her absolute glee is evident and sets the tone for the monologue.

Performers have perhaps always been among the most

accurate of observers, leaving volumes of history, both private and public. Fanny Kemble, the noted Anglo-American Shakespearan actress, made her debut in 1829, hoping—successfully as it turned out—to revive her family's fortune. Her disillusionment and intense frustration with the mechanics of the stage and with fellow actors have been experienced by many a performer. Kate Ryan's reminiscences of her years at Boston's Museum Theatre comfortably balance narrative objectivity and personal warmth in a manner that makes me suspect that she was very good at her art. Sharing a Boston locale is Enrico Caruso's outrageous courtship of Billie Burke, the woman who was to marry Flo Ziegfeld and star as Glinda, the good witch, in *The Wizard of Oz*.

Umm Kulthum, until her death in 1975 a singer of traditional religious music and the most beloved of Egyptian performers, tells disturbing and recognizable stories of audience difficulties that would make the most secure performer shiver.

Fanny Burney
(Madame Frances D'Arblay)
Pursued by the King

Kew Palace, *Monday, February 2nd.*
Sir Lucas Pepys still persisting that exercise and air were absolutely necessary to save me from illness, I have continued my walks, varying my gardens from Richmond to Kew, according to the accounts I received of the movements of the king. For this I had her Majesty's permission. . . .

This morning, when I received my intelligence of the king from Dr. John William, I begged to know where I might walk in safety. "In Kew Gardens," he said, "as the king would be in Richmond."

"Should any unfortunate circumstance," I cried, "at any time occasion my being seen by his Majesty, do not mention my name, but let me run off without call or notice."

This he promised. Everybody, indeed, is ordered to keep out of sight.

Taking, therefore, the time I had most at command, I strolled into the gardens. I had proceeded, in my quick way, nearly half the round when I suddenly perceived, through some trees, two or three figures. Relying on the instructions of Doctor John, I concluded them to be workmen and gardeners, yet tried to look sharp, and, in so doing, as they were less shaded, I thought I saw the person of his Majesty.

Alarmed past all possible expression, I waited not to know more, but turning back, ran off with all my might. But what was my terror to hear myself pursued!—to hear the voice of the king himself loudly and hoarsely calling after me, "Miss Burney! Miss Burney!"

I protest I was ready to die. I knew not in what state he

might be at the time; I only knew the orders to keep out of his way were universal; that the queen would highly disapprove any unauthorised meeting, and that the very action of my running away might deeply, in his present irritable state, offend him. Nevertheless, on I ran, too terrified to stop, and in search of some short passage, for the garden is full of little labyrinths, by which I might escape.

The steps still pursued me, and still the poor hoarse and altered voice rang in my ears; more and more footsteps resounded frightfully behind me,—the attendants all running to catch their eager master, and the voices of the two Doctor Willises loudly exhorting him not to heat himself so unmercifully.

Heavens, how I ran! I do not think I should have felt the hot lava from Vesuvius,—at least, not the hot cinders,—had I so run during its eruption. My feet were not sensible that they even touched the ground.

Soon after I heard other voices, shriller, though less nervous, call out, "Stop! stop! stop!"

I could by no means consent; I knew not what was purposed, but I recollected fully my agreement with Doctor John that very morning that I should decamp if surprised, and not be named.

I knew not to what I might be exposed, should the malady be then high, and take the turn of resentment. Still, therefore, on I flew; and such was my speed, so almost incredible to relate or recollect, that I fairly believe no one of the whole party could have overtaken me, if these words, from one of the attendants, had not reached me, "Doctor Willis begs you stop!"

"I cannot! I cannot" I answered, still flying on, when he called out, "You must ma'am; it hurts the king to run."

Then, indeed, I stopped,—in a state of fear really amounting to agony. I turned around; I saw the two doctors had got the king between them, and three attendants of

Doctor Willis's were hovering about. They all slackened their pace, as they saw me stand still. . . . .

As they approached, some little presence of mind happily came to my command; it occurred to me that, to appease the wrath of my flight, I must now show some confidence. I therefore faced them as undauntedly as I was able, only charging the nearest of the attendants to stand by my side.

When they were within a few yards of me, the king called out, "Why did you run away?"

Shocked at a question impossible to answer, yet a little assured by the mild tone of his voice, I instantly forced myself forward to meet him. . . . I fairly think I may reckon it the greatest effort of personal courage I have ever made.

The effort answered; I looked up, and met all his wonted benignity of countenance, though something still of wildness in his eyes. Think, however, of my surprise to feel him put both his hands around my two shoulders, and then kiss my cheek!

I wonder I did not really sink, so exquisite was my affright when I saw him spread out his arms. Involuntarily, I concluded he meant to crush me; but the Willises, who have never seen him till this fatal illness, not knowing how very extraordinary an action this was from him, simply smiled and looked pleased, supposing, perhaps, it was his customary salutation.

He now spoke in such terms of his pleasure in seeing me that I soon lost the whole of my terror; astonishment to find him so nearly well, and gratification to see him so pleased, removed every uneasy feeling, and the joy that succeeded, in my conviction of his recovery, made me ready to throw myself at his feet to express it.

Lady Augusta Stanley
The Duke of Wellington's Funeral

Posted from Windsor, *Nov. 20, 1852*

By three the carriages were on the move, at half-past four we dressed—at 5:30 we started on foot to Thomas's near Picadilly, which was already occupied by spectators—standing in the mud and darkness, perfectly good humoured, civil and decorous. "Master Bruce" as his maid calls him, was asleep—Fred and I *en attendant* the carriage watched the tide of human life pouring down towards St. Pauls and the City. The beautiful soldiers, etc.

The carriages came, . . . took us up and proceeded. The balconys were all hung with black, and the seats covered. Every creature, rich and poor, had at least an attempt at mourning, and even at that early hour you heard no rude, rough jokes, or indecorous noise among the crowds. The Police everywhere carrying and helping ladies across, and facilitating instead of impeding everything. The throng so well managed, so quiet, setting down so clever and rapid. A moment only we were uncertain about our places, but we immediately found them over the West door, and beautiful the view was from where we sat. We were very comfortable and perfectly cool and at our ease. Gradually the immense Cathedral filled, and nothing was so interesting and fine as seeing all those handsome men and uniforms—from every Regiment in the Service. The colours blended well with the black and white dresses of the choristers, and when the whole was filled made it more magnificent than anything I could have conceived. The gas lighting produced very striking effects, and the beautiful sunshine that found its way in as the morning cleared added to it instead of marring it. When the head of the procession reached the

Cathedral the bands commenced to play the Dead March, and the effect was wonderful. The music seemed to swell and die away and commence at intervals. The great bell tolled, the cannon was heard in the distance, and solemnly the various bodies, deputations and illustrious men marched up and took their places. The priests and the choir received the coffin at the door and preceded it chanting as it was slowly moved up the long space to the Dome, on a black bier. There it was placed on a pedestal, and the service proceeded. Not a breath was to be heard, and with the deepest emotion the whole congregation joined in the solemn service, repeating as with one voice the response to the Lord's Prayer. Poor Lord Douro was quite upset, so were many more, and our poor dear Prince was perfectly overcome.

The silence, the order, the deep feeling of the whole could not fail to impress the most careless. . . . It was indeed glorious—dear, dear old man—how worthy of him, and what a dignity the love of him seemed to impart to a whole nation!

Queen Victoria in Mourning

Windsor Castle, *Dec. 19th, 1861*

The Queen was wonderful: saw several people; was able to speak, to weep freely, and was preserved from saying one doubting repining word. All she could not bear, she said, was to hear it said that it was in wrath God so acted. She felt that the God whose law of love and truth had been so deeply engraved in the heart of that adored husband, is a God of love, and that in love He had taken her treasure.

Darling, I can not tell you what this cloud is; this dark, overwhelming cloud—no ray of light seemed to pierce it. To me it felt amost as if we were being cast off, till she spoke of what had been his views of life, his teaching and training of herself, how he had often wondered at her clinging to the present as she did, how he had done everything always with his whole heart, had rejoiced in his work, but had ever felt that there was no rest or real joy here, and was ever ready and willing to depart, and how last March he had more particularly led her to think likewise, guided her feet to the entrance to the dark valley, and left her words, some written and some engraved on her memory only, to help her through every bitter and agonising circumstance connected with the last sad days and duties.

Darling, how I see and feel that this was not without a purpose of love, and I feel it still. I feel also our God is leading and teaching her Himself, that His ways are not as ours, and that His channels of access to the heart are more diversified than we can understand. Therefore I look on and watch with humble thankfulness all that she is doing, seeing every day more and more how vain is the help of man; how impossible to convey to another human heart and mind what is in one's own; even for the most holy and wise to find access to the spirit of another. It is through

this absorbing human love, this love bestowed on one
whose worthiness I, even, had only conceived of, that God
has educated this beautiful, simple, childlike, truthful soul.

Lady Mary Wortley Montagu
Overlooking Constantinople

Here, at my window, I at once survey,
The crowded city and resounding sea;
In distant views the Asian mountains rise,
And lose their snowy summits in the skies;
Above these mountains proud Olympus tow'rs,
The parliamental seat of heavenly pow'rs.
New to the sight my ravished eyes admire
Each gilded crescent and each antique spire,
The marble mosques, beneath whose ample domes
Fierce warlike sultans sleep in peaceful tombs . . . .
One little spot the tenure small contains,
Of Greek nobility the poor remains;
Where other Helens, with like powerful charms,
Had once engaged the warring world in arms;
Those names which royal ancestors can boast,
In mean mechanic arts obscurely lost;
Those eyes a second Homer might inspire,
Fixed at the loom, destroy their useless fire:
Grieved at a view, which struck upon my mind
The short-lived vanity of humankind.

In gaudy objects I indulge my sight,
And turn where Eastern pomp gives gay delight;
See the vast train in various habits dressed,
By the bright scimitar and sable vest
The proud vizier distinguished o'er the rest!

Six slaves in gay attire his bridle hold,
His bridle rich with gems, and stirrups gold:
His snowy steed adorned with costly pride,
Whole troops of soldiers mounted by his side,
These top the plumy crest Arabian courtiers guide.
With artful duty all decline their eyes,
No bellowing shouts of noisy crowds arise;
Silence, in solemn state, the march attends,
Till at the dread divan the slow procession ends.
   Yet not these prospects all profusely gay,
The gilded navy that adorns the sea,
The rising city in confusion fair,
Magnificently formed, irregular,
Where woods and palaces at once surprise,
Gardens on gardens, domes on domes arise,
And endless beauties tire the wand'ring eyes,
So soothe my wishes, or so charm my mind,
As this retreat secure from humankind.
No knave's successful craft does spleen excite,
No coxcomb's tawdry splendour shocks my sight,
No mob-alarm awakes my female fear,
No praise my mind, nor envy hurts my ear,
Ev'n fame itself can hardly reach me here;
Impertinence, with all her tattling train,
Fair-sounding flattery's delicious bane;
Censorious folly, noisy party rage,
The thousand tongues with which she must engage
Who dares have virtue in a vicious age.

Ellen Terry
America

The stores in New York are now the most beautiful in the world, and the women are dressed to perfection. They are as clever at the *demi-toilette* as the Parisian, and the extreme neatness and smartness of their walking-gowns are very refreshing after the floppy, blowsy, trailing dresses, accompanied by the inevitable feather boa of which English girls, who used to be so tidy and "tailor-made," now seem so fond. The universal white "waist" is very pretty and trim on the American girl. It is one of the distinguishing marks of a land of the free, a land where "class" hardly exists. The girl in the store wears the white waist; so does the rich girl on Fifth Avenue. It costs anything from seventy-five cents to fifty dollars!

London when I come back from America always seems at first like an ill-lighted village, strangely tame, peaceful and backward. Above all, I miss the sunlight of America, and the clear blue skies of an evening.

"Are you glad to get back?" said an English friend.

"Very."

"It's a land of vulgarity, isn't it?"

"Oh yes, if you mean by that a wonderful land—a land of sunshine and light, of happiness, of faith in the future!" I answered. I saw no misery or poverty there. Every one looked happy. What hurts me on coming back to England is the *hopeless* look on so many faces; the dejection and apathy of the people standing about in the streets. Of course there is poverty in New York, but not among the Americans. The Italians, the Russians, the Poles—all the host of immigrants washed in daily on the bosom of the Hudson—these are poor, but you don't see them unless you go Bowery-ways, and even then you can't help feeling that in

their suffering there is always hope. The barrow man of
today is the millionaire of tomorrow! Vulgarity? I saw little
of it. I thought that the people who had amassed large
fortunes used their wealth beautifully.

Elizabeth Barrett Browning
Italy

I felt the wind soft from the land of souls;
The old miraculous mountains heaved in sight,
One straining past another along the shore,
The way of grand dull Odyssean ghosts,
Athirst to drink the cool blue wine of seas
And stare on voyagers. Peak pushing peak
They stood: I watched, beyond that Tyrian belt
Of intense sea betwixt them and the ship,
Down all their sides the misty olive-woods
Dissolving in the weak, congenial moon
And still disclosing some brown convent tower
That seems as if it grew from some brown rock,
Or many a little lighted village, dropped
Like a fallen star upon so high a point,
You wonder what can keep it in its place
From sliding headlong with the waterfalls
Which powder all the myrtle and orange groves
With spray of silver. Thus my Italy
Was stealing on us. Genoa broke with day,
The Doria's long pale palace striking out,
From green hills in advance of the white town,
A marble finger dominant to ships,
Seen glimmering through the uncertain grey of dawn.

And then I did not think, 'My Italy',
I thought 'My father!' O my father's house,
Without his presence!—Places are too much,
Or else too little, for immortal man—
Too little, when love's May o'ergrows the ground;
Too much, when that luxuriant robe of green
Is rustling to our ankles in dead leaves.
'Tis only good to be or here or there,
Because we had a dream on such a stone,
Or this or that,—but, once being wholly waked
And come back to the stone without the dream,
We trip upon't,—alas, and hurt ourselves;
Or else it falls on us and grinds us flat,
The heaviest gravestone on this burying earth.

Susan Hale
To Miss Mary B. Dinsmoor

Weimar, *February 19, 1873*

In the first place, the Bed. You have none of you any true conception of it, and Lucretia has hinted that she thinks she might like it,—not she! There's a total absence of *tuck in* to the German bed, which no effort can remedy, and I have spoiled my best nail trying for it in vain. (By the way they take not the slightest interest in fingernails.) Lucretia thinks she would like the feather bed on top, but the thing is, it is so very on top, while underneath every blast of heaven howls and whistles all night, as they do round Park Street corner. First comes a sort of cold flap-jack, too small and stiff to tuck down, and on top the feather bed . . . *a* is the feather bed; *b*, the cold flap-jack; *c*, a vacuum visited by the winds of heaven; *d*, the Victim.

I may add that this preparation is just the thing for chill-blains, and that we are all suffering therewith the torments of the d————d. In the morning I am awaked, in this receptacle, by the clatter of the door. I sleep in a little dark closet, but that I like,—the little door stands open into the big room, and Frau Baier, *Morgen früh*, comes in to make the fire. Her idea is to do it softly. Her first care is to shut the little door, which has a peculiar squawk only attainable in Germany. She then clatters away at the fire and leaves. There's a clumsy great lock on the big door and a handle like a stop-cock which kills your hand and spoils your glove. In about ten minutes Mrs. Baier comes in again to look at the fire, and goes out again. In about five minutes Mrs. Baier comes in to get my boots to clean. After five minutes more she comes in to bring back my boots. That is all she comes, unless she forgets something, in which case she comes once for each thing she forgets. Oh, no, let me tell you, she opens the little door with a squeak and comes into my closet and stealthily takes my water pitcher to fill, and brings it back with another squeak and clatter.

Quarter of an hour later Elise begins. She don't practise stealthiness, but advisedly makes as much noise as possible. You'd think it was somebody falling off a house with a sewing-machine and trunk, five stories into the street,—but it's only Elise with my bath-tub,—a regular wash-tub, which by great persistence I have attained to, although all Weimar thinks me insane, and Mrs. Baier, wherever we go, tells that I wash myself all over in cold water every morning. "Yes," said an elderly lady last evening, "when one is so *gewohnt* it is necessary. I used to wash myself once but I have got over it—" much as you'd speak of a person who, having acquired the fatal habit of smoking, is obliged to leave it off gradually, and not of a sudden. I don't mean to say but what they are clean and neat enough,—

as a general thing I think they always wash their faces once a day and their hands, say, twice a week, when they are going to a party, but not so often with soap.

Well, Elise bangs the tub down at the foot of the bed, stops and takes a good stare at me, and goes off. Shuts the little door, squeak; shuts big door, clatter. Comes back with a pail full of water, and *da capo*,—stare, shut little door, squeak, shut big door, clatter. Third time, second pail of water, squeak, clatter.

When I am pretty sure the coast is clear I come out, draw to the little door and proceed to bathe. It is generally then that the postman comes. Walks in (to the big room only) without knocking, and leaves letter on the table. My dear, they never any of them knock! and I can't teach them to. I can only suppose that the reason is that they are determined to come in whether I want them to or not, and therefore think knocking a useless affectation; for if the door is locked they stand rattling away at the handle until I come out of bed, or bath, or nap, or whatever, and let them in. That's a bother, so now I have given up locking the door.

Sylvia Ashton-Warner
from *I Passed This Way*

I'd soon found the railway station a few blocks along. The express train had a way of passing through Hastings late afternoons and I was enthralled at the drama there. Things happened in the station that didn't happen in the windows of shops. The comings and goings of crowds of people, the glad greetings and kisses when the long train puffed steaming to a stop, the talk and luggage and interaction, the urgent bell ringing to warn the travellers of the train's imminent departure and suddenly the change to partings and tears. I'd sit on a seat on the platform, loiter at the waiting room door and watch and feel it all, indeed become it all hearing in mind the sentimental song Mumma had taught us in school, "Upon a railway station stood a little child one night. The last train was just leaving and the bustle at its height."

This song continued through several verses, every word of which I know, describing how the station-master asks her what she's doing there on her own to which she replies that her mother died when she was born, Sir, and her father had just left for heaven. She's concerned that he might be lonely travelling all that way on his own so, "Give me a ticket to heaven please before the last train has gone."

More than once I risked forfeiting my evening meal in order to be here. I'd come by myself as it didn't draw the others. I was attracted to that station at that time of day as one is pulled to any drama on or off the stage. Long dress, bare feet, severely plaited hair and freckles, I'd lurk, loiter, linger in that place looking up widely about me, intensely agog; absorbing the flashing exposed emotions, compulsively living them through, catching them myself contagiously. In fact the station-master did look upon me but only in curiosity. He didn't say Go away.

Which was all right on warm days but when they were cold there was a price to pay, like a ticket to heaven. Some large red lumps appeared on my legs which the doctor said were rheumatic so I couldn't walk and lay on a bed. They pulled this camp stretcher out in the kitchen at Mrs. Lawson's place. Having at last achieved the distinction of being genuinely ill I found I didn't appreciate it. In mind I kept my appointments at the station whenever I heard the engine's whistle, examining the eyes of these who arrived seeking the eyes of those who met them; the eyes of a young lady upon a young man as he climbed down from the train, thrilling with excitement at their kiss. From my stretcher amid the surrounding hubbub of the household I'd respond to the volcanic life at that station as I heard the fateful trains arrive and depart, actually hearing the engine.

These legs kept me bedded for quite some time, but before the lumps were wholly gone, the moment I could bear my feet on the floor even with the aches still in them I all but crawled along the street towards the railway station, resting on the kerb of the gutter often as the lights turned up around me, coatless in the cold lit street to keep my vigil with the train. "Crawled" is not too far off target either as a word, for I couldn't climb the ramp to the platform itself but again sat on the kerb of the footpath below in the gathering glamorous dusk. "The last train was just leaving and the bustle at its height." Up on the platform lights flashing, people flashing, emotion flashing in the miracle of reality. I felt it all as well as my legs, hearing the clang of the boarding bell, the guard's whistle and the hysterical shriek of the engine. It was some time before I was able to come again.

Isadora Duncan
D'Annunzio

For many years I was prejudiced against him on account of my admiration for Duse, whom I imagined he had not treated well, and I refused to meet him. A friend had said to me, "May I bring D'Annunzio to see you?" and I replied, "No, don't, for I shall be very rude to him if I see him." But in spite of my wishes, he entered one day, followed by D'Annunzio.

Although I had never seen him before, when I saw this extraordinary being of light and magnetism I could only exclaim, "*Soyez le bienvenue; comme vous êtes charmant!*"

When D'Annunzio met me in Paris in 1912, he decided he would make my conquest. This was no compliment, as D'Annunzio wanted to make love to every well-known woman in the world and string them round his waist as the Indian strings his scalps. But I resisted on account of my admiration for Duse. I thought I would be the only woman in the world who would resist him. It was a heroic impulse.

When D'Annunzio wants to make love to a woman, every morning he sends a little poem to her with a little flower expressing the poem. Every morning at 8 o'clock I received this little flower, and yet I held to my heroic impulse!

One night (I had a studio then in the street near the Hotel Byron), D'Annunzio said to me with a peculiar accent:

"I will come at midnight."

All day long I and a friend of mine prepared the studio. We filled it with white flowers, with white lilies: all the flowers that one brings to a funeral. And we lit myriads of candles. D'Annunzio was *ébloui* at the sight of this studio, which was like a Gothic chapel, with all those candles burning and all those white flowers. He came in and we received

him and led him to a divan heaped with cushions. First I
danced for him. Then I covered him with flowers and put
candles all round him, treading softly and rhythmically to
the strains of Chopin's Funeral March. Gradually, one by
one, I extinguished all the candles, leaving alight only those
at his head and feet. He lay as if hypnotised. Then, still
moving softly to the music, I put out the light at his feet.
But when I advanced solemnly towards the one at his head,
with a tremendous effort of will-power he sprang to his feet
and with a loud shriek of terror rushed from the studio,
while the pianist and I, helpless with laughter, collapsed
in each other's arms.

Fanny Kemble
from *The Journal of Frances Anne Butler*

Wednesday, 5th [New York]:—At half-past five, went to
the theatre. The play was *Romeo and Juliet;* the house not
good. Mr. ——played Romeo. I acted like a wretch, of
course; how could I do otherwise? Oh, Juliet! vision of the
south! rose of the garden of the earth! was this the glorious
hymn that Shakespeare hallowed to your praise? was this
the mingled strain of Love's sweet going forth, and Death's
dark victory, over which my heart and soul have been
poured out in wonder and ecstasy?—How I do loathe the
stage! these wretched, tawdry, glittering rags, flung over
the breathing forms of ideal loveliness; these miserable,
poor, and pitiful substitutes for the glories with which poetry has invested her magnificent and fair creations—the
glories with which our imagination reflects them back again.
What a mass of wretched mumming mimicry acting is!
Pasteboard and paint, for the thick breathing orange groves

of the south; green silk and oiled parchments, for the solemn splendour of her noon of night; wooden platforms and canvas curtains, for the solid marble balconies, and rich dark draperies of Juliet's sleeping chamber, that shrine of love and beauty; rouge, for the startled life-blood in the cheek of that young passionate woman; an actress, a mimicker, a sham creature, me, in fact, or any other one, for that loveliest and most wonderful conception, in which all that is true in nature, and all that is exquisite in fancy, are moulded into a living form. To *act* this! to *act* Romeo and Juliet! horror! horror! how I do loathe my most impotent and unpoetical craft! . . .

In the last scene of the play, I was so mad with the mode in which all the preceding ones had been perpetrated, that, lying over Mr. ——'s corpse, and fumbling for his dagger, which I could not find, I, Juliet, thus apostrophised him,—Romeo being dead—"Why, where *the* devil *is* your dagger, Mr. ——?" What a disgusting travesty. On my return home, I expressed my entire determination to my father to perform the farce of Romeo and Juliet no more.

Kate Ryan
from *Old Boston Museum Days*

Every theater possesses a stage cat, and the Museum cat, not unlike her kind, made her début and many unexpected reappearances, usually selecting the time during an emotional scene. She would take the center of the stage, blink her approval of the audience, and then proceed to wash her face; or at other times, she would stalk on cautiously, and then make a sudden dash for an exit that was not an exit. I hardly know which method the audience enjoyed most; but I am quite sure the actor who happened to be on the stage at the time suffered much discomfort. But regardless of this, the cat would reach a place of safety and there remain, despite the efforts of the stage hands, who made appealing calls to lure her from the spot. Even the rats could not disturb Puss's equilibrium . . . and before the renovation of the theater, we had many rats. They never feared our intrusion, and I believe they knew each member of the company; Mrs. Vincent's stamping and "ssshing" didn't dismay them in the least. Miss Clark declared that one old fellow always came down the stairs to witness every first-night performance. Her dressing-room in those days was up one flight from the stage, and rickety old stairs they were! Miss Clark said she could hear him majestically thudding over those stairs and back again. I saw him once; he was very grizzled and gray. He was most considerate and would always step aside,—slowly, not hurriedly. Although I didn't exactly fear him, yet somehow I didn't enjoy meeting him, and was glad when he and his kind passed out with the ramshackle stairs and the old dressing-rooms.

Billie Burke
from *With a Feather on My Nose*

Caruso began coming to the theater every night when he was not singing in the opera, and every night there would come hurtling down from his gilded box a vast bouquet of American Beauty roses which were the fashion then, to the amusement of the audience. I suspect that if our play had not been a good play those proper Bostonians would have come anyway, just to see Caruso throw the roses.

Enrico would send back notes almost as flowery as his bouquets, but I avoided meeting him for a while. It was not long, though, before we were introduced at a luncheon thoughtfully arranged by a mutual friend. Immediately after that he began to call on me at the old Touraine and to fall on one knee and ask me to marry him. That man, I promise you, was very impetuous. He not only played in opera, he lived it.

"Leesten, leetle ba-bee," he would plead. "I seeng you the most lovely aria in all music." And he would fill his great chest and pour forth golden notes in such crescendo that the whole apartment trembled. He would sing anywhere. Once, when he was smitten with overwhelming passion for an unknown and considerably startled girl in the midst of Grand Central Station, he opened up with an aria *there* and caused many commuters to miss their trains.

We often took long walks along the Charles. There Caruso would declare his adoration; but first, he would test his "Mi-mi." He had to know if his "Mi-mi" was there before any other consideration.

Then he would announce:

"Ah, my Mi-mi she is there. Billee, I love you."

We had many suppers together. Caruso loved spaghetti, of course, and delighted to arrange parties at which he would consume enormous quantities between his declarations of passion. Caruso was always accompanied by his entourage, like European royalty or an American crooner, and his people were, of course, mostly Italian. My entourage would consist chiefly of Harvard boys, embryonic brain-trusters, who would object violently to my going out with anyone else; they had their own ideas about parties. But Caruso insisted, volubly brushing aside objections as if they did not exist, and away we would go.

Our patient special waiter would beam at us. "Ah, I see we are fourteen tonight," he would grin. Fourteen or forty, it made no whit of difference to Enrico Caruso. He made love and ate spaghetti with equal skill and no inhibitions. He would propose marriage several times each evening.

Naturally, I did not take him seriously. I treated him as if he were a great, mischievous baby and said "Pouf" to his rather overpowering brand of love-making. I am afraid that I mistreated this great artist. My! Suppose I had taken him seriously!

Umm Kulthum
from *The Umm Kulthum Nobody Knows*

I remember particularly one of the first nights when I sang in the Casino des Sports in Maydan al-Mahattah (called Maydan Bab al-Hadid today). I began that night at ten o'clock with the song "Glory to Him Who Was Sent to Us to Bring Mercy to Whoever Hears and Sees." Soon some members of the audience shouted for me to stop and sing instead, "Draw the Curtains, So We Can Enjoy Ourselves." I shook my head and went on with my religious music. But the voices which objected to the songs of the Prophet got louder and louder and I could hardly sing above the noise. I still carried on, but the matter did not end there. A few members of the audience jumped on the stage and tried to pull the curtains shut on me. At this point, I lost my temper. I felt that whoever came to the Casino that night knew what to expect, for the sign outside the door bore my name and the kind of songs I would sing; there were plenty of places in the Maydan where the kind of popular song they were demanding was being sung. I was so angry I began to shout insults back at the men who came toward me from the audience. I was hardly aware at all of what I was saying until I felt my father slapping me. I burst into tears.

That was the first time my father had ever slapped me at all, let alone in front of an audience! I wept because I knew I was right and my father knew I was right. But he had slapped me in front of the angry audience to please them, to calm them down, for he had then seen the evil on their faces as they approached the stage. He was afraid the men would hurt me, for they were very drunk. So he took the initiative in punishing me instead of letting them do it, to save me further pain, but also, I think, to give me a lesson in good behavior. Whatever the circumstances, he said, the audience was always right. We were performers and could not insult those who came to hear us. After all, hadn't my great teacher, Shaykh Abu al-'lla, been forced off the stage by an unfriendly audience and had to listen to 'Abd al-Latif al-Banna instead of himself? Had he lost his temper? No. I had to learn, said my father. But it was not easy. . . .

Even in the countryside, sometimes, we would find drunken audiences like this. Once I was singing in a village close to the town of Mit al-'Amil in the province of Dakhaliyah. The concert was in the reception hall of the *umdah*, or mayor, a very large hall which was full. That night I recognized many faces in the audience, for, during the years I had sung in villages and towns throughout the countryside, people who really wanted to hear *tawashih*, or religious songs, had learned what to expect from me. This was *our* audience, built up over several years. But that night, in addition to our audience, there was a small group reminiscent of the drunk Cairo audiences. These people were a minority, but they were there.

"Glory to Him . . . ," I began. Suddenly a man stood up in the audience screaming, "What's this? Are we in a place of mourning? Has somebody died? We came here to be gay. We want to feel happy!"

"Glory to Him who was sent to us to bring mercy . . . ," I continued.

The man started in again. "This is nonsense," he shouted in a louder voice. "We want to feel lighthearted. I want to hear 'Oh, My Love!' "

I continued to sing, and other members of the audience tried to mollify the man.

But in an instant the atmosphere was suddenly charged with electricity, for the drunken man ran out into the middle of the aisle, took a pistol out of his pocket, and began to wave it in the air threateningly.

"All those who don't want to hear 'Oh, My Love,' " he shouted, "get out!"

There was a moment of silence. People began scurrying quickly out of their chairs, and I faced an empty hall. Obviously this man with the gun was someone important, but we had no idea who he was until later, when we discovered he was the son of the *umdah*.

"All right, now you sing what I want you to sing!" he screamed pointing his gun at me.

"I'll sing what I want!" I answered, trying to be polite and calm.

My father, who had moved closer to me, said quickly, "Calm yourself, my son. Don't be upset."

"I'm not upset," said the man in a shrill voice. "But she has to sing 'Oh, My Love' for me. She has to give me some pleasure. That's what I paid for."

"Yes, yes, my dear son," said my father, "but look. You want to be happy and gay and you are waving a gun around?"

"That's the only way to get what I want with that girl," he said.

I heard my father sigh. "All right, sir, at your service," he answered. "We'll sing everything you want. But first you must calm down. Now, my daughter, sing for him. If we must, we must, and trust the rest to God!"

I refused. My refusal wasn't a sign of courage, it was stubbornness and pride and a strong belief that I was doing the right thing. I don't remember even thinking about the gun.

"Oh, ho, so you're not going to sing for me, the son of the *umdah*, eh?" cried the man in a frenzy. "Well, we'll see about that," and he tried to steady the gun in his shaking, drunken hand.

"She'll sing! She'll sing!" my father's voice was shaking now. "But be patient, for God's sake, be patient."

And God must truly have saved us, for at that moment, someone we knew came quietly into the back of the hall, crept up behind the drunken son of the *umdah*, and seized the loaded gun. Later we discovered that our friend had been simply passing through the village on his way back to Tammay, had seen the sign with my name on it, and had come late to the concert on the chance that it was not yet finished. Thanks to him, to chance, to God's mercy, to who knows what, we survived.

4
WITNESSES TO WAR
Introduction

As more and more war material came to my attention, I understood that the phenomenon of women in war is as specific as it is eternal. It is most often about enduring, carrying on with the necessities of daily life in the face of danger, disorientation, and death. But it is also, in special circumstances, about taking an active part, protecting, healing, even fighting—as a woman or, disguised, as a man among men.

The American Revolution, to Margaret Hill Morris and Elizabeth Sandwith Drinker, is really about invasion—of home, family, and the familiar by foreigners; whether Hessians or British, it's all one. A Philadelphia Quaker, Drinker is contemplative, surprised at disturbance, whereas Morris seems to have been more involved, facing enemy officers in person during the British drive from New Brunswick, New Jersey, through her own village of Burlington, to Philadelphia. Deborah Sampson Gannett sought escape from her life as a Massachusetts farm girl by enlisting. She served for three years in the Uxbridge regiment of the Continental army as Robert Shurtleff, and was described by her commanding officer thus: "He had the confidence of his officers, did his duty as a faithful and good soldier, and was honorably discharged [from] the army of the United States." Although her experience has been theatricalized by time and form and was meant to be performed on stages throughout the Northeast, the speech is rousing and energetic, if a bit short on specifics.

Similar in tone is Margaret E. Breckenridge's article of nearly a century later condemning the secessionists, but it also has a specific political purpose. A devoted nurse, she sought extra opportunities to work at every turn, sometimes to the detriment of her own health, and was quoted as saying: "Shall men come here by tens of thousands, and fight, and suffer, and die, and shall not some women be willing to die to sustain and succor them?" The southern viewpoint is expressed by Georgia girl Eliza Frances Andrews, curiously in conflict with her own father, a Yankee sympathizer.

Emma Adair's excerpt, from Joanna L. Stratton's *Pioneer Women*, gives a feeling of the upset and confusion caused by the Civil War on the frontier near John Brown's home base as bodies, fugitives, soldiers, and seemingly whole armies scatter across the countryside. Mrs. John Harris and Mrs. A. H. Hoge spearheaded parallel efforts to provide the Union army with all needed supplies, medicine, food, et cetera, by means of the Ladies' Aid Society and the United States Sanitary Commission, and both were on the spot to see a great deal of suffering and be moved by it. Mrs. Hoge used her experiences to raise support for her efforts, and so there is about her speech a more politically canny calculation. A completely different note is struck by Mrs. Belle Reynolds, a young newlywed who followed the army to be near her husband, as she finds herself cooking breakfast in the midst of what later became known as the battle of Pittsburgh Landing. The contrasting danger and domesticity make her diary material especially evocative.

In tune with the extreme misery that has been associated with most records of World War I is May Sinclair's finely etched ambulance ride across the war-torn Belgian countryside. It is reflective, gentle, moving, and requires utmost simplicity in the telling.

There is a wonderful theatricality about Anaïs Nin's World War II encounter with the grounded aviator, offering the actor the rare opportunity to speak for the gunner him-

self, using his words and speech patterns, and then to pull
back and comment. The last line is a perfect expression of
the way in which war, even from a distance, pollutes the
smallest, simplest, and best things in life.

Diana Barnato Walker is herself an aviatrix—she flew
Spitfires for the RAF from 1941 to the end of the war—
and so her perspective is much more immediate and personal. The intimate details of her story, as told in Shelley
Saywell's *Women in War*, create a vulnerability that is as
appealing as it is terrifying. Even more startlingly vivid is
Ida Dobrzanska Kasprzak's experience of the 1944 Warsaw
uprising. As one of the forty thousand women resisting the
Nazis as a soldier in the Polish Home Army, Kasprzak was
an officer in charge of a crew of women medics when the
events she describes took place, and her story serves as a
simple and profound spiritual affirmation, without benefit
of religious overtones or direct mention of God.

Dellie Hahne's interview from Studs Terkel's *The Good
War* is propelled by emotion—associations with the past,
anger at the politics and the lies, and, as if she only realizes
it as she is speaking, grief for her brother and her mother,
who was destroyed by his death. As with most highly
charged monologues, restraint is crucial.

Lynn Bower was an army nurse in Vietnam, and she
describes her early experience at the 93rd Evac at Longbinh
as a sickening series of first contacts with the dying young.
Her anger, fueled by horror and a sense of complete futility,
is open and almost violent.

In recent years, Latin American women have had especially active roles in their countries' revolutions and sub-
sequent politics. Daisy Zamora became Vice-Minister of
Culture in the Nicaraguan National Reconstruction government she helped create by participating in the vividly
described 1978 battle for the National Palace. The poem
that ends the selection adds an important human touch to

the otherwise unrelenting brutality of the revolution. In Argentina, the late seventies and early eighties were marked by thousands of disappearances engineered by the oppressive military junta, until the restoration of civilian rule in 1983. The pain of Nellie Bianchi's search for her missing son is controlled, organized into restraint by the chronology, the carefully detailed list of events—where she went, when, to whom she spoke, what she was told.

Margaret Hill Morris
from her *Diary*

Dec. 16, 1776: This day we began to feel a little like ourselves again. This day there was no appearance of the formidable Hessians. Our friends began to show themselves abroad. Several called to see us; amongst the number was one (Dr. Odell) esteemed by the whole family, and *very intimate* in it; but the spirit of the devil still continued to rove through the town in the shape of Tory-hunters. A message was delivered to our intimate friend, informing him a party of armed men were on the search for him— his horse was brought, and he retired to a place of safety. Some of the gentlemen who entertained the foreigners were pointed out to the gondola men. Two worthy inhabitants were seized upon and dragged on board. From the 13th to the 16th we had various reports of the advancing and retiring of the enemy. Parties of armed men rudely entered the houses in town, and a diligent search was made for Tories. Some of the gondola gentry broke into and pillaged Richard Smith's house on the bank. About noon this day a very terrible account of thousands coming into town and now actually to be seen on Gallows Hill. My incautious son caught up the spyglass, and was running towards the mill to look at them. I told him it would be liable to misconstruction, but he prevailed upon me to let him gratify his curiosity. He went, but returned much dissatisfied, for no troops could he see. As he came back poor Dick took the glass and, resting it against a tree, took a view of the fleet. Both of these were observed by the people on board, who suspected it was an enemy that was watching their motions. They manned a boat, and sent her on shore. A loud knocking on my door brought me to it. I was a little fluttered and kept locking and unlocking that I might get my ruffled face a little composed. At last I opened it, and half a dozen men, all armed, demanded the keys of the empty house. I asked what they wanted there; they said to search for a d———d Tory who had been spying at them from the mill. The name of a Tory, so near to *my own door* seriously alarmed me, for a poor refugee, dignified by that name, had claimed the shelter of my roof, and was at that very time concealed, like a thief in an auger hole. I rung the bell violently—the signal agreed on if they came to search—and when I thought he had crept into the hole, I put on a very simple look, and cried out, "Bless me, I hope you are not Hessians. Say, good men are you the Hessians"? "Do we look like Hessians," asked one of them rudely. "Indeed I don't know." "Did you ever see a Hessian?" "No, never in my life; but they are *men*, and you are men, and may be Hessians, for anything I know. But I'll go with you into Col. Cox's house, though indeed it was my son at the mill. He is but a boy, and meant no harm. He wanted to see the troops." So I marched at the head of them, opened the door, and searched every place; but we could not find the Tory—strange where he could be. We returned—they, greatly disappointed—I, pleased to think *my house* was not suspected. The captain, a smart little fellow named Shippen, said he wished he could see the spyglass. Sarah Dillwyn produced it, and very civilly desired his acceptance of it, which I was sorry for, as I often amused myself in looking through it. They left us, and searched James Verree's and the next two houses, but no Tory could they find. This transaction reached the town, and Col. Cox was very angry and ordered the men on board. In the evening I went to town with my refugee and placed him in other lodgings. I was told today of a design to seize upon a young man in town, as he was deemed a Tory. I thought a hint would be kindly received and, as I came back, called on a friend of his, and told him. Next day he was out of the reach of the gondolas.

Elizabeth Sandwith Drinker
A Day of Great Confusion

Sept. 25, 1777:—This has been, so far, a day of great confusion in the city, though in respect to ourselves we have experienced no injury, and but little fright. Enoch Story was the first who informed us this morning that the English were within four or five miles of us. We have since heard they were by John Dickinson's place. They are expected by some this evening in the city. Most of our warm people* have gone off, though there are many who continue here that I should not have expected. Things seem very quiet and still. Should any be so wicked as to attempt firing the town, rain, which seems to be coming on, may Providentially prevent it. A great number of the lower sort of people are gone out to them. G. Napper went. I hear he brings word that he spoke to Galloway, who told him that the

*warm people: rebels

inhabitants must take care of the town tonight. They would be in in the morning. As it rained, they fixed their camp within two miles of the city for the night. It is now near 11 o'clock. It has been raining for several hours, which I look upon as a remarkable favor, as it's said that tarred faggots are laid in several outhouses in different parts, with mischievous intent. Numbers met at the State House since 9 o'clock to form themselves into different companies to watch the city. All things appear peaceable at present. The watchmen crying the hour without molestation.

The Blazing Fleet

Nov. 21, 1777:—I was awakened this morning before 5 o'clock by the loud firing of cannon, my head aching very badly. All our family were up but little Molly, and a fire made in the parlour more than an hour before day. All our neighbours were also up and, I believe, most in town. The Americans had set their whole fleet on fire, except one small vessel and some of the gondolas, which passed by the city in the night. The firing was from the *Delaware* vessel that lay at Cooper's Point, upon the gondolas. Billy counted eight different vessels on fire at once. One lay near the Jersey shore, opposite our house. We heard the explosion of four of them when they blew up, which shook our windows greatly. We had a fair sight of the blazing fleet from our upper windows.

Deborah Sampson Gannett
An Address Delivered
at the Federal-Street Theatre, Boston

Wrought upon at length by an enthusiasm and frenzy that could brook no control, I burst the tyrant bonds which held my sex in awe, and clandestinely, or by stealth, grasped an opportunity, which custom and the world seemed to deny, as a natural privilege. And whilst poverty, hunger, nakedness, cold and disease had dwindled the American armies to a handful—whilst universal terror and dismay ran through our camps, ran through our country—while even Washington himself, at their head, though like a god, stood, as it were, on a pinnacle tottering over the abyss of destruction, the last prelude to our falling a wretched prey to the yawning jaws of the monster aiming to devour—I threw off the soft habiliment of my sex, and assumed those of the warrior, already prepared for battle.

Thus I became an actor in that important drama, with an inflexible resolution to persevere through the last scene; when we might be permitted and acknowledged to enjoy what we had so nobly declared we would possess, or lose with our lives—freedom and independence!—when the philosopher might resume his research unmolested; the statesman be disembarrassed by his distracting theme of national politics; the divine find less occasion to invoke the indignation of heaven on the usurpers and cannibals of the inherent rights and even existence of man; when the son should again be restored to the arms of his disconsolate parent, and the lover to the bosom of her, for whom indeed he is willing to jeopard his life, and for whom alone he wishes to live!

A new scene and a new world now opened to my view; the objects of which now seemed as important as the transition before me seemed unnatural. It would, however, be a weakness in me to mention the tear of repentance, or of that of temerity, from which the stoutest of my sex are, or ought not to be, wholly exempt on extreme emergencies, which many times involuntarily stole into my eye, and fell unheeded to the ground before I had reached the embattled field, the ramparts, which protected its internal resources—which shielded youth, beauty, and the delicacy of that sex at home, which perhaps I had forfeited in turning volunteer in their defense. Temerity: when reflections on my former situation, and this new kind of being, were daggers more frightful than all the implements of war; when the rustling of every leaf was an omen of danger, the whisper of each wind, a tale of woe! If then the poignancy of thought stared me thus haggardly in the face, found its way to the inmost recesses of my heart, forcibly, in the commencement of my career—what must I not have anticipated before its close!

The curtain is now up. A scene opens to your view. . . .

Margaret E. Breckenridge
from *The Princeton Standard, 1862*

England has her standing army ready at her sovereign's call, but England never saw what we have seen. She never saw the hills and valleys start to life with armed men; and from the eastern seaboard, the northern hills, the western prairies, and the sunny plains and mountain sides which rebellion thought to claim, saw the growing streams pour inward to a common centre, leaving in their track the deserted workshop, the silent wheel, the idle tool, and the ungathered harvest. All was forgotten but the danger threatening the country in which each man was a sovereign, the city which belonged alike to all, and the rulers whom the right of suffrage had proclaimed the people's choice. Is not this as it should be? Surely they only who govern themselves can fight heartily and bravely for the preservation of that noble right of self-government.

There is a legend of a holy man, to whom God spoke at midnight, and said, "Rise, and write what I shall tell thee;" but he answered, "Lord, I have no light." And God said, "Rise, and write as bid thee, and I will give thee light." So he obeyed. His fingers sought the pen, and as he touched it to the parchment, his hand glowed with light that streamed from under it, and illumined all the chamber. So it has been with us. It was the voice of God that roused us to see the peril which menaced liberty and union. It was only for the rescue of such liberty and such a Union as ours that a nation could have been so roused; and therefore from this very uprising come new light and strength; for that Union must be worth our lives and fortunes the possibility of whose destruction has called a nation to its feet. Yes, good seceding brothers, the Union is worth all that we can give; "there are many things dearer to a nation than even blood and treasure," and we must bring you home like the prodigal, and restore to you all that you have madly flung away, whatever it may cost us. You may hug to your bosoms the narrow liberties and loose-twisted union of your new Confederacy for a little while, but your waking will come as surely as ours. O, if he who stirred the people with his war-cry a hundred years ago, could come back now, and, standing where he stood then, gaze upon the ruins you have made, do you not think he would lift his hand to Heaven once more, praying, "If this is liberty, O give me death!"

Eliza Frances Andrews
from *The War-Time Journal of a Georgia Girl, 1864–65*

May 7, Sunday:— . . . But even if father does stick to the Union, nobody can accuse him of being a sycophant or say that he is not honest in his opinions. He was no less a Union man in the days of persecution and danger for his side than he is now. And though he still holds to his love for the Union—if there is any such thing—he has made no indecent haste, as some others have done, to be friends with the Yankees, and he seeks no personal advantage from them. He has said and done nothing to curry favor with them, or draw their attention to his "loyalty," and he has not even hinted to us at the idea of paying them any social attentions. Poor father, it is his own house, but he knows too well what a domestic hurricane *that* would raise, and though he does storm at us sometimes, when we say too much, as if he was going to break the head of the last one of us, he is a dear, good, sweet, old father, after all, and I am ashamed of myself for my undutiful conduct to him. I know I deserve to have my head cracked, but oh! I do wish that he was on our side! He is too good a man to be in the same political boat with the wretches that are plundering and devastating our country. He was right in the beginning, when he said that secession was a mistake, and it would be better to have our negroes freed in the Union, if necessary, than out of it, because in that case, it would be done without passion, and violence, and we would get compensation for them—but now the thing is done, and there is no use talking about the right or the wrong of it. I sympathize with the spirit of that sturdy old heathen I have read about somewhere, who said to the priests who were trying to convert him, that he would rather stick to his own gods and go to hell with his warrior ancestors, than sit down to feast in heaven with their little starveling band of Christians. That is the way I feel about Yankees; I would rather be wrong with Lee and his glorious army than right with a gang of fanatics that have come down here to plunder and oppress us in the name of liberty.

Emma Adair
*Fred Brown's Body**

Our cabin was the first one on the main road to escape being burned, which my father attributed to our having given refuge to a family from Boston, a Mr. Babb, his wife and three children, several of whom were quite sick. The father, Mr. Babb, was very sick, but my mother and Mrs. Babb insisted on his trying to get out of the house. He protested that he would be killed anyway, but between them they got him to his feet and out of the house and into the brush north of the cabin.

When the enemy came they placed their cannon directly in front of our home. The men surrounded the house and many crowded inside. The screams of the terrified children were no doubt disconcerting, for after making sure there were no men about they exclaimed, "Oh well, we will not kill women and children but if we get hold of any men, we'll put this over their heads mighty quick," and they shook out a rope. They then departed, taking with them a number of head of cows and calves.

All that day, the body of Fred Brown had lain in the burning sun by the roadside. Settlers living south of the Pottawatomie had watched the burning of the town from the high hills and when they saw that the enemy had departed, they hastened in to help gather up the wounded and the dead.

Fred Brown's body was brought into the north part of our cabin. Someone reported that David Garrison was lying dead in a deep ravine some distance to the southeast. By this time, it was night and the wolves were howling terribly. My father said no time was to be lost, so he and my brother

*Emma Adair was a niece of Captain John Brown. Fred Brown, the first victim on the day of the battle of August 30, 1856, was John Brown's son.

went in search of the body. An old man who lived in the neighborhood consented to go with them on the condition that my father go first and carry the lantern. They were fortunate in finding the body undisturbed by the wolves, and it was brought to the cabin and placed beside that of Fred Brown.

Their funeral, with that of those who were killed in town, was held the following afternoon. All of the bodies, except Mr. Williams, were placed in the same grave on the high ground to the southwest of town. Afterwards, they were removed to a lot given for the purpose by Charles Foster, and here a few years later in 1877 on the anniversary of the battle of August 30, the monument to their memory and to the memory of John Brown was dedicated.

Mrs. John Harris
from *Letters*

I just recall an instance of filial devotion on the part of a young boy, who sickened and died on his way to Poolesville the last month. He was extemely delicate, almost childish in appearance and expression. When told that he must be very quiet, that his physician thought he should have rested at Washington, and not come on with his regiment, he replied, "Yes, I thought I ought to stay there; I felt awful bad and weak like; but it seemed so much like giving up." Then he burst into tears, and his delicate frame quivered with emotion, as he added, "My mother is weakly, and is trying to educate my little brother and sister, and I helped her; and now that I must die, what will she do?" After a time he grew calm, and said, "I will try and leave her where she said she left me all the time—in the arms of our heav-

enly Father. If I die, he can and will take care of her and
her children." All this was said with many interruptions,
for he was very weak. He languished a few days, and slept
in Jesus. This is not an uncommon experience.

Passing over the battle-ground of the 9th, such sights as
might cause the general pulse of life to stand still met our
eyes.

Stretched out in every direction, as far as the eye could
reach, were the dead and dying. Much the larger proportion must have died instantly—their positions, some with
ramrod in hand to load, others with gun in hand as if about
to aim, others still having just discharged their murderous
load. Some were struck in the act of eating. One poor fellow
still held a potato in his grasp. Another clutched a piece of
tobacco; others held their canteens as if to drink; one
grasped a letter. Two were strangely poised upon a fence,
having been killed in the act of leaping it. How my heart
sickens at the recollection of the appearance of these men,
who had left their homes in all the pride of manly beauty.

When they kissed their loved ones, and bade farewell,
a gush of pride, mixed with the sadness of the parting, may
have swelled the hearts of mothers, wives, and sisters, as
they gazed upon the manly forms, in their bright, new
uniforms, and for a time the perils of the soldier may have
been forgotten. Now, how changed! Begrimed with dust,
heads and bodies bloated and blackened, a spectacle of
sickening horror, objects of loathing, the worm already
preying upon them!

Mrs. A. H. Hoge
from *Ladies' Address at the Packer Institute, Brooklyn, Spring, 1865*

For ten days I stood in the little storehouse of the Commission, dealing out life, and health, and happiness . . . as convalescent soldiers, that we should call skeletons at home, by dint of canes and crutches, and friendly hands, came in solemn procession to receive for themselves these treasures. "Will you have a few soft crackers? Shall I give you an onion? Perhaps you would like a lemon." "A lemon!" replied one, "just let me look at and smell one; I believe 'twould cure me." "How about some home-made gingerbread?" That always brought the gushing tears, and was, without fail, just like wife's or mother's.

One poor fellow, who was obliged to seize both railings to support himself up the narrow stairway, opened his battered haversack, and drew forth a small paper of coffee. Said he, "I know you don't sell anything here; but I thought, if I could change this coffee I've saved from my rations for a little green tea, I'd get an appetite. If I could only get a cup of tea like mother made, I believe I should get well." I motioned back the parcel, for I could not speak, and gave him a little package containing white sugar, and a lemon, some green tea, two herrings, two onions, and some pepper. He looked at the parcel a moment, and said, "Is that *all* for me?" I bowed assent. He covered his pinched face with his thin hands, and burst into a low, sobbing cry. I laid my hand upon his shoulder, and said, "Why do you weep?" "God bless the women!" he sobbed out; "what should we do but for them?"

Mrs. Belle Reynolds
from her *Diary*

April 17, 1862:—On Sunday morning at sunrise we heard the roll of distant musketry; but supposing it to be the pickets discharging their pieces, we paid no attention to it. In about an hour after, while preparing breakfast over the camp fire, which Mrs. N. and I used in common, we were startled by cannon balls howling over our heads. Immediately the long roll was beaten, and orders came from the commanding officer of the brigade to fall in. Knowing my husband must go, I kept my place before the fire, that he might have his breakfast before leaving; but there was no time for eating, and though shells were flying faster, and musketry coming nearer, compelling me involuntarily to dodge as the missiles shrieked through the air, I still fried my cakes, and rolling them in a napkin, placed them in his haversack, and gave it to him just as he was mounting his horse to assist in forming the regiment. His last words to me, as he rode away, were, "What will you do, Belle?" I little knew then what I should do; but there was no time to hesitate, for shells were bursting in every direction about us. Tents were torn in shreds, and the enemy, in solid column, was seen coming over the hill in the distance. Mrs. N. and I, thinking we might have time to pack our trunks, were doing so, when Lieutenant Williams, acting quartermaster, passing by, saw us, apparently regardless of the flying missiles. "For God's sake," exclaimed he, "run for the river; the rebels are coming!" We were by this time convinced of their close proximity; for we had scarcely left when a shell shot passed through headquarters.

May Sinclair
Field Ambulance in Retreat
(*Via Dolorosa, Via Sacra*)

I

A straight flagged road, laid on the rough earth,
A causeway of stone from beautiful city to city,
Between the tall trees, the slender, delicate trees,
Through the flat green land, by plots of flowers, by black
  canals thick with heat.

II

The road-makers made it well
Of fine stone, strong for the feet of the oxen and of the
  great Flemish horses,
And for the high wagons piled with corn from the
  harvest.
And the labourers are few;
They and their quiet oxen stand aside and wait
By the long road loud with the passing of the guns, the
  rush of armoured cars, and the tramp of an army on
  the march forward to battle;
And, where the piled corn-wagons went, our dripping
  Ambulance carries home
Its red and white harvest from the fields.

III

The straight flagged road breaks into dust, into a thin
  white cloud,
About the feet of a regiment driven back league by
  league,
Rifles at trail, and standards wrapped in black funeral
  cloths.

Unhasting, proud in retreat,
They smile as the Red Cross Ambulance rushes by.
(You know nothing of beauty and of desolation who have
    not seen
That smile of an army in retreat.)
They go: and our shining, beckoning danger goes with
    them,
And our joy in the harvests that we gathered in at
    nightfall in the fields;
And like an unloved hand laid on a beating heart
Our safety weighs us down.
Safety hard and strange; stranger and yet more hard
As, league after dying league, the beautiful, desolate
    Land
Falls back from the intolerable speed of an Ambulance in
    retreat
On the sacred, dolorous Way.

Anaïs Nin
The Grounded Aviator

The next day we met at the beach. The grounded aviator
was there. We were introduced. We took a walk along the
beach. John began to talk: "I've had five years of war as a
rear-gunner. Been to India a couple of years, to North
Africa, slept in the desert, crashed several times, made
about a hundred missions, saw all kinds of things. Men
dying, men yelling when they're trapped in burning planes.
Their arms charred, their hands like the claws of animals.

The first time I was sent to the field after a crash . . . the smell of burning flesh. It's sweet and sickening, and it sticks to you for days. You can't wash it off. You can't get rid of it. It haunts you. We had good laughs, though, laughs all the time. We laughed plenty. We would commandeer prostitutes and push them into the beds of the guys who didn't like women. We had drunks that lasted several days. I like that life. India. I'd like to go back. This life here, what people talk about, what they think, bores me. I liked sleeping in the desert. I saw a black woman giving birth. She worked in the fields carrying dirt for a new airfield. She stopped carrying dirt to give birth under the wing of a plane, just like that, and then bound the kid in some rags and went back to work. Funny to see the big plane, so modern, and this half-naked woman giving birth and then continuing to carry dirt in pails for an airfield. You know, only two of us came back alive of the bunch I started with. My buddies always warned me: 'Don't get grounded; once you're grounded, you're done for.' Well, they grounded me, too. Too many rear-gunners in the service. I didn't want to come home. What's a civilian life? Good for old maids. It's a rut. It's drab. Look at this: the young girls giggle, giggle at nothing. The boys are after me. Nothing ever happens. They don't laugh hard and they don't yell. They don't get hurt, and they don't die, and they don't laugh either."

There was a light in his eyes I could not read, something he had seen but would not talk about.

We walked tirelessly along the beach, until there were no more homes, no more cared-for gardens, no more people, until the beach became wild.

"Some die silent," he continued, as if obsessed. "You know by the look in their eyes that they are going to die. Some die yelling, and you have to turn your face away and not look into their eyes. When I was being trained, you know, the first thing they told me: 'Never look into a dying man's eyes.' "

"But you did," I said, suddenly understanding the expression of his eyes. I could see him clearly at seventeen, not yet a man, with the delicate skin of a girl, the finely carved features, the small straight nose, the mouth of a woman, a shy laugh, something very tender about the face and body, looking into the eyes of the dying.

I saw him two or three times, and then he disappeared. He was in the hospital with a bout of malaria.

I returned to New York. The sea at Easthampton had not renewed me. It was not the same sea.

Diana Barnato Walker
Holding the Line, Britain, 1939–45

I remember one day before I could instrument-fly, I was flying on a lovely summer day, everything was all right, and suddenly I was in a cloud, just like that. It was my first time in a cloud. I did all the things I had been told, but I was very close to the ground and slightly off course. I'd just come off leave and was still wearing a skirt and stockings. I thought, "I can't bail out because I'll look so silly coming down in a skirt with my stockings and panties showing." It was so stupid; I should have bailed out. I broke at treetop level and thought this was too low. It was pouring with rain. Thank God I saw a little plane landed on a grass airfield that was covered in water. It was not a good idea to land in water in a Spitfire because the flaps would get caught and break and the plane could nose over, but I had no choice. I landed it all right and taxied in. It was teeming with rain. I shut off just near a Nissen hut, and a very tall man came out of the hut with a huge camouflaged cape over his head and walked over to the side of the airplane, putting up the cape to keep me dry. I got out of the cockpit and my knees collapsed, I was so frightened. I couldn't let him know that, so I pretended I had kneeled down to get my bag out of the plane. When we went into the hut I stole a glance at the bulletin board to see where I was—I didn't want to ask.

Ida Dobrzanska Kasprzak
Uprising, Poland, 1939–45

Out in the streets we were open targets, dodging bullets, with no time to shoot anyone. The Germans had a big gun they called Big Bertha. They placed it on the railway bridge aiming down at us in the streets below. A lot of people in the area were wounded. We were sent out there to bring them in. People were screaming and moaning. My girl-friend and I spotted a man severely wounded in the head. She grabbed his legs and I grabbed his arms and we ran through the streets. He was a huge man, he must have weighed two hundred pounds. We were running, and I saw a piece of shrapnel fly into her leg. Blood was running down, and I wanted to scream at her to put him down. Just at that moment I saw a piece of metal coming straight towards my stomach. There was a gap of about six inches between his head and my stomach, and it was coming straight towards us. I thought, My God, what can I do? If I drop him he will die as soon as his head hits the pavement. I was petrified. All this occurred in split seconds, of course. Then, just as the shrapnel came within an inch of my stomach it fell down, between me and the wounded man's head. It was as though someone had punched it from above. I screamed "Dunca, stop running, put him down gently." I ran back and picked up the shrapnel. It was still hot. I carried it with me through the uprising, and always felt as though I was not alone, that somebody was helping me. I still have it today.

Dellie Hahne
Forty Years Later

The good war? That infuriates me. Yeah, the idea of World War Two being called a good war is a horrible thing. I think of all the atrocities. I think of a madman who had all this power. I think of the destruction of the Jews, the misery, the horrendous suffering in the concentration camps. In 1971, I visited Dachau. I could not believe what I saw. There's one barracks left, a model barracks. You can reconstruct the rest and see what the hell was going on. It doesn't take a visit to make you realize the extent of human misery.

I know it had to be stopped and we stopped it. But I don't feel proud, because the way we did it was so devious. How many years has it been? Forty years later? I feel I'm standing here with egg on my face. I was lied to. I was cheated. I was made a fool of. If they had said to me, Look, this has to be done and we'll go out and do the job . . . we'll all get our arms and legs blown off but it has to be done, I'd understand. If they didn't hand me all this shit with the uniforms and the girls in their pompadours dancing at the USO and all those songs—"There'll Be Bluebirds over the White Cliffs of Dover"—bullshit!

If only we had a different approach, that's all I'm asking for. If you have to live through a war, be truthful. Maybe you have to get people to fight a war, maybe you have to lie to them. If only they'd said that this isn't the greatest of all worlds, and there's graft and corruption in Washington, and kids are going without milk so some asshole can take a vacation in Florida. If they'd done that, I wouldn't feel so bad.

My brother was killed. Not even overseas. He was killed in North Carolina on a flight exercise. It ruined my mother, because she just worshipped my brother. He was the only boy. I don't think she ever recovered from it.

Lynn Bower
Twilight Zone, Vietnam, 1965–72

The troops were pulling out and there were none between us and Saigon. It wasn't a very comforting thought, but it wasn't Tet. The first day I arrived I was told I was needed in the ER for triage. I went in. It was a big room near the chopper pad. There were things like sawhorses to put the litters on, and next to each one were IV stands.

There was no time to adjust. They called "litter" and I rushed to the stand, and oh my God . . . they brought him in. He was sandy haired, very fair skinned, with freckles. He looked like half the boys I knew in Minnesota. He looked so young. I started cutting off his fatigues and took his blood pressure and put the number on his forehead or his arm, I can't remember. I went to start the IV, and then someone said, "Lieutenant, you can't start that IV, it isn't going to do him any good." I said, "I have to get it in." He repeated, "It's not going to do him any good. He's dead."

I couldn't see it. He was a bit rumpled, but he was in his fatigues. His eyes were shut and he was quiet, but . . . I had never seen anybody young die. Then they rolled him over and his whole backside was gone. I couldn't believe it. I remember the room started spinning. I was saying, "No, no. I'll just get this IV in and he'll be all right." He was just too young. I wanted to be sick. The captain came over and said, "Let's put you at the desk for a while. You can do paperwork." So I sat at the desk, feeling a little better. Later in the afternoon they brought in some guys who'd hit a land mine. Five of them were young, and they had their sergeant with them. He was crying. I had never seen anybody older cry.

I was confused. He had been there for two tours, yet he was crying. Their faces were so dirty. I had never seen anybody really dirty in a hospital before. They had black camouflage on their faces, and I remember because his tears were coming through this black stuff.

They brought them in on litters. Not one of them lived, except the sergeant. I was at the desk and I didn't have to do anything physical. I had to write the death pacts; there was a seventeen-year-old and a twenty-three-year-old, and it was his birthday that day. There was a nineteen-year-old who'd been set to go home the very next day. That was why they were coming in. They were taking him to Ben Hoa. He was going home.

I was sitting there, and I got angrier and angrier. I thought, "Who is going to tell their parents what happened to their children? They sent real people off to Vietnam, and they are getting back a body bag. They are so young, so young, God. What are they doing here?"

Nellie Bianchi
The Kidnappings

After my son was kidnapped I went to Famaillá to ask for him. I didn't know anything about it being a secret camp then. For me it was a police headquarters and I went there to speak to the chief. I spoke to a colonel, I think. He told me, "I don't have any bad news for you, if I had I would tell you. I have the young Bianchi and I'm going to take a statement from him and after that he'll be released. Go home and be calm. If he hasn't done anything nothing will happen to him." I didn't believe him. I left that place with a feeling of death inside me.

A bit later the father of another boy who had been kidnapped the same night as my son came to tell me some bodies had been found in the south of Tucamán and did I want to go with him to identify them. I went. There were five bodies, two boys and three girls, completely naked but unrecognizable. They had shot them so many times they were completely disfigured. When I saw them I went into a state of shock. I couldn't tell if my son was one of them. I didn't think my son was there. I spoke to a military officer and I was crying and shouting—I don't know how nothing happened to me—and he said, "But your son wasn't there." "So you know where he is, you are responsible, why are you lying?" I shouted. He said nothing. Every time I went to the army they always said come back tomorrow, next week. Once one of them told me, "Your son is being held under PEN.* Be calm and come back next week. I'll have

*PEN, *Poder Ejecutivo de la Nación:* PEN prisoners were those held at the disposal of the Executive Power. The Argentine constitution places no time limit on such detentions.

more information." I went back the next week and he denied that he'd ever said it and said they knew nothing about a Bianchi.

Daisy Zamora
Trapped in the Cross-Fire

The action was a success even though our preparation had been pretty rudimentary. Our plan was to destroy the station in ten minutes and in fact we were able to burn it to the ground in seven. But we did make a serious error in planning. We hadn't discovered that there was an EEBI* barracks nearby. The guards came out of their barracks, crossed the highway and began to take their positions. The comrade in charge of our squadron told Dionisio to cover our retreat. He said we'd have to try to get to the nearby houses. Dionisio was firing from behind the car and I was trying to make my way out, moving from position to position.

At one point when the two of us were together, I asked Dionisio what he thought our chances of escape were. "Look," he said, "forget it. There's no way out of this. We're surrounded. I don't see how we can break the circle they've thrown around us. So be prepared to die." We calculated between 150 and 200 guards in all. So that's just what we did, prepared to die.

We tried to save as much ammunition as we could, defending our positions and waiting for the Guard to move

*EEBI, *Escuela de Entrenamiento Basico de Infanteria:* Infantry Basic Training School. A special, repressive force of Green Beret-type troops headed by Dictator Anastasio Somoza's son.

in and finish us off. It was probably the other attacks that saved us. If ours had been an isolated action I don't think we could have escaped. But the Guard seemed disoriented. We heard their commander ordering them to advance, but they didn't. We could hear gunfire over by San Judas—the attack spot nearest us—and we realized that battles were taking place in different parts of the city.

I don't know why, but suddenly there seemed to be a sort of truce. No shots were fired. Five of us moved toward a small rocky area. We thought we were the only survivors and decided our best move was to try joining up with the comrades over at San Judas. We made our way through a hilly area behind us. The trail was very difficult, practically straight up. We spent all night trying to get through. At one point we came close to some houses but a couple of dogs smelled us coming from a kilometre away and barked every time we moved closer. That was as far as we made it that night.

There was a beautiful moon over the hills. I cursed it being so bright. One of the Guard's helicopters passed overhead but they didn't see us. We were all exhausted. I volunteered for the first guard duty. I spent the whole night awake. At dawn I woke the rest of the comrades. I had an idea how we might get away. I suggested I go out to the highway. I thought that being a woman they might believe me if I said I had been caught in the middle of the previous night's battle. If that worked I might be able to get help.

We discussed my plan. The comrades claimed that it would be obvious I had taken part in the battle. We were all dressed the same, dark pants and shirts. And that wasn't as much of a problem as the blood I'd got all over my clothing from bandaging that comrade's arm. The blood, combined with the mud I'd picked up from crawling along the ground, made an awful mess. The others thought the plan too risky but I was firm in my decision. Dionisio said

he wouldn't let me go alone, that he'd come with me. And
that's what happened. We went together, pretending we
were a couple who had been trapped in the cross-fire.

To Dionisio, Comrade

Nearer ourselves than we ourselves
now.
More than when flooded with objects we moved
among those people
                              always outsiders.

We have nourished with life words
never spoken before.
Nothing said now, without sustenance.
No longer can I write you passive poems
shaded by locust trees and garden's willows.

I have no window now to look upon the sun
                        lighting gentians.
Our life is different today. That life
we always spoke about
and slowly came to live.

Now that we are ourselves
                    with thousands of brothers and sisters.

Part II

ACTOR

5
POLEMICS

Introduction

The monologues in this section most fully address the issue of scale in performance. Whether or not they were actually spoken in public, all of them sound as if they are being delivered to a multitude, perhaps even generations into the future. Further, the women represented herein are not speaking, or writing, merely for themselves. Rather, each raises issues or represents principles that have a bearing on the lives of thousands or millions.

The reign of Egyptian Queen Hatshepsut is usually dated near the turn of the fifteenth century B.C., although controversial historian Immanuel Velikovsky has produced interesting evidence suggesting the possibility that she was the Queen of Sheba of King Solomon's day. In any case, her time was one of unprecedented peace and prosperity, immortalized in the inscriptions on the four pink Assuan granite obelisks she had installed at the temple of the god Amun at Karnak. In these inscriptions, for the edification of her then and future subjects, she glorifies the god, sings the praises of her earthly father and herself—as woman and king, the legitimate heir to the throne, and describes the composition of the obelisks and the rich gilding she has had applied to them.

If many have dramatized Joan of Arc's life and actions, her own words, as transcribed from the 1431 trial that led to her being burned at the stake, seem to speak most clearly and simply for the dedication of her life to God and country. I have compiled these excerpts from several sources to be used as a single monologue. There is a disjointed quality to the text because much of it is in response to the inquisitors' questions, so the actor has the useful option of imagining both interrogators and questions.

Anne Boleyn's and Anne Askewe's verses were also written near the time of their appointed executions. Boleyn, second wife of King Henry VIII and mother of Queen Elizabeth I, was charged with adultery and incest; she was beheaded in 1536. Whether the poem attributed to her was actually written by her is subject to question, but it does have an appealing directness. A less well known figure but unquestionably the author of the inspired vision *Like as the Armed Knight*, Anne Askewe, twenty-six, was found guilty of heresy and burnt at the stake ten years after Anne Boleyn's execution. She was described by a contemporary writer, a Mr. Loud: "I must needs confess of Mrs. Askewe, now departed to the Lord, that the day afore her execution, and the same day also, she had an angel's countenance and a smiling face; though when the hour of darkness came, she was so racked, that she could not stand, but was holden up between two serjeants." On being fastened to the stake, she was asked to recant, the royal pardon being offered her if she would do so. Her reply was "I do not come here to deny my Lord and Master."

Much as her father, King Henry VIII, had done, Elizabeth I fancied herself a poet. *Oh Fortune!*, a resentful indictment of her oppressors, was written before she became queen when, a victim of court politics, she was kept prisoner at Woodstock by her predecessor, Queen ("Bloody") Mary.

Education, frequently a topic central to women's concerns in the eighteenth and nineteenth centuries, informs the next three selections. First, Lady Montagu responds to her daughter's request for advice as to how to bring up her rather numerous family. Her notions on this subject are full of the clear but cold common sense which was one of her most striking characteristics. Especially noteworthy is the stoical recommendation to repress maternal anxiety and tenderness and prepare for the inevitable disappointments of a large family. Then, in our second excerpt from the semi-autobiographical epic *Aurora Leigh*, Elizabeth Barrett Browning catalogues her heroine's education, ending with a wry denunciation of the worth of women's "work." Miss Wentworth's story tells how she was coaxed into becoming a teacher. This narrative, being the culmination of her little book, *Life's Lessons*, was meant to provide a model of how to find a "high vocation" in this difficult and distracting world.

Partly because of her association with Dr. Johnson, who employed her as a reader and translator, Mary Wollstonecraft gained a position of some influence in English literary circles, and her *A Vindication of the Rights of Women* serves not merely as an outraged reply to the writings of French philosopher Jean-Jacques Rousseau, but also as a defense of the prerogative of every individual to flourish in his or her own right. The birth of her daughter Mary in 1797—she would become the second wife of the poet Shelley—proved fatal to her.

More recent advocates of women's rights include Boston's Maria W. Stewart, the first American-born woman to speak in public, and New York's suffragette Susan B. Anthony. Stewart addresses a great many issues, including Black heritage and the role of women in religion and history with graciousness and sensitivity in her 1833 farewell speech, *What If I Am a Woman?* Anthony's *On Woman's Right to Suffrage* was delivered in 1873, in response to her arrest the previous year for casting a ballot in the presidential election. It is a model of logic imbued with passion.

Deceptively dispassionate is Merle Woo's newsreel-style poem, *Whenever You're Cornered, the Only Way Out Is to Fight*. Be advised that under the cool, objective format must crouch genuine rage.

Queen Hatshepsut
Monument to Amun

I have built this monument with a loving heart for my father
   Amun;
Initiated in his secret of creation,
Acquainted with his beneficent power,
I did not forget his laws.
My majesty knows his divinity,
I acted under his command;
It was he who led me,
I contrived nothing without him.
It was he who gave directions,
I did not sleep because of his temple,
I did not stray from his commands.
My heart was at his disposal,
I entered into the designs of his heart.
I did not turn my back to the city of the Almighty,
Rather did I turn my face to it.
I know that his is the land of light on earth,
The exalted hill of creation,
The Sacred Eye of the Almighty,
His favorite, the place that bears his beauty,
That calls his followers.

It is I, the King himself who speaks:
I declare before future multitudes,
Who shall see the monument I made for my father,
Who shall speak in discussion,
Who shall look to posterity—
It was as I sat in the palace,
And thought of my maker,
That my heart caused me to make for him

Two obelisks of silvered gold,
Whose peaks would touch the heavens.
Now my heart hesitates,
Thinking what will people say,
They who shall see my monument in later years,
And speak of my deeds.
I swear, as I am loved of Re,
As Amun, my father, favors me,
As I am refreshed with life and sovereignty,
As I wear the white crown,
As I display the red crown,
As I rule this land like the son of Isis,
As I am mighty like the son of Nut,
As Re takes his rest in the ship of night,
As he awakes in the ship of day,
As he joins his two mothers in the god's ship,
As heaven endures, as his creation lasts,
As I shall be eternal like an undying star,
So these two great obelisks,
Without seam, without join,
Gilded with electrum by my majesty for my father Amun,
In order that my name may endure in this temple,
For everlasting eternity.
Say of this, "How like her it is,
She is devoted to her father!"
Lord Amun knows me well,
He made me ruler of Black Land and Red Land as reward,
No one rebels against me in all lands.
All foreign lands are my subjects,
He placed my border at the limits of heaven,
What Aten encircles labors for me.
He gave it to him who came from him,
Knowing I would rule it for him.
I am his daughter in very truth,

Who serves him, who knows his laws.
My reward from my father is my sovereignty,
On the Horus throne of all the living, eternally like Re.

Joan of Arc
Statements

Among my own people, I was called Jehanette; since my coming into France, I am called Jehanne.

I was born in the village of Domremy. My father's name is Jacques d'Arc, my mother's Isabelle.

As long as I lived at home, I worked at common tasks about the house, going but seldom afield with our sheep and other cattle. I learned to sew and spin: I fear no woman in Rouen at sewing and spinning.

As to my schooling, I learned my faith, and I was rightly and duly taught to do as a good child should.

From my mother I learned "Our Father," "Hail Mary," and "I believe." And my teaching in my faith I had from her and from no one else.

It is now seven years since the saints appeared to me for the first time. It was a summer day, around the hour of noon. I was scarcely thirteen years old, and I was in my father's garden. I heard a voice on my right, from the direction of the church; and I saw at the same time an apparition framed in brightness. It had the appearance of a beautiful and virtuous man, winged, surrounded on all sides by great light and accompanied by heavenly angels. It was the archangel Michael. He seemed to me to have a powerful voice, and I, still a young child, was terrified of this vision, unsure that it was really an angel. It was only after hearing that voice three times that I recognized it to be his. He taught me and showed me so many things that I finally believed firmly that it was he. I saw him—him and the angels—with my own eyes, as clearly as I see you—you, my judges.

Concerning my father and mother and what I have done since I took the road to France I will willingly swear to tell the truth. But the revelations which have come to me from God I have never told or revealed to anyone, except to Charles, my King. Nor would I reveal them if I were to be beheaded. A week from today I shall have learned whether I may reveal them.

I will not say the "Our Father" for you unless you will hear me in confession.

I protest against being kept in chains and irons.

I do not accept your prohibition. And if I escape from prison, no one can accuse me of breaking my faith, for I have pledged it to no one.

It is true that I have wished, and that I still wish, what is permissible for any captive: to escape!

Queen Anne Boleyn
Defiled Is My Name Full Sore

Defiled is my name full sore,
   Through cruel spite and false report,
That I may say, for evermore,
   Farewell, my joy! adieu, comfort!
For wrongfully ye judge of me,
   Unto my fame a mortal wound;
Say what ye list, it will not be,
   Ye seek for that cannot be found.

O Death! rock me on sleep!
   Bring me a quiet rest:
Let pass my very guiltless ghost
   Out of my careful breast:
Toll on the passing bell,
Ring out the doleful knell,
Let the sound my death tell,
   For I must die,
   There is no remedy,
   For now I die.

Farewell my pleasures past,
   Welcome my present pain;
I feel my torments so increase,
   That life cannot remain.
Cease now the passing bell,
Rung is my doleful knell,
For the sound my death doth tell:
   Death doth draw nigh,
   Sound my end dolefully,
   For now I die.

Anne Askewe
Like as the Armed Knight

Like as the armed knight
   Appointed to the field,
With this world will I fight,
   And faith shall be my shield.

Thou say'st, Lord, whoso knock,
   To them wilt thou attend;
Undo therefore the lock,
   And thy strong power send.

I am not she that list
   My anchor to let fall;
For every drizzling mist,
   My ship substantial.

Not oft I use to write
   In prose nor yet in rhyme,
Yet will I show one sight
   That I saw in my time.

I saw a royal throne
   Where Justice should have sit,
But in her stead was one
   Of moody cruel wit.

Absorb'd was righteousness
   As of the raging flood:
Satan in his excess
   Suck'd up the guiltless blood.

Then thought I, Jesus, Lord,
   When thou shalt judge us all,

Hard is it to record
    On these men what will fall.

Yet Lord, I thee desire,
    For that they do to me,
Let them not taste the hire
    Of their iniquity!

—————

Queen Elizabeth I
Oh Fortune!

Oh, Fortune! how thy restless wavering state
    Hath fraught with cares my troubled wit!
Witness this present prison, whither fate
    Could bear me, and the joys I quit:
Thou causedest the guilty to be loos'd
From bands, wherein are innocents inclos'd:
    Causing the guiltless to be strait reserv'd,
    And freeing those that death had well deserv'd.
But by her envy can be nothing wrought,
So God send to my foes all they have thought.

Lady Mary Wortley Montagu
Thoughts on Education
(Response to a request for advice
from her daughter, Lady Bute)

My Dear Child:—People commonly educate their children as they build their houses, according to some plan they think beautiful, without considering whether it is suited to the purposes for which they are designed. Almost all girls of quality are educated as if they were to be great ladies, which is often as little to be expected, as an immoderate heat of the sun in the north of Scotland. You should teach yours to confine their desires to probabilities, to be as useful as is possible to themselves, and to think privacy (as it is) the happiest state of life. I do not doubt your giving them all the instructions necessary to form them to a virtuous life, but 'tis a fatal mistake to do this without proper restrictions. Vices are often hid under the name of virtues, and the practice of them followed by the worst of consequences. Sincerity, friendship, piety, disinterestedness, and generosity are all great virtues, but, pursued without discretion, become criminal. I have seen ladies indulge their own ill humour by being very rude and impertinent, and think they deserved approbation by saying, "I love to speak truth." One of your acquaintance made a ball the next day after her mother died, to show she was sincere. I believe your own reflection will furnish you with but too many examples of the ill effects of the rest of the sentiments I have mentioned, when too warmly embraced. They are generally recommended to young people without limits or distinction, and this prejudice hurries them into great misfortunes, while they are applauding themselves in the noble practice (as they fancy) of very eminent virtues.

I cannot help adding (out of my real affection to you), I

wish you would moderate that fondness you have for your children. I do not mean you should abate any part of your care, or not do your duty to them in its utmost extent; but I would have you early prepare yourself for disappointments, which are heavy in proportion to their being surprising. It is hardly possible, in such a number, that none should be unhappy; prepare yourself against misfortune of that kind. Strictly speaking, there is but one real evil—I mean, acute pain; all other complaints are so considerably diminished by time, that it is plain the grief is owing to our passion, since the sensation of it vanishes when that is over.

There is another mistake usual in mothers: If any of their daughters are beauties, they take great pains to persuade them that they are ugly, or at least that they think so, which the young woman never fails to believe springs from envy, and is, perhaps, not much in the wrong. I would, if possible, give them a just notion of their figure, and show them how far it is valuable. Every advantage has its price, and may be either over or undervalued. It is the common doctrine of (what are called) good books, to inspire a contempt of beauty, riches, greatness, etc., which has done as much mischief among the younger of our sex as an over-eager desire of them.

Elizabeth Barrett Browning
An Englishwoman's Education

I learnt the collects and the catechism,
The creeds, from Athanasius back to Nice,
The Articles, the Tracts *against* the times
(By no means Bonaventure's "Prick of Love"),
And various popular synopses of
Inhuman doctrines never taught by John,
Because she liked instructed piety.
I learnt my complement of classic French
(Kept pure of Balzac and neologism)
And German also, since she liked a range
Of liberal education,—tongues, not books.
I learned a little algebra, a little
Of the mathematics,—brushed with extreme flounce
The circle of the sciences, because
She misliked women who are frivolous.
I learnt the royal genealogies
Of Oviedo, the internal laws
Of the Burmese empire,—by how many feet
Mount Chimborazo outsoars Teneriffe,
What navigable river joins itself
To Lara, and what census of the year five
Was taken at Klagenfurt,—because she liked
A general insight into useful facts.
I learnt much music,—such as would have been
As quite impossible in Johnson's day
As still it might be wished—fine sleights of hand
And unimagined fingering, shuffling off
The hearer's soul through hurricanes of notes
To a noisy Tophet; and I drew . . . costumes
From French engravings, nereids neatly draped
(With smirks of simmering godship): I washed in

Landscapes from nature (rather say, washed out).
I danced the polka and Cellarius,
Spun glass, stuffed birds, and modelled flowers in wax,
Because she liked accomplishments in girls.
I read a score of books on womanhood
To prove, if women do not think at all,
They may teach thinking (to a maiden aunt
Or else the author),—books that boldly assert
Their right of comprehending husband's talk
When not too deep, and even of answering
With pretty "may it please you," or "so it is"—
Their rapid insight and fine aptitude,
Particular worth and general missionariness,
As long as they keep quiet by the fire
And never say "no" when the world says "ay,"
For that is fatal,—their angelic reach
Of virtue, chiefly used to sit and darn,
And fatten household sinners,—their, in brief,
Potential faculty in everything
Of abdicating power in it: she owned
She liked a woman to be womanly,
And English women, she thanked God and sighed
(Some people always sigh in thanking God),
Were models to the universe. And last
I learnt cross-stitch, because she did not like
To see me wear the night with empty hands
A-doing nothing. So, my shepherdess
Was something after all (the pastoral saints
Be praised for't), leaning lovelorn with pink eyes
To match her shoes, when I mistook the silks;
Her head uncrushed by that round weight of hat
So strangely similar to the tortoise-shell
Which slew the tragic poet.

                              By the way,
The works of women are symbolical.

We sew, prick our fingers, dull our sight,
Producing what? A pair of slippers, sir,
To put on when you're weary—or a stool
To stumble over and vex you . . . "curse that stool!"
Or else at best, a cushion, where you lean
And sleep, and dream of something we are not
But would be for your sake. Alas, alas!
This hurts most, this—that, after all, we are paid
The worth of our work, perhaps.

Miss Wentworth
from *Life's Lessons*

"How fortunate you are in having these little children about you," said Miss Elliott to me one day; "children are always interesting."

"Do you think so? I am not fond of children."

"Oh, yes, pardon me, my dear Miss Wentworth, I am sure you are fond of children; you looked so pleased yesterday when little Fanny threw her arms around your neck, and kissed you for showing and explaining to her the pictures in your album. I am sure you are fond of children, though you may not know it yourself."

And so I was; but the habit of repeating the contrary assertion had prevented my really perceiving the interest which had lately been awakened in me towards the children, and I envied Miss Elliott the power she possessed of transforming them into tractable and intelligent beings.

Half with the desire of imitating her, and half as an experiment upon my own power of winning their love, I made efforts to interest and amuse them, none of which went unnoticed or unencouraged. She would remark to me

how delighted the children were with my music, and my
little drawings for their scrap-books; and, above all, she
endeavoured to raise me in the opinion of the children, by
referring them to me for explanations of things that came
within my province, so that my self-respect was raised, and
I began to feel a before unknown pleasure in this application
of attainments, which for so long had lain neglected and
useless.

Gradually dawned upon my mind the perception of the
high vocation which it was in my power to fill, in the education of these children. They were naturally intelligent
and quick. There was nothing wrong in their dispositions
but what resulted from bad management and over-indulg-
ence. What a noble employment would then be the ex-
panding of their intellects, the exercising of their faculties,
and the gradual softening of their tempers and manners!
Miss Elliott thought this, and she led me to perceive how
much in so doing I should increase my own happiness, and
how, the opportunity for such usefulness having once become manifest, and the power of performing it acknowledged, its fulfillment became a religious duty.

Mary Wollstonecraft
from *A Vindication of the Rights of Woman*

Women are, therefore, to be considered either as moral beings, or so weak that they must be entirely subjected to the superior faculties of men.

Let us examine this question. Rousseau declares, that a woman should never, for a moment feel herself independent, that she should be governed by fear to exercise her *natural* cunning, and made a coquettish slave in order to render her a more alluring object of desire, a *sweeter* companion to man, whenever he chooses to relax himself. He carries the arguments, which he pretends to draw from the indications of nature, still further, and insinuates that truth and fortitude the cornerstones of all human virtue, shall be cultivated with certain restrictions, because with respect to the female character, obedience is the grand lesson which ought to be impressed with unrelenting rigour.

What nonsense! When will a great man arise with sufficient strength of mind to puff away the fumes which pride and sensuality have thus spread over the subject! If women are by nature inferior to men, their virtues must be the same in quality, if not in degree, or virtue is a relative idea; consequently, their conduct should be founded on the same principles and have the same aim.

Connected with man as daughters, wives, and mothers, their moral character may be estimated by their manner of fulfilling those simple duties; but the end, the grand end of their exertions should be to unfold their own faculties, and acquire the dignity of conscious virtue. They may try to render their road pleasant; but ought never to forget, in common with man, that life yields not the felicity which can satisfy an immortal soul. I do not mean to insinuate, that either sex should be so lost, in abstract reflections or distant views, as to forget the affections and duties that lie before them, and are in truth, the means appointed to produce the fruit of life; on the contrary, I would warmly recommend them, even while I assert, that they afford most satisfaction when they are considered in their true subordinate light.

Maria W. Stewart
from *What If I Am a Woman?*

What if I am a woman; is not the God of ancient times the God of these modern days? Did he not raise up Deborah to be a mother and a judge in Israel? Did not Queen Esther save the lives of the Jews? And Mary Magdalene first declare the resurrection of Christ from the dead? Come, said the woman of Samaria, and see a man that hath told me all things that ever I did; is not this the Christ? St. Paul declared that it was a shame for a woman to speak in public, yet our great High Priest and Advocate did not condemn the woman for a more notorious offense than this; neither will he condemn this worthless worm . . . Did St. Paul but know of our wrongs and deprivations, I presume he would make no objection to our pleading in public for our rights . . .

Among the Greeks, women delivered the oracles. The respect the Romans paid to the Sybils is well known. The Jews had their prophetesses. The prediction of the Egyptian women obtained much credit at Rome, even unto the emperors. And in most barbarous nations all things that have the appearance of being supernatural, the mysteries of religion, the secrets of physic, and the rites of magic, were in the possession of women.

If such women as are here described have once existed, be no longer astonished, then, my brethren and friends, that God at this eventful period should raise up your own females to strive by their example, both in public and private, to assist those who are endeavoring to stop the strong current of prejudice that flows so profusely against us at present. No longer ridicule their efforts, it will be counted for sin. For God makes use of feeble means sometimes to bring about his most exalted purposes.

In the fifteenth century, the general spirit of this period is worthy of observation. We might then have seen women preaching and mixing themselves in controversies. Women occupying the chairs of Philosophy and Justice; women haranguing in Latin before the Pope; women writing in Greek and studying in Hebrew; nuns were poetesses and women of quality divines; and young girls who had studied eloquence would, with the sweetest countenances and the most plaintiff voices, pathetically exhort the Pope and the Christian princes to declare war against the Turks. Women in those days devoted their leisure hours to contemplation and study. The religious spirit which has animated women in all ages showed itself at this time. It has made them, by turns, martyrs, apostles, warriors, and concluded in making them divines and scholars. . . .

What if such women as are here described should rise among our sable race? And it is not impossible; for it is not the color of the skin that makes the man or the woman, but the principle formed in the soul. Brilliant wit will shine, come from whence it will; and genius and talent will not hide the brightness of its lustre. . . .

Men of eminence have mostly risen from obscurity; nor will I, although a female of a darker hue, and far more obscure than they, bend my head or hang my harp upon willows; for though poor, I will virtuous prove. And if it is the will of my Heavenly Father to reduce me to penury and want, I am ready to say: Amen, even so be it.

Susan B. Anthony
On Woman's Right to Suffrage

Friends and fellow citizens:—I stand before you to-night under indictment for the alleged crime of having voted at the last presidential election, without having a lawful right to vote. It shall be my work this evening to prove to you that in thus voting, I not only committed no crime, but, instead, simply exercised my *citizen's rights*, guaranteed to me and all United States citizens by the National Constitution, beyond the power of any State to deny.

The preamble of the Federal Constitution says:

"We, the people of the United States, in order to form a more perfect union, establish justice, insure *domestic* tranquillity, provide for the common defense, promote the general welfare, and secure the blessings of liberty to ourselves and our posterity, do ordain and establish this Constitution for the United States of America."

It was we, the people; not we, the white male citizens; nor yet we, the male citizens; but we, the whole people, who formed the Union. And we formed it, not to give the blessings of liberty, but to secure them; not to the half of ourselves and the half of our posterity, but to the whole people—women as well as men. And it is a downright mockery to talk to women of their enjoyment of the blessings of liberty while they are denied the use of the only means of securing them provided by this democratic-republican government—the ballot.

For any State to make sex a qualification that must ever result in the disenfranchisement of one entire half of the people is to pass a bill of attainder, or an *ex post facto* law, and is therefore a violation of the supreme law of the land. By it the blessings of liberty are for ever withheld from women and their female posterity. To them this government has no just powers derived from the consent of the governed. To them this government is not a democracy. It is not a republic. It is an odious aristocracy; a hateful oligarchy of sex; the most hateful aristocracy ever established on the face of the globe; an oligarchy of wealth, where the rich govern the poor. An oligarchy of learning, where the educated govern the ignorant, or even an oligarchy of race, where the Saxon rules the African, might be endured; but this oligarchy of sex, which makes father, brothers, husband, sons, the oligarchs over the mother and sisters, the wife and daughters of every household—which ordains all men sovereigns, all women subjects, carries dissension, discord and rebellion into every home of the nation.

Webster, Worcester and Bouvier all define a citizen to be a person in the United States, entitled to vote and hold office.

The only question left to be settled now is: Are women persons? And I hardly believe any of our opponents will have the hardihood to say they are not. Being persons, then, women are citizens; and no State has a right to make any law, or to enforce any old law, that shall abridge their privileges or immunities. Hence, every discrimination against women in the constitutions and laws of the several States is to-day null and void, precisely as is every one against negroes.

Merle Woo
Whenever You're Cornered,
the Only Way Out Is to Fight

Karen, comrade and sister poet, sends me this news
    article
about a woman warrior.
She includes a note that says:
    "We've got her philosophy and her strength, too.
    "We'll get them all by the ears and let them have
        it."

The article is one I've been wanting
to slip into speeches, talks, poems, conversations.
The images we get from reality—
Those fighting-back images in the face of great adversity.

I saw another news article of the Voting Rights marchers.
Their banner, red, black and green—for Black liberation,
carried by Carrie Graves of Richmond, VA—mother of
    five teenagers.
Carrie says:
    "My arms are tired, my feet have blisters,
        but I'm fired up!"

So, what is *this* article?
The reporter must have loved writing it, the way it came
    out:

Beijing

    A crippled grandmother caught a leopard by the
    ears, dragged it to the ground and then helped kill it
    with her bare hands, official reports said Tuesday.

Qi Deying, who can barely walk because her feet were bound from birth, was gathering herbs with her niece and grandchildren on a mountain in North China's Shaanxi Province when the six-foot leopard attacked her and sank his teeth into her arm.

But the animal soon realized he had bitten off more than he could chew.

The 77-year-old Qi grabbed the leopard by the ears, wedged its jaw shut with her right shoulder and forced it to the ground, the Shaanxi Daily said.

Their bodies locked in combat, the grandmother and the leopard rolled more than 120 feet down the mountainside, bouncing off rocks before coming to rest in a wheatfield.

Qi called out to her grandchildren, who were hiding behind a boulder, to come to her aid. They tore branches off a tree and helped her beat the animal to death.

Qi, only bruised, told the paper: "Whenever you're cornered, the only way out is to fight."

6
CHOICES
Introduction

Not all of life's choices are prompted by adversity, but one does get a sense from these nineteen selections that the very act of choosing can be painful, or at best highly disruptive.

The distinction between freedom and bondage is rarely as well documented as in these first selections. During the latter portion of the nineteenth century, the prostitution business in San Francisco and elsewhere was fed by a continuous influx of young girls imported from the Orient and indentured into a particularly nasty form of slavery. Loi Yau's *Agreement* is a bill of sale typical of the period, meticulous in its detail. Jane Johnson's *Affidavit* records the opposite route, a woman seizing her freedom when opportunity presents itself. Both monologues should be read simply and steadily, with few or no pauses. The run-on quality suggested by the punctuation of Johnson's speech especially reinforces this.

The difficulties of growing up amidst the relatively oppressive mores of nineteenth-century Scotland are presented in the *Daily Diary* of Marjorie Fleming, who died of meningitis in 1811, before her tenth birthday. At once naive and cunning, she was a favorite of Mark Twain's, and he wrote of her that she "was made out of thunder-storms and sunshine, and not even her little perfunctory pieties and shop-made holiness could squelch her spirits or put out her fires for long."

School is Susan Hale's bugbear, as she exhaustively enumerates every curricular detail of her voyage upon the "sea of education." Kate Ryan's brush with the world of the dance, although told in a memoir and so lacking the impertinence of Hale's letter, benefits from a sense of calm nostalgia.

There is nothing calm about Helen Ward Brandreth's "courtship diary." She fully captures the confusions, dilemmas, and guilts that can be such a major part of a twenty-year-old's experience. Member of a prominent Ossining ("Sing Sing"), New York family, she writes with a rare immediacy, confessing her errors to Fanny Fern, the name she has given her diary, quite likely inspired by novelist Sarah Willis Parton who wrote under that name.

If not always actively at odds with their social environment, many women seem to be nevertheless engaged in a struggle to define and understand it. Thus Mrs. Mary Robinson is astonished to find her own comfortable standing in such contrast to that of the once accomplished, now wretched Mrs. Lorrington, who succumbed to drink. And Jane Carlyle, in a merry speculation on "principles," admires a famous murderer for his triumph of character, thereby redefining herself and placing herself somehow beyond the social pale as well.

Joanna L. Stratton's *Voices from the Kansas Frontier,* as her book *Pioneer Women* is subtitled, speak of genuine hardship and courage. There is a sense here of character being shaped by environment and great pride is taken in the accomplishments of family. These are stories that have been told again and again, and, hardship notwithstanding, there is a joy in the telling that needs to be present at all times.

Harsher still is Martha Martin's story of survival in the Alaskan wilderness in the 1920s. Pregnant, separated from her husband by an avalanche that nearly kills her and leaves her seriously wounded, she manages to enjoy the role of a female Crusoe, sending out challenges to the world at large and eating her illegal otter liver with gusto.

In Donna Redmond's story we meet another kind of survivor, also proud, but challenged now by the people and attitudes of the new urban culture. She's pugnacious, secure in her world, and speaks with a conversational ease in rich contrast to the powerful statements she makes.

Studs Terkel's oral histories are a tremendous resource for both monologues and plain human understanding. Although *Working* has been adapted for the musical stage, I am including a portion of hooker Roberta Victor's indictment of American women. In my teaching of public speaking and other disciplines, she has been a favorite among my students, and men as well as women have chosen to speak her words.

In *The Great Divide*, Terkel interviews people on the down side, at odds with "the American Dream." Carolyn Nearmyer's life is the threatened farm that surrounds her, and that presence, even to her daughter's peeking in during the interview, is the source of her anger and fear. For Jean Gump, too, the feisty grandmother with a mission—she occupied a missile silo, detail is important, and her story is filled with a rich humor born of absurd contrasts.

Dr. Jane Hodgson also has a mission, the care of other women, and it is her anger that drives her to acts of courage. But note that this is a very specific anger, fed by her experiences of Catholicism and understood through the vocabulary of the medical profession. For Zahrah Muhammad, a rural Moroccan woman, courage lies in choosing a husband rather than accepting the one chosen for her. Her story is bursting with action and color, clearly conveying the woman's determination, energy, and humor.

Isolation, elected or imposed, requires its own brand of courage. During a student demonstration and the ensuing violence, militant revolutionary Carmen Prado must deny herself open solidarity with her compatriots. Unbeknownst to the young student who tried to defend Prado until "she discovered I was a cop," Prado was in fact a member of the FSLN working undercover as a policewoman in the National Guard.

Loi Yau
An Agreement to Assist a Young Girl

Because she became indebted to her mistress for passage, food, etc., and has nothing to pay, she makes her body over to the woman, Sep Sam, to serve as a prostitute to make out the sum of five hundred and three dollars. The money shall draw no interest, and Loi Yau shall serve four and one-half years. On this day of agreement, Loi Yau receives the sum of five hundred and three dollars in her own hands. When the time is out, Loi Yau may be her own master, and no man shall trouble her. If she runs away before the time is out, and any expense is incurred in catching her, then Loi Yau must pay the expense. If she is sick fifteen days or more, she shall make up one month for every fifteen days. If Sep Sam shall go back to China, then Loi Yau shall serve another party till her time is out; if, in such service, she should be sick one hundred days or more, and cannot be cured, she may return to Sep Sam's place. For a proof of this agreement, this paper.

Dated second, sixth month of the present year.

Jane Johnson
Affidavit and Testimony,
State of New York,
City and County of New York, July 1855

Jane Johnson being sworn, makes oath and says—

My name is Jane—Jane Johnson: I was the slave of Mr.
Wheeler of Washington; he bought me and my two children, about two years ago, from Mr. Cornelius Crew, of
Richmond, Va.; my youngest child is between six and seven
years old, the other between ten and eleven; I have one
other child only, and he is in Richmond; I have not seen
him for about two years; never expect to see him again;
Mr. Wheeler brought me and my two children to Philadelphia, on the way to Nicaragua, to wait on his wife; I
didn't want to go without my two children, and he consented to take them; we came to Philadelphia by the cars;
stopped at Mr. Sully's, Mr. Wheeler's father-in-law, a few
moments; then went to the steamboat for New York at 2
o'clock, but were too late; we went into Bloodgood's Hotel;
Mr. Wheeler went to dinner; Mr. Wheeler had told me in
Washington to have nothing to say to colored persons, and
if any of them spoke with me, to say I was a free woman
traveling with a minister; we staid at Bloodgood's till 5
o'clock; Mr. Wheeler kept his eye on me all the time except
when he was at dinner; he left his dinner to come and see
if I was safe, and then went back again; while he was at
dinner, I saw a colored woman and told her I was a slave
woman, that my master had told me not to speak to colored
people, and that if any of them spoke to me to say that I
was free; but I am not free; but I want to be free; she said:
"poor thing, I pity you;" after that I saw a colored man and
said the same thing to him, he said he would telegraph to
New York, and two men would meet me at 9 o'clock and

take me with them; after that we went on board the boat, Mr. Wheeler sat beside me on the deck; I saw a colored gentleman come on board, he beckoned to me; I nodded my head, and could not go; Mr. Wheeler was beside me and I was afraid; a white gentleman then came and said to Mr. Wheeler, "I want to speak to your servant, and tell her of her rights;" Mr. Wheeler rose and said, "If you have anything to say, say it to me—she knows her rights;" the white gentleman asked me if I wanted to be free; I said "I do, but I belong to this gentleman and I can't have it;" he replied, "Yes, you can, come with us, you are as free as your master, if you want your freedom come now; if you go back to Washington you may never get it;" I rose to go, Mr. Wheeler spoke, and said, "I will give you your freedom," but he had never promised it before, and I knew he would never give it to me; the white gentleman held out his hand and I went toward him; I was ready for the word before it was given me; I took the children by the hands, who both cried, for they were frightened, but both stopped when they got on shore; a colored man carried the little one, I led the other by the hand. We walked down the street till we got to a hack; nobody forced me away; nobody pulled me, and nobody led me; I went away of my own free will; I always wished to be free and meant to be free when I came North; I hardly expected it in Philadelphia, but I thought I should get free in New York; I have been comfortable and happy since I left Mr. Wheeler, and so are the children; I don't want to go back; I could have gone in Philadelphia if I had wanted to; I could go now; but I had rather die than go back. I wish to make this statement before a magistrate, because I understand that Mr. Williamson is in prison on my account, and I hope the truth may be of benefit to him.

Marjory Fleming
from *Daily Diary, 1810*

I confess that I have been
more like a little young
Devil then a creature for
when Isabella went up
to stairs to teach me religion and my multi-
plication and to be good
and all my other lessons
I stamped with my feet
and threw my new hat
which she made on the
ground and was sulky and
was dreadfuly passionate
but she never whipped me
but gently said Marjory
go into another room and
think what a great crime
you are committing
letting your temper
git the better of you
but I went so sulkely that
the Devil got the better of me
but she never whip
me so that I think I would
be the better of it and the
next time that I behave
ill I think she should do it . . . .

The weather is very mild
& serene & not like winter
A sailor called here to say

farewell, it must be dread-
full to leave his native country
where he might get a wife
or perhaps me, for I love
him very much & with
all my heart, but O I
forgot Isabella forbid me to
speak about love . . .
. . . Isabella is always reading &
writing in her room & does not
come down for long & I wish every
body would follow her example
& be as good as pious & virtuous as
she is & they would get husbands
soon enough, love is a very
papithatick thing as well as
troubelsom & tiresome but O
Isabella forbid me to speak
about it . . .

Susan Hale
School-Days

Sunday Evening, *October 14, 1849*

I am now fairly launched on the sea of education, or school. I go daily from nine till two. You may be interested in knowing my course of study. In the first place, I write an abstract every Sunday of the sermon of Sunday morning. This is for Monday morning's lesson. At school I learn a lesson from "Viri Romae" and recite in Colburn's "Mental Arithmetic." I don't *study* the lessons in this latter branch, but we are supposed to know it by intuition, and every day are plied with it by Mr. Emerson. We get up and down in this class. I vary, being sometimes within three of the head, occasionally, though rarely, equally near the foot, of the class. We learn an evening lesson in zoology for every day but Monday and Saturday. The book is Agassiz and Gould's "Zoology" and treats of diverse subjects referring to the animal kingdom—such as the vertebrate animals, mollusks, mammals, etc., and if you were here I could logically expound to you that man, as well as many other *vertebrate* animals, is possessed of a *carpus* and a *metacarpus*, also a *tarsus* and a *metatarsus*. This highly instructive and interesting work is replete with pictures. . . . I study "Viri Romae" every day but Friday and Saturday. Friday is French day, and then I study a French translation book called Bonnechose's "History of France," and next week I am to begin Ollendorf's Exercises. Saturday we learn poetry, and as soon as we have recited that, we are at liberty to go home, so that yesterday I got home before eleven. Other days I do not get home till after two sometimes. Professor Gould comes several times a week to give us lectures, and explains what we have gone over in zoology, and brings with him in a bundle monkeys' skulls, and *Polypi*, a marine animal. . . .

Kate Ryan
The Little Red Shoes

At one time I was ambitious to become a ballet dancer. The idea presented itself after seeing the Rigl Sisters dance, and on my way home, I saw stage dancing advertised at fifty cents a lesson. After considering the matter carefully, I decided to make the plunge, and invested one dollar in two lessons. During the interview a pair of spangled red shoes was presented to my view; for another dollar I might possess them. Though they were much worn,—though carefully darned,—and my feet were somewhat cramped in them, nevertheless they were little red shoes with spangles. To me they were very beautiful,—and for one dollar they would be my very own! On my next visit I bought them, but I had some difficulty in enjoying my little red shoes, as my family were not aware of my ambition to become a ballet dancer. After retiring to my room at night, I would place them first on the chair near my bed, so I could admire them by lamplight, then tie them on the bedpost, and often even get out of bed after I had put out my light, and strike a match in order again to admire them. Several falls in the seclusion of my chamber, however, convinced me that nature never intended me for a ballet dancer.

Helen Ward Brandreth
"I have determined to keep a journal.
I shall call it Fannie Fern."

Vine Cottage, *Sept. 17th, 1882*

Dear Fan:—At the Theatre Party Thursday night I saw Jim and his Mother! O dear, every time I get satisfied without him I meet him again and then I realize what I have lost out of my life. It made me miserable to see him; twice they played, "We sat by the river, you and I, in the sweet summertime long ago!" Poor Sweetheart, it was hard on us both. He came to Sing Sing next day, but I did not see him. Only I was so unhappy! O how I longed to send for him, to put my arms around his neck and be forgiven, but I *could* not. What a mistake my life has been. I wish now I had married him in "80" before I ever saw Zete or mistrusted my Sweetheart or myself. I know I would have made it up if I had been sure of him. Ralph says he is sure he cares for me, but he did act dreadfully with Miss Howard and then he rarely wrote me and never even sent me a line at Christmas or my birthday. Little things but they all count. I hope after a time I won't care; only now I am miserable. I don't know what I want for I don't suppose I would marry him even now. The Cavalry is so terribly hard. I have lost faith in everything, myself included. I utterly despise myself! O dear, I am such a *fool!* How could I have been in love with *two* men, and yet I have been miserable about them both. However, I honestly believe I have gotten over my fancy for Zete. I wish I were entirely different. I am so weak. O! I blame myself bitterly for the way I have acted. I never told you much about the way I acted with John Shober. I am so ashamed of it and I knew how wrong it was at the time, but he used to beg me so. He held my hand ever so many times; once he caught me in his arms;

and twice, another time, he kissed my hair. But worse than anything else is that one night when his head was close to my arm, I bent and kissed it twice. O it is so dreadful. How could I so far forget myself. I hate fast women and I intended to keep myself pure and free from stain. And yet *how* I have fallen! It must have been because I trusted in my own strength, and did not beg God to help me. Oh, I have fallen so far short of what I reached after. I have drifted away from God and am growing a wicked, careless woman. I hope and pray I will become different. To think of one of Mother's children doing such a thing! How grieved she would have been. It must be a dreadful sin for I worry so about it. I have made a vow that with God's help I will never let a man so much as touch my hand again.

Mrs. Mary Robinson
A Propensity to Intoxication

Shortly after my mother had established herself at Chelsea, on a summer's evening, as I was sitting at the window, I heard a deep sigh, or rather a groan of anguish, which suddenly attracted my attention. The night was approaching rapidly, and I looked toward the gate before the house, where I observed a woman evidently labouring under excessive affliction; I instantly descended and approached her. She, bursting into tears, asked whether I did not know her. Her dress was torn and filthy; she was almost naked; and an old bonnet, which nearly hid her face, so completely disfigured her features that I had not the smallest idea of the person who was then almost sinking before me. I gave her a small sum of money, and inquired the cause of her apparent agony. She took my hand and pressed it to her lips. "Sweet girl," she said, "you are still the angel I ever knew you!" I was astonished. She raised her bonnet—her fine dark eyes met mine. It was Mrs. Lorrington. I led her into the house; my mother was not at home. I took her into my chamber, and, with the assistance of a lady who was our French teacher, I clothed and comforted her. She refused to say how she came to be in so deplorable a situation, and took her leave. It was in vain that I entreated her to let me know where I might send to her. She refused to give me her address, but promised that in a few days she would call on me again. It is impossible to describe the wretched appearance of this accomplished woman! The failing to which she had now yielded, as to a monster that would destroy her, was evident even at the moment when she was speaking to me. I saw no more of her; but to my infinite regret, I was informed some years after that she had died, the martyr of a premature decay, brought on by the indulgence of her propensity to intoxication, in the workhouse of Chelsea!

Jane Welsh Carlyle
Letter to John Sterling

My very *beau-idéal* of manhood is that Paul Giordano; could I hear the like of him existing anywhere in these degenerate times, I would, even at this late stage of the business— send him—my picture! and an offer of my heart and hand for the next world, since they are already disposed of in this. Ah! what a man that must be, who can strangle his young, beautiful wife with his own hands, and, bating one moment of conventional horror, inspire not the slightest feeling of aversion or distrust! When a man strangles his wife nowadays he does it brutally, in drink, or in passion, or in revenge; to transact such a work coolly, nobly, on the loftiest principles, to strangle with dignity because the woman "was unworthy of him", that indeed is a triumph of character which places Giordano above all the heroes of ancient and modern times; which makes me almost weep that I was not born two centuries earlier, that I might have been—his mistress—not his wife!

S. N. Hoisington
Wolves at the Door

A man by the name of Johnson had filed on a claim just west of us, and had built a sod house. He and his wife lived there two years, when he went to Salina to secure work. He was gone two or three months, and wrote home once or twice, but his wife grew very homesick for her folks in the east, and would come over to our house to visit mother.

Mother tried to cheer her up, but she continued to worry until she got bed fast with the fever. At night she was frightened because the wolves would scratch on the door, on the sod and on the windows, so my mother and I started to sit up nights with her. I would bring my revolver and ammunition and axe, and some good-sized clubs.

The odor from the sick woman seemed to attract the wolves, and they grew bolder and bolder. I would step out, fire off the revolver and they would settle back for a while when they would start a new attack. I shot one through the window and found him lying dead in the morning.

Finally the woman died and mother laid her out. Father took some wide boards that we had in our loft and made a coffin for her. Mother made a pillow and trimmed it with black cloth, and we also painted the coffin black.

After that the wolves were more determined than ever to get in. One got his head in between the door casing and as he was trying to wriggle through, mother struck him in the head with an axe and killed him. I shot one coming through the window. After that they quieted down for about half an hour, when they came back again. I stepped out and fired at two of them but I only wounded one. Their howling was awful. We fought these wolves five nights in succession, during which time we killed and wounded four gray wolves and two coyotes.

When Mr. Johnson arrived home and found his wife dead and his house badly torn down by wolves he fainted away. . . . After the funeral he sold out and moved away.

Annette Lecleve Botkin
An Undependable Sort of Bird

It was the last of July, and my father was thinking of the long winter ahead, and perhaps the blizzards to come. And at that time there was not a tree in sight. The little four-room frame house (at that time the only frame house in the county) had to be kept warm, for there were a couple of little children already in the home and the stork was expected to make his appearance again in a short time. So my father arose early and started on his all-day trip to Mule Creek to get a load of wood. Mule Creek was about seventeen miles away.

He had no sooner gotten out of sight, than my mother knew that the stork, being an undependable sort of bird, had decided that it was time to leave his precious bundle. Now that was a terrifying situation. Alone with two babies, one four and the other eighteen months, not a neighbor that could be called, no doctor to be gotten.

So my brave mother got the baby clothes together on a chair by the bed, water and scissors and what else was needed to take care of the baby; drew a bucket of fresh water from a sixty-foot well; made some bread-and-butter sandwiches; set out some milk for the babies. And when Rover had orders to take care of the babies he never let them out of his sight, for at that time any bunch of weeds might harbor a rattlesnake.

So, at about noon the stork left a fine baby boy. My

father arrived home about dusk with a big load of wood and congratulating himself that he would at least have some wood to burn on very cold days. My mother, having fainted a number of times in her attempt to dress the baby, had succeeded at last; and when my father came in he found a very uncomfortable but brave and thankful mother, thankful that he had returned home with the precious wood, and that she and the baby were alright.

Lavina Gates Chapman
Blow the Building Down

The first Presbyterian Church was built at Lindsey, and they received as many contributions from the Methodists as from the Presbyterians. They got the church enclosed and the Methodists were to have every alternate sabbath. They needed more money to furnish the building, so they nailed boards to the windows and decided to raise what was needed by giving a dance and had all in readiness when I told them I would pray to the Lord to blow the building down rather than to dedicate it with a dance. Oh, the burden that was in me that day, and it was as beautiful a day as I ever saw, but just before night there came up a storm and laid the building down to the ground.

So they wanted us to give more money. Well, they got the building up again and, of course, would still have their dances now in spite of the elements. Another beautiful day and the cooking and preparations were all done. Of course a few do not amount to much, but we could talk to God and he had said, "Whatsoever you ask it shall be, do we ask in faith, believing," and I asked that the building might be blown to the four winds.

Oh, such a beautiful day as it had been. All was in readiness and I said, "Lord, Lord, will you let them dedicate it with a dance?" Just before dark a storm came and some of the church went east, some north, some west and some south, the ground where the church had stood was swept as clean as if it had been swept and they never got the pieces together again. Houses were moved off their foundations and the next morning it was a sad little town. The pieces that were found were collected together and sold to the highest bidder. Brother Cooper who lives on Pipe Creek has some of the boards in his house now. A piece of one of those boards would be a relic to me.

Martha Martin
The Sea Otter

I killed a sea otter today. I actually did kill a sea otter. I killed him with the ax, dragged him home, and skinned him. I took his liver out, and ate part of it. I'm going to eat the rest of it, and his heart, too. His liver was quite large, bigger than a deer's, and it had more lobes to it. It was very good liver, and I enjoyed it.

Most of today was devoted to the sea otter; getting the hide off was a real task. It's a lovely skin, the softest, silkiest, thickest fur I have ever seen. I am going to make a robe for my baby out of the beautiful fur. My darling child may be born in a lowly cabin, but she shall be wrapped in one of the earth's most costly furs.

It was such a splendid piece of luck. Lucky in more ways than one. The otter might have killed me, although I have never heard of such a thing.

This morning I went to the woods to gather a load of

limbs. As I was coming home with them, I saw the tide was nearly out, and I thought I'd walk over to the bar and take a look at the boat. . . . I was going along, swinging the ax in my left hand, managing the crutch with the right hand, . . . not thinking of anything in particular, when right beside me I heard a bark. It was like a dog bark; not a bow-wow bark, more of a yip. I looked around and saw a huge creature reared up on its haunches. I saw its white teeth.

Without thinking, I swung the ax at the side of its head, saw it hit, felt the jar in my arm, heard the thud. As I swung the ax, I turned and tried to run. I was so terrified the thing would nab me from behind that I could hardly move. I glanced over my shoulder to see how close it was. It hadn't budged from where it dropped. . . .

I got down on my knees and examined it from one end to the other. First off, I noticed the lovely fur. I took off my glove and ran my fingers through the nice silky coat. I decided right then I would have the skin. I saw it as a baby blanket. . . .

It is very much against the law to kill a sea otter. Right now I don't care a rap for law. I'd like to have a picture of a game warden who could arrest me now. I am safe enough from the law, and I think I always will be. Under the circumstances I doubt if any judge would send me to jail for what I have done. . . .

I dragged my kill home, and was a long time doing so. I'll bet the creature weighed a hundred pounds. I worked and worked, rested, pulled, and dragged, rested some more, and by and by I reached the cabin with my prize. . . .

The head was a mess, so I just cut the skin at the neck line and let the head fur go. I chopped off the feet and threw them in the stove. After I got the legs and sides skinned, I turned the otter on his belly and worked the skin off his back down to the tail. I had more trouble with that tail than I did with all the rest of the animal. I wanted it for a neckpiece, and I tried to get the bony tail out without slitting the skin. It can't be done. . . .

My hands got awful cold examining the innards, rather smelly, too. I had let the fire go down, and there wasn't enough hot water for me to scrub properly. I made up the fire, washed a little, and then sat down to rest and gloat over my wonderful sea-otter fur. . . .

Donna Redmond
I'm Proud to Be a Hillbilly

Okay, I'm White. If all I have to make me feel better than anybody else is a freak of nature, I ain't got a whole hell of a lot going for me. I'm White, I'm proud to be White. I've got it a whole hell of a lot easier than if I was black, yellow, red, or anything else. But I'm also proud to be a *woman*. I don't want to run a Euclid earth-mover. I just want to be a woman and have a man that has sense enough to treat me like an equal.

There's some kind of courage and independence in a woman who's had to work hard all her life. Like the women around here. Even if you've got a man, it's not easy.

One girl VISTA told me recently that I don't know anything about life because I had never been to college, never been to New York City. Said I didn't know anything about what's *really* going on, like campus riots and all that crap. I may live in my own litle world, but as far as knowing anything about life, that's a bunch of bull. Cause you just don't get pregnant, get married at fifteen, get divorced, work to support your kids and yourself without knowing a *little* bit about where it's really at. And I don't care if she *has* hitchhiked all over the country. Anybody that's got damn little enough sense to get out and hitchhike these days ain't too up on what's happening.

"VISTA: Take a year out from living to decide what you want to do . . ." at the expense of the poor people and the taxpayers. What are they going to change anyway? These folks here know who they are and where they're going. Ain't going to go nowhere except where they been for the past sixty years.

Maybe you just get hard. I mean *strong*. But I don't think there are any women around that are more *woman* than hillbilly women. When things aren't like they should be, you don't sit around and cry and say, "I'm frail, I'm soft, I just can't handle it," or sling around ten-dollar words. You just do whatever has to be done.

I *need* a man. But not to depend on. I want a friend I can share everything with. I'd like to have a man to come home to me and sit down and eat beans and potatoes with me every night. We wouldn't have to starve. I can still work too.

I want a man that's as big as I am. A man I can't walk over. Someone who is willing to share the good and the bad. When I find him, I don't care if he digs outhouse holes for a living, I'm going to live with him.

If I caught a woman messing around with my man, I'd beat the hell out of her. If I wanted him bad enough. And then, if he was cooperating, I'd beat the hell out of him.

Roberta Victor
Hooker

A hustler is any woman in American society. I was the kind of hustler who received money for favors granted rather than the type of hustler who signs a lifetime contract for her trick. Or the kind of hustler who carefully reads women's magazines and learns what it is proper to give for each date, depending on how much money her date or trick spends on her.

The favors I granted were not always sexual. When I was a call girl, men were not paying for sex. They were paying for something else. They were either paying to act out a fantasy or they were paying for companionship or they were paying to be seen with a well-dressed young woman. Or they were paying for somebody to listen to them. They were paying for a *lot* of things. Some men were paying for sex that *they* felt was deviant. They were paying so that nobody would accuse them of being perverted or dirty or nasty. A large proportion of these guys asked things that were not at all deviant. Many of them wanted oral sex. They felt they couldn't ask their wives or girl friends because they'd be repulsed. Many of them wanted somebody to talk dirty to them. Every good call girl in New York used to share her book and we all knew the same tricks.

We knew a guy who used to lie in a coffin in the middle of his bedroom and he would see the girl only once. He got his kicks when the door would be open, the lights would be out, and there would be candles in the living room, and all you could see was his coffin on wheels. As you walked into the living room, he'd suddenly sit up. Of course, you screamed. He got his kicks when you screamed. Or the guy who set a table like the Last Supper and sat in a robe and sandals and wanted you to play Mary Magdalene.

I was about fifteen, going on sixteen. I was sitting in a coffee shop in the Village, and a friend of mine came by. She said, "I've got a cab waiting. Hurry up. You can make fifty dollars in twenty minutes." Looking back, I wonder why I was so willing to run out of the coffee shop, get in a cab, and turn a trick. It wasn't traumatic because my training had been in how to be a hustler anyway.

I learned it from the society around me, just as a woman. We're taught how to hustle, how to attract, hold a man, and give sexual favors in return. The language that you hear all the time—"Don't sell yourself cheap," "Hold out for the highest bidder," "Is it proper to kiss a man good night on the first date?" The implication is it may not be proper on the first date, but if he takes you out to dinner on the second date, it's proper. If he brings you a bottle of perfume on the third date, you should let him touch you above the waist. And go on from there. It's a marketplace transaction.

Somehow I managed to absorb that when I was quite young. So it wasn't even a moment of truth when this woman came into the coffee shop and said, "Come on." I was back in twenty-five minutes and I felt no guilt.

Carolyn Nearmyer
Family Farmer

I tend to live in a lot of fear. Every time my husband goes out, supporting other farmers, stopping a foreclosure sale, or something like that, I am so scared that he's going to make too many waves and someone is going to take a shot at him. Every time he's gone, I can't sleep. I stay up until he gets home.

My eight-year-old senses this, too. A lot of times, she cannot sleep and she'll come downstairs and want to know if daddy is home. Then it reflects in my mind: what if he doesn't come home?

This was a house that my in-laws lived in and their folks. They always took so much pride in it. Today this house needs painting really bad. The ceilings and everything else needs repair.

Whenever you have to feed your hogs or buy chicken feed, that's gotta come first. You just don't have any money for leisure stuff. We used to go out and eat every once in a while when times were better, like in the seventies. We'd go to the harness races, which we enjoy. Now we buy all our clothes at garage sales, and I mean *all*. Hand-me-down clothes.

This is my husband's terrain, it sure is. My blood, sweat, and tears have only been here for twenty-three years, where his is double that, because he was born here. I've seen him get up before daylight—like when he was planting just this spring—and he wouldn't get home until nine at night. He doesn't mind the hard work, to him, it's a pleasure. What is so heartbreaking about the whole thing is that he doesn't get any reward for it.

(Cary peeks through the door.)

She plays a very important role because she has to. It's

not just something she hears about and goes on with a normal eight-year-old's life. It is something she lives day to day. When we were going through our foreclosure, I was really concerned about her because she couldn't sleep at night, just nervous, really flighty all the time.

You bet she was aware of it. She saw her father when they came to repossess our grain truck. As soon as the wrecker was pulling it out of the driveway, she was standing out there watching her dad cry. He couldn't stop 'em and there was nothing she could do to stop 'em. That's hard on kids. They shouldn't have to go through that at that age. She was watching for us, to make sure the cops didn't come. If the lights were coming down the road, she'd run in the house and tell us. She brought her tricycle on the porch 'cause she was afraid the sheriff would take it, too. I re-assured her that it was paid for and after you have something paid for it's yours. She didn't understand that.

Whenever the deputy came out to take our stuff away from us, I asked him, "How can you go home and face your family?" I happen to know he has an eight-year-old girl too. I said, "How can you sleep tonight, knowing that someday this could be you?" You don't have to be a farmer. This is not just a farm crisis.

He said, "If I didn't do it, somebody else would be here. To me, it's just a job." Auctioneers at foreclosures say that, too: "If we don't sell 'em out, someone else'll get the profits. I might just as well do it." To me, that's heartless people. I wouldn't do that to somebody just because I needed the money. Money to me is just not that important. If we can pay the light bill and have food on the table, that's it. We know in our hearts that we're doing a good job raising our kids, teaching them decency and right from wrong. We've always taught them to respect the flag and respect author-ities and obey the law. I still make sure Cary stands up to the flag and pays honor. But if the sheriff comes out here and takes your stuff away—I mean, how are these kids supposed to say, Okay, you're the sheriff, go ahead and take it? It does hurt me, it really does.

Jean Gump
Swords into Plowshares

We commemorated the crucifixion of Christ by entering a missile silo near Holden, Missouri. We hung a banner on the outside of the chain-link fence that read: SWORDS INTO PLOWSHARES, AN ACT OF HEALING. Isaiah 2, from Scriptures: We will pound our swords into plowshares and we will study war no more.

It's a Minuteman II silo, a first-strike weapon. There are 150 of these missiles. If one of these missiles were to leave the ground, it would decimate an area of seventy-two miles. And all the children and others. We wanted to make this weapon inoperable. We succeeded.

We carried three hammers, a wire clipper, three baby bottles with our blood, papers with an indictment against the United States and against the Christian church for its complicity. Ken Ripito, who is twenty-three, and Ken Moreland, who is twenty-five, went with me. The other two went to another silo about five miles away.

It is going to be the citizens that will have to eliminate these weapons. They were built by human hands. People are frightened of them, yet view them as our Gods of Metal. It is a chain-link fence with barbed wire on top. We have become so accustomed to these monstrosities that there are no guards. It is nondescript. If you were passing it on the road, you would see this fence. The silo itself is maybe a foot or two out of the earth. It looks like a great concrete patio. It's very innocuous.

To get through the fence, we used a wire clipper. We had practiced in the park the day before. Once we were in, I proceeded to use the blood and I made a cross on top of the silo. Underneath, I wrote the words, in black spray paint: DISARM AND LIVE.

We sat down and waited in prayer. We thanked God, first of all, that we were alive. We expected a helicopter to come over and kill us terrorists. We thanked God for our successful dismantling, more or less, of this weapon. We assumed the responsibility for our actions and we waited to be apprehended.

About forty minutes later, the soldiers arrived in an armored vehicle. There was a machine-gun turret at the top. The commander used a megaphone and said, "Will all the personnel on top of the silo please leave the premises with your hands raised?" So all of us "personnel" left the silo. I was concerned because it would be difficult getting out of that little hole in the fence with our hands up. We made it fine.

They put the men up against the fence in a spread-eagle position. They asked the female—myself—to "take ten steps and stand with your hands raised." I did it for a few minutes and my fingers were beginning to tingle. I put my hands down. The soldier said, "You must put your hands up." I said, "No, I have a little funny circulation." He said, "You must put your hands up." I said, "Shoot me." He chose not to, which I thought was good.

I said, "I'll compromise with you. I will raise my hands for five minutes and I will put them down for five minutes." He said, "You can't put them down." I said, "But I will." It was hysterical.

Dr. Jane Hodgson
On Probation

I *was* concerned about losing my license after my conviction. I was on probation and I had to be darned careful what I did. I could still refer patients out, and I did continue to refer them to New York and California. But I didn't *dare* perform an abortion, even on patients who were obviously spontaneously aborting. Practicing good gynecology in a strong Catholic community is not easy, and I'd run into problems early in my practice. I had used St. Joseph's Hospital for quite a while. I remember taking care of a woman who was a good Catholic. She'd already had twelve spontaneous abortions; she wanted a pregnancy desperately and I wanted to help her. This woman was in her thirteenth pregnancy. We thought we had it made—she was over four months. She came into my office with no symptoms of labor and I examined her and realized that the fetus was hanging by the cord in her vagina and that she could expel the whole sac at any time and hemorrhage.

So I got her in my car and took her to St. Joseph's and scheduled her for surgery to remove the placenta and terminate her pregnancy. We were waiting for the operating room to be ready, and the priest came up to her bedside and they told me, He canceled your surgery. They thought I was deliberately aborting her. I was *so* incensed at the idea that he could go in and cancel my orders. I put her in my car and took her to a Protestant hospital. I later got that priest by the nape of the neck, I had him up against a wall, and I said, If you *ever* interfere in my practice again, I'll have you sued for practicing medicine without a license. I was so *angry* with him; and he got transferred shortly after that and he was out of my hair. After a while you get to the point of frustration and you can't even be reasonable in your dislike of people like that. This male-dominated hierarchy and what it has inflicted on the women of their church! They don't realize what agony they put women through. I had so many Catholic patients and dried their tears and tried to teach them to use rhythm. When I think of the basal temperature charts I've gone over with women and tried to figure out when and if they got pregnant, or how they could avoid pregnancy!

Zahrah Muhammad
from *"My Life,"*
An Extended Interview by Susan S. Davis

The man I married before that—I didn't stay with him. My mother gave me to that man when I was still small; my mother hadn't remarried yet. My father died, God bless his soul, and my mother gave me while I was still small. And that man would bring one big basket of grapes and he brings henna (the leaves, for dye) and he brings things. . . . I take it and I dump it all out and I let the chicken eat that stuff; he ate it all up! And if he brought meat, I didn't want to eat it. When he had the wedding, I ran away and went to this woman's home and stayed with her; it was in the same village.

They came and caught me; they brought me back. I ran away again, and they slapped me into irons, on my legs they put a chain—on my legs they put iron rings like those for animals. A girl friend helped me and we took them off one leg and I hung it around my neck and I had the iron ring in my hand and I ran away from the village until I got to the farm. It was the farm on which that Christian lived;

the Christian who took my father's land. When that Christian saw that iron on my leg, he took it off. And he telephones Meknes and took me away from that man . . . that's that. From that time, I never went near that man again; that was it. That man didn't take *anything* from me. Well, that was it. When I stayed with my mother a little while, my mother married and we went to Meknes.

Carmen Prado
If We Stay Together They Can't Hurt Us

Just before I left the police something happened that I'll never forget. A few of us were sent as "plainclothes" informers to a student demonstration. We were to find out who was armed, who the big shots were, who did most of the shouting, and so on. We were to get all the information we could. I stayed toward the back of the march. A woman near me was carrying a flag and for some reason she dropped it. Someone grabbed me and said, "Here, take the flag." He thought I was a student. I was the last one in the row. Behind us were the guards. They were from other stations and didn't know me.

We began to march. "Shout, comrade," they yelled at me. The policewoman beside me whispered, "Prado, drop the flag." She knew, as I did, that the students would be trapped between them and the guards following behind. That was when those of us undercover tried to get out. But as I tried to get away the guards started lobbing tear gas. The policewoman grabbed me but so did one of the students. "No comrade," the student said, "if we stay together they can't hurt us." It was horrible. Everyone was running to escape the tear gas, the shots, the arrests. . . . The police were out to get me because they had seen me with the flag. Just when a guard was about to strike me the student grabbed me, and she got hit instead of me. I was trying to find my way out and this young woman was taking the beating meant for me. Through all this the woman kept clutching onto me. The results was that we both got beaten. Finally the students were all rounded up and brought to the station. By that time the police had sorted out who I was.

It was awful when we got to the station. The police-women had to register the women students and by chance I got the woman who had tried to defend me. She didn't say a word. All the sweetness in her face vanished when she saw who I was. She just kept glaring at me, not saying anything. Such hate in her eyes. Just imagine, she had taken a beating for me only to discover I was a cop. I've never seen her again but sometimes I walk around hoping I'll bump into her so I can let her know, now that we can speak freely, that we were on the same side.

7
FRIENDS, LOVERS AND WIVES

Introduction

The word "friend" has many meanings, and Gareth Owen's inventory of schoolday relationships seems to include quite a few of them, each summarily rejected, leaving our heroine lonely but unbowed. I have heard this piece read many times, by men as well as women, and it works best when the next "friend" is the audience.

Sei Shōnagon's meticulous guidelines for a lover's early morning departure ring as true today as they must have done in tenth-century Japan, when at the age of twenty-seven she became lady-in-waiting to the fifteen-year-old Empress Sadako. And what a striking contrast is her down-to-earth pragmatism to Heloise's towering passion, cast in the courtly medieval tradition that exalted distance between lovers. The romance of Heloise and Abelard is the tragic model of secret love, exposure, ruin and final separation, set amidst the convoluted church politics of twelfth-century France. Her words exalt the epistolary form to such a degree that she seems intoxicated not only by Abelard's words but by the actual physical presence of his letters as well. Her prefatory salutation, which I have chosen not to include in the selection, states for all time the breadth of her love in terms that are especially useful to the actor: "To her Lord, her Father, her Husband, her Brother; his Servant, his Child, his Wife, his Sister, and to express all that is humble, respectful and loving to her Abelard, Heloise writes this."

The counterpoint between the worldly and the sublime continues with Aphra Behn's *In Imitation of Horace*, a seduction at once intensely sensual and self-consciously lit-

erary, scrupulously mindful of Roman and other antecedents to the form. Elizabeth Tollet's fiercely protective
Winter Song pledges romance and warm comfort amid the
bleakest, most savage of landscapes, while Mirra Lokhvitskaya plumbs a mythic Russian "underworld" in a mes-
merizing spell that entices her lover away from the merely
human surface world. The three poems share a quality of
enchantment—the beloved is bound in a hermetic world
of consistent and powerful imagery from which no possibility of escape exists.

More practical and more immediate in scope are the next
three pieces, all dealing with promises and their consequences. Adelaide Procter wistfully questions her intended, apparently on the eve of their wedding, at first
demanding assurances, then, intercepting his reply, choosing to "risk it all" without the answers she fears. In *Were
I but His Own Wife*, the nineteenth-century Irish poet
Ellen Downing expresses her longing in a gentle, lyrical
oath that promises flowers, harps, healing, and protection
from the sorrows of the world. And in Lady Gregory's magnificent translation of the anonymous Gaelic *Grief of a
Girl's Heart*, the very fabric of the universe is imperiled
by a promise betrayed.

Anne Bradstreet is considered colonial America's first
woman poet, and her expansive cosmology when writing
to her absent husband is reminiscent of John Donne's meta-
physical intricacies. Her work seems almost purposely difficult, a complex treasure map riddled with arcane clues,
and therein lies its special interest. For her, even the most
mundane concerns are placed within the grand web of celestial influences, and anything of lesser scale, small or
underplayed, must be avoided in the presentation.

Absence, actual or anticipated, has certainly inspired
more writing than contented domestic life has ever done.
Lynne Yamaguchi Fletcher's *After Delivering Your Lunch*

comes near a recipe for grief, the meticulous attention to the details of food preparation and service helping to keep back the tears for her dying husband. In *Eleanor*, a fictional biography of Eleanor Roosevelt, Rhoda Lerman explores the thresholds of patience, monotony, guilt, denial, and love itself in a vigil over the fevered Franklin. Both selections are dominated by the presence, just out of frame perhaps, of the dying person, a highly dramatic presence that colors and distorts the speaker's world.

Even death, of course, does not sever truly powerful ties, and in her *Epitaph* for Sir William Dyer, his widow promises to join her "dearest dust." Mary Shelley, too, writes in her journal to the departed Shelley himself. She examines what is left of her life through the lens of his absence, and then grudgingly accepts that new lonely life, releasing him with a fond "Good night!" Her lament that she cannot join him in death is a poignantly apt quote from his own work *Adonais*, an elegy on the death of John Keats.

Memory is the subject of Christina Rossetti's search for personal history, *The First Day*. The trap to be avoided here is excessive privacy and introspection, a dreamy surrender to the personal past. Instead, search actively for the past, almost as if it were a puzzle, in pieces, physically present in the objects around you.

Gareth Owen
Friends

When first I went to school
I walked with Sally.
She carried my lunch pack,
Told me about a book she'd read
With a handsome hero
So I said,
"You be my best friend."
After break I went right off her.
I can't say why
And anyway I met Joan
Who's pretty with dark curls
And we sat in a corner of the playground
And giggled about the boy who brought the milk.
Joan upset me at lunch,
I can't remember what she said actually,
But I was definitely upset
And took up with Hilary
Who's frightfully brilliant and everything
And showed me her history
Which I considered very decent.
The trouble with Hilary is
She has to let you know how clever she is
And I said,
"You're not the only one who's clever you know,"
And she went all quiet and funny
And hasn't spoken to me since.
Good riddance I say
And anyway Linda is much more my type of girl;
She does my hair in plaits
And says how pretty I look,
She really says what she thinks

And I appreciate that.
Nadine said she was common
When we saw her on the bus that time
Sitting with three boys from that other school,
And I had to agree
There was something in what she said.
There's a difference between friendliness
And being cheap
And I thought it my duty
To tell her what I thought.
Well she laughed right in my face
And then pretended I wasn't there
So I went right off her.
If there's one thing I can't stand
It's being ignored and laughed at.
Nadine understood what I meant,
Understood right away
And that's jolly nice in a friend.
I must tell you one thing about her,
She's rather a snob.
I get the feeling
She looks down on me
And she'll never come to my house
Though I've asked her thousands of times.
I thought it best to have it out with her
And she went off in a huff
Which rather proved my point
And I considered myself well rid.

At the moment
I walk home on my own
But I'm keeping my eyes open
And when I see somebody I consider suitable
I'll befriend her.

Sei Shōnagon
On Parting

It is important that a lover should know how to make his departure. To begin with, he ought not to be too ready to get up, but should require a little coaxing: "Come, it is past daybreak. You don't want to be found here . . ." and so on. One likes him, too, to behave in such a way that one is sure he is unhappy at going and would stay longer if he possibly could. He should not pull on his trousers the moment he is up, but should first of all come close to one's ear and in a whisper finish off whatever was left half-said in the course of the night. But though he may in reality at these moments be doing nothing at all, it will not be amiss that he should appear to be buckling his belt. Then he should raise the shutters, and both lovers should go out together at the double-doors, while he tells her how much he dreads the day that is before him and longs for the approach of night. Then, after he has slipped away, she can stand gazing after him, with charming recollections of those last moments. Indeed, the success of a lover depends greatly on his method of departure. If he springs to his feet with a jerk and at once begins fussing round, tightening in the waist-band of his breeches, or adjusting the sleeves of his Court robe, hunting-jacket or what not, collecting a thousand odds and ends, and thrusting them into the folds of his dress, or pulling in his over-belt—one begins to hate him.

Heloise
To Abelard

I have your picture in my room; I never pass it without stopping to look at it; and yet when you are present with me I scarce ever cast my eyes on it. If a picture, which is but a mute representation of an object, can give such pleasure, what cannot letters inspire? They have souls; they can speak; they have in them all that force which expresses the transports of the heart; they have all the fire of our passions, they can raise them as much as if the persons themselves were present; they have all the tenderness and the delicacy of speech, and sometimes even the boldness of expression beyond it.

We may write to each other; so innocent a pleasure is not denied us. Let us not lose through negligence the only happiness which is left us, and the only one perhaps which the malice of our enemies can never ravish from us. I shall read that you are my husband and you shall see me sign myself your wife. In spite of all our misfortunes you may be what you please in your letter. Letters were first invented for consoling such solitary wretches as myself. Having lost the substantial pleasures of seeing and possessing you, I shall in some measure compensate this loss by the satisfaction I shall find in your writing. There I shall read your most sacred thoughts; I shall carry them always about with me, I shall kiss them every moment; if you can be capable of any jealousy let it be for the fond caresses I shall bestow upon your letters, and envy only the happiness of those rivals.

Aphra Behn
In Imitation of Horace [ode v, lib. 1]

I

What mean those Amorous Curls of Jet?
  For what heart-Ravisht Maid
Dost thou thy Hair in order set,
  Thy Wanton Tresses Braid?
And thy vast Store of Beauties open lay,
That the deluded Fancy leads astray.

II

For pitty hide thy Starry eyes,
  Whose Languishments destroy:
And look not on the Slave that dyes
  With an Excess of Joy.
Defend thy Coral Lips, thy Amber Breath;
To taste these Sweets lets in a Certain Death.

III

Forbear, fond Charming Youth, forbear,
  Thy words of Melting Love:
Thy Eyes thy Language well may spare,
  One Dart enough can move.
And she that hears thy voice and sees thy Eyes
With too much Pleasure, too much Softness dies.

IV

Cease, Cease, with Sighs to warm my Soul,
  Or press me with thy Hand:
Who can the kindling fire control,
  The tender force withstand?
Thy Sighs and Touches like wing'd Lightning fly,
And are the Gods of Loves Artillery.

Elizabeth Tollet
Winter Song

Ask me no more my truth to prove,
What I would suffer for my love;
With thee I would in exile go
To regions of eternal snow;
O'er floods by solid ice confin'd,
Through forests bare, with northern wind;
While all around my eyes I cast,
Where all is wild, and all is waste.
If there the timorous stag you chase,
Or rouse to fight a fiercer race,
Undaunted, I thy arms would bear,
And give thy hand the hunter's spear.
When the low sun withdraws his light,
And menaces an half-year's night,
The conscious moon and stars above
Shall guide me with my wandering love.
Beneath the mountain's hollow brow,
Or in its rocky cells below,
Thy rural feast I would provide,
Nor envy palaces their pride;
The softest moss should dress thy bed,
With savage spoils about thee spread;
Whilst faithful love the watch should keep,
To banish danger from thy sleep.

Mirra Lokhvitskaya
Tsarina of the Underworld

No, I've no need for the sun, nor the brilliant azure,
No desire for rustling leaves, nor singing birds;
All is inconstant, treacherous, and deceitful—
Leave the world—leave evil and suffering.
We'll live in the depths of an impenetrable cavern—
  The entrance blocked behind us by a boulder,
And, in place of nuptial torches, multicolored fires
Of rubies, sapphires, and diamonds will flash in the
  gloom . . .
There earthly cares and storms will not touch
Our happiness—we'll guard it jealously,
In that night of our mute, subterranean kingdom—
We will be two, and love will bind us . . .
I will reveal to you the mystery . . . O, look deep into my
  eyes!
Do you know who I am? I—tsarina of the underworld! . . .
The zealous, old gnomes obey me alone—
It is they who have carved our cave in the cliff . . .

Adelaide Anne Procter
A Woman's Question

Before I trust my fate to thee,
  Or place my hand in thine,
Before I let thy future give
  Color and form to mine,
Before I peril all for thee, question thy soul to-night for
    me.

I break all slighter bonds, nor feel
  A shadow of regret:
Is there one link within the Past
  That holds thy spirit yet?
Or is thy faith as clear and free as that which I can
    pledge to thee?

Does there within thy dimmest dreams
  A possible future shine,
Wherein thy life could henceforth breathe,
  Untouch'd, unshar'd by mine?
If so, at any pain or cost, O, tell me before all is lost.

Look deeper still. If thou canst feel,
  Within thy inmost soul,
That thou hast kept a portion back,
  While I have stak'd the whole;
Let no false pity spare the blow, but in true mercy tell
    me so.

Is there within thy heart a need
  That mine cannot fulfill?
One chord that any other hand
  Could better wake or still?

Speak now—lest at some future day my whole life wither
    and decay.

Lives there within thy nature hid
    The demon-spirit Change,
Shedding a passing glory still
    On all things new and strange?
It may not be thy fault alone—but shield my heart
    against thy own.

Couldst thou withdraw thy hand one day
    And answer to my claim,
That Fate, and that to-day's mistake—
    Not thou—had been to blame?
Some soothe their conscience thus; but thou wilt surely
    warn and save me now.

Nay, answer not,—I dare not hear,
    The words would come too late;
Yet I would spare thee all remorse,
    So, comfort thee, my fate—
Whatever on my heart may fall—remember, I would risk
    it all!

Ellen Mary Patrick Downing
Were I but His Own Wife

Were I but his own wife, to guard and to guide him,
  'Tis little of sorrow should fall on my dear;
I'd chant my low love-verses, stealing beside him,
  So faint and so tender his heart would but hear;
I'd pull the wild blossoms from valley and highland,
  And there at his feet I would lay them all down;
I'd sing him the songs of our poor stricken island,
  Till his heart was on fire with a love like my own.

There's a rose by his dwelling,—I'd tend the lone
    treasure,
  That he might have flowers when the summer would
    come;
There's a harp in his hall,—I would wake its sweet
    measure,
  For he must have music to brighten his home.
Were I but his own wife, to guide and to guard him,
  'Tis little of sorrow should fall on my dear;
For every kind glance my whole life would award him,
  In sickness I'd soothe and in sadness I'd cheer.

My heart is a fount welling upward forever!
  When I think of my true-love, by night or by day,
That heart keeps its faith like a fast-flowing river
  Which gushes forever and sings on its way.
I have thoughts full of peace for his soul to repose in,
  Were I but his own wife, to win and to woo;
O sweet, if the night of misfortune were closing,
  To rise like the morning star, darling, for you!

Anonymous
Grief of a Girl's Heart

O Donal Oge, if you go across the sea,
Bring myself with you and do not forget it;
And you will have a sweetheart for fair days and market
    days,
And the daughter of the King of Greece beside you at
    night.

It is late last night the dog was speaking of you;
The snipe was speaking of you in her deep marsh.
It is you are the lonely bird through the woods;
And that you may be without a mate until you find me.

You promised me, and you said a lie to me,
That you would be before me where the sheep are
    flocked;
I gave a whistle and three hundred cries to you,
And I found nothing there but a bleating lamb.

You promised me a thing that was hard for you,
A ship of gold under a silver mast;
Twelve towns with a market in all of them,
And a fine white court by the side of the sea.

You promised me a thing that is not possible,
That you would give me gloves of the skin of a fish;
That you would give me shoes of the skin of a bird;
And a suit of the dearest silk in Ireland.

O Donal Oge, it is I would be better to you
Than a high, proud, spendthrift lady:
I would milk the cow; I would bring help to you;

And if you were hard pressed, I would strike a blow for
    you.

You have taken the east from me; you have taken the
    west from me,
You have taken what is before me and what is behind
    me;
You have taken the moon, you have taken the sun from
    me,
And my fear is great that you have taken God from me!

Anne Bradstreet
A Letter to Her Husband, Absent upon Publick Employment

My head, my heart, mine Eyes, my life, nay more,
My joy, my Magazine of earthly store,
If two be one, as surely thou and I,
How stayest thou there, whilst I at *Ipswich* lye?
So many steps, head from the heart to sever
If but a neck, soon should we be together:
I like the earth this season, mourn in black,
My Sun is gone so far in's Zodiack,
Whom whilst I 'joy'd, nor storms, nor frosts I felt,
His warmth such frigid colds did cause to melt.
My chilled limbs now nummed lye forlorn;
Return, return sweet *Sol* from *Capricorn;*
In this dead time, alas, what can I more
Then view those fruits which through thy heat I bore?
Which sweet contentment yield me for a space,
True living Pictures of their Fathers face.
O strange effect! now thou art *Southward* gone,

I weary grow, the tedious day so long;
But when thou *Northward* to me shalt return,
I wish my Sun may never set, but burn
Within the *Cancer* of my glowing breast,
The welcome house of him my dearest guest.
Where ever, ever stay, and got not thence,
Till natures sad decree shall call thee hence;
Flesh of thy flesh, bone of thy bone,
I here, thou there, yet both but one.

Lynne Yamaguchi Fletcher
After Delivering Your Lunch

Empty-handed, I return home
along the same path above the Kamo's west bank.
I am trying to whistle, that sort of day.
Today the nurse will try feeding you,
her chopsticks efficient, insistent;
you will clench your face, swallow.
This last week I have watched every mouthful
feed the bandage thickening around your neck.

I stop to choose three persimmon leaves,
slide them into a breast pocket, walk
past the steps descending to river
to where the crooked limb of the middle-aged pine,
like the entrance to a tea room, asks everyone to bend.
This time before I duck I clasp
the rough bark to my cheek, lean into the wind.

The leaves, one red, two yellow,
garnish a Kutani plate I brought you from summer one
    year.
I arrange the fish on them, three bites
now twelve translucent morsels you can swallow.
A cobalt-brushed porcelain dish holds five young spinach
    leaves,
boiled to peak color in salted water, chopped fine,
    mounded.
I add six drops of soy sauce.
Into a bowl smaller than your cupped hand
I slip a cube of tofu;
into a second, muskmelon ripe to melting,
the softest, juiciest bits.
I think I know just how little you will eat, how few
times I can watch you swallow.
Tonight, in the shopping bag I delivered your lunch in,
dishes will rattle as I carry your leftovers home in a cab.

Rhoda Lerman
from *Eleanor*

I remember the soldiers going over No-Man's-Land, re-
citing as they took the German bullets. Fourteen times
fourteen, to be or not to be. The lead moves slowly, deep-
ening in his limbs. Do rub his muscles. Do feed him solids.
Don't. Do. Whom fire doth spare, sea doth drown. Whom
sea spares, pestilent air doth send to clay, whom war
'scapes, sickness takes away. And the mackerels float fer-
menting silver-bellied on their backs in green pools at the
water's edge.

"His mind, Louis?"

"Let's not make decisions. Let's not ask questions, Eleanor. We have too much work to do. Worry about your own mind."

"If only he'd taken off the wet bathing suit, Louis."

"It's more than that. One thing I understand, Eleanor, is being sick. Let's get to work."

And so, as if being organized would help, Louis and I made up a schedule for the water after the local doctor came and warned us of dehydration, a danger I had forgotten, I was so stricken. And since I was to sleep in Franklin's room during the night, it became my duty to make certain he had water every hour and every hour I dragged myself more and more slowly from the cot to the washstand to the bed to his lips. Some nights I dreamed I had already awoken, gone to the washstand, to the bed, to his lips, and back to my cot and I would somehow cut through the dream and force myself up. Nothing existed except that fever. Once I slept through the night until I heard Franklin call for water. His head was a fiery stone and his lips were bleeding. I who had lived on dreams vowed I would never dream again as long as I lived. My dreams had nearly killed him.

I prayed. "I will look up to the hills, from whence comes my help." From whence comes my help became a question. I did not pray. But it happened so suddenly, I said to no one, a sudden storm. A cobalt sky, lightning filling the bowl of mountains. There is always that sense of yet another suddenness, waiting in the wings and sweeping in just before the curtains go down. There, my dear. You may rest now. It is over. See, the sky is blue, dear girl, and a gentle rain to cleanse your hands and see, the gulls again skim the bay and even the suicidal bellies of the mackerel turned up dead six-deep on the shore in some horror of nature beyond ken, even the mackerels will be restored and turn again on their bellies, verily, and go back to the sea, and your husband will stand and walk and run and come alive just as soon as the mackerels turn over. Just as soon as the lights dim and intermission is over.

Mary Shelley
My Beloved Shelley

May 31.—The lanes are filled with fireflies; they dart between the trunks of the trees, and people the land with earth-stars. I walked among them tonight, and descended towards the sea. I passed by the ruined church, and stood on the platform that overlooks the beach. The black rocks were stretched out among the blue waters, which dashed with no impetuous motion against them. The dark boats, with their white sails, glided gently over its surface, and the star-enlightened promontories closed in the bay: below, amid the crags, I heard the monotonous but harmonious, voices of the fishermen.

How beautiful these shores, and this sea! Such is the scene—such the waves within which my beloved vanished from mortality.

The time is drawing near when I must quit this country. It is true that, in the situation I now am, Italy is but the corpse of the enchantress that she was. Besides, if I had stayed here, the state of things would have been different. The idea of our Child's advantage alone enables me to keep fixed in my resolution to return to England. It is best for him—and I go.

Four years ago, we lost our darling William; four years ago, in excessive agony, I called for death to free me from all I felt that I should suffer here. I continue to live, and

thou art gone. I leave Italy and the few that still remain to
me. That, I regret less; for our intercourse is [so] much
chequered with all of dross that this earth so delights to
blend with kindness and sympathy, that I long for solitude,
with the exercise of such affections as still remain to me.
Away, I gainsay the pure attachment which chiefly clings
to them, because they knew and loved you—because I
knew them when with you, and I cannot think of them
without feeling your spirit beside me.

I cannot grieve for you, beloved Shelley; I grieve for thy
friends—for the world—for thy Child—most for myself,
enthroned in thy love, growing wiser and better beneath
thy gentle influence, taught by you the highest philosophy—your pupil, friend, lover, wife, mother of your children! The glory of the dream is gone. I am a cloud from
which the light of sunset has passed. Give me patience in
the present struggle. *Meum cordium cor!* Good night!

> I would give
> All that I am to be as thou now art!
> But I am chain'd to time, and cannot thence depart!*

*Percy Bysshe Shelley, *Adonais*, XXVI, 233–35.

Lady Catherine Dyer
Epitaph on the Monument of
Sir William Dyer at Colmworth, 1641

My dearest dust, could not thy hasty day
Afford thy drowsy patience leave to stay
One hour longer: so that we might either
Sit up, or gone to bed together?
But since thy finished labour hath possessed
Thy weary limbs with early rest,
Enjoy it sweetly: and thy widow bride
Shall soon repose her by thy slumbering side.
Whose business, now, is only to prepare
My nightly dress, and call to prayer;
Mine eyes wax heavy and the day grows old,
The dew falls thick, my blood grows cold.
Draw, draw the closéd curtains; and make room:
My dear, my dearest dust; I come, I come.

Christina Rossetti
The First Day

I wish I could remember the first day,
First hour, first moment of your meeting me;
If bright or dim the season, it might be
Summer or winter for aught I can say.
So unrecorded did it slip away,
So blind was I to see and to foresee,
So dull to mark the budding of my tree
That would not blossom yet for many a May.

If only I could recollect it! Such
A day of days! I let it come and go
As traceless as a thaw of bygone snow.
It seemed to mean so little, meant so much!
If only now I could recall that touch,
First touch of hand in hand!—Did one but know!

8
DAUGHTERS, SISTERS
AND MOTHERS

Introduction

So much of the lives of families seems to be built on letting go; departures and transformations, changes through growth and changes by death.

Emily Dickinson's letters dealing with her father's death are infused with as much a sense of transformation as of loss. Each of the pieces shifts in tone about midway, as her perspective changes and she samples a broader vision—of idealized gardens, "Home," and immortality itself.

For the former slave, "Puss," the recollection of her mother's last day on earth is one glorious captured moment, full of pride, respect, and the fighting spirit that is her legacy. Lucille Clifton's *Memoir* is an even richer statement of family history and Black pride, funny and scary at the same time, pivoting around her father's tall tale of seduction, murder, and punishment. There is a marvelous opportunity here to play Daddy, to take on some elements of his speech or behavior, and then to drop it all for the personal commentary that follows.

In *The Warriors* the two Native American sisters share memories of their Uncle Ralphie in an easy, reassuring manner that scarcely prepares the listener for the magnitude of the lesson they have learned from him, making this selection especially effective as a teaching tool.

Wintermelons, Marian Yee's good-bye to her Chinese heritage and her mother, is a curious mix of memory, hard tactile detail, and estrangement. Recollections of lovemaking contrast with images of gardening, rendered immediate through repeated references to palms of hands. And Karen

Wolman's Jewish mother in *Telling Mom* is an expert at "parental density." How aware is she really?

The forms by which mothers communicate with their young children are inventive and, by necessity, most often entertaining. I have chosen to include a selection of what I believe are lesser known anonymous rhymes and proverbs from the Victorian collection, *Pinafore Palace*, to be used not only as recitations for children, but also as refreshing transitional pieces for adult presentations, even for auditions. They tend to be disarmingly artless and wise, and most are so broadly lyrical that they inspire a degree of fun and flamboyance uncommon in most other types of monologue material. Some, like *I had a little pony* and *Solomon Grundy* are mostly about sounds and repetitions. Others present games or paradoxes, sometimes—as with *Three children sliding on the ice*—involving unexpected hints of darkness. The simplest and grandest is *Our Mother*, a lovely salute to the natural mother of us all. Other poems for children that share many of these qualities include Christina Rossetti's *Who has seen the Wind*, a teasing quiz; Abbie Farwell Brown's punning *Learning to Play;* and Eliza Lee Follen's *The New Moon*, a nursery rhyme that achieves a scale to which, unfortunately, only children usually aspire.

Dinah Craik's *Philip, My King* is an adoring anthem to her baby boy, projecting an exemplary life as well loved of woman, a leader among men, and spiritually triumphant, while Mirra Lokhvitskaya's *My Sky* takes a gentler, more mystical approach to the same subject.

One of the few pioneer women to become literate, Jane Cannary Hickock looked up words in her dictionary in order to write to her daughter. Her unposted letters—she arranged to have them given to Janey only after her own death—are a treasure trove for monologue hunters, filled with the concerns, observations, feelings, and facts that give a true sense of time and place, shot through with dramatic pathos. They are a great story, nothing short of mythic, and each installment is all the more riveting for being true.

Emily Dickinson
Father Does Not Live with Us Now

We were eating our supper the fifteenth of June, and Austin came in. He had a despatch in his hand, and I saw by his face we were all lost, though I didn't know how. He said that father was very sick, and he and Vinnie must go. The train had already gone. While horses were dressing, news came that he was dead. Father does not live with us now—he lives in a new house. Though it was built in an hour it is better than this. He hasn't any garden because he moved after gardens were made, so we take him the best flowers, and if we only knew he knew, perhaps we could stop crying.

The Last Afternoon that My Father Lived

The last Afternoon that my Father lived, though with no premonition—I preferred to be with him, and invented an absence for Mother, Vinnie being asleep. He seemed peculiarly pleased as I oftenest stayed with myself, and remarked as the Afternoon withdrew, he "would like it not to end." His pleasure almost embarrassed me and my Brother coming—I suggested they walk. Next morning I woke him for the train—and saw him no more. His Heart was pure and terrible and I think no other like it exists. I am glad there is Immortality—but would have tested it myself—before intrusting him.

Home is so far from Home, since my Father died.

Anonymous
Oral Testimony of a Former Slave

My mother was the smartest black woman in Eden. She was as quick as a flash of lightning, and whatever she did could not be done better. She could do anything. She cooked, washed, ironed, spun, nursed and labored in the field. She made as good a field hand as she did a cook. I have heard Master Jennings say to his wife, "Fannie has her faults, but she can outwork any nigger in the country. I'd bet my life on that."

The one doctrine of my mother's teaching which was branded upon my senses was that I should never let anyone abuse me. "I'll kill you, gal, if you don't stand up for yourself," she would say. "Fight, and if you can't fight, kick; if you can't kick, then bite." Ma was generally willing to work, but if she didn't feel like doing something, none could make her do it. At least, the Jennings couldn't make, or didn't make her.

On the day my mother died, she called pa and said . . . "Go tell Master Jennings to come in, and get all the slaves too."

Pa went and returned in five minutes with old master.

"Fannie, are you any worse?" said old master.

"No, no, Master Jennings, no worse. But I'm going to leave you at eight o'clock."

"Where are you going, Fannie," Master Jennings asked as if he didn't know that ma was talking about dying.

Ma shook her head slowly and answered, "I'm going where there ain't no fighting and cussing and damning."

"Is there anything that you want me to do for you, Fannie?"

Ma told him that she reckoned there wasn't much of anything that anybody could do for her now. "But I would like for you to take Puss . . . she always called me Puss . . . and hire her out among ladies, so she can be raised right. She will never be any good here, Master Jennings."

A funny look came over Master Jennings' face, and he bowed his head up and down. All the hands had come in and were standing around with him.

My mother died just about eight o'clock.

Lucille Clifton
from *Generations: A Memoir*

"Harvey Nichols was a white man," my Daddy would say, "who come South after the war to make money. He brought his wife and family down and bought himself a house and everything. And it was close to the Sale place and all the slaves had stayed there after emancipation because they said the Sales was good people, but they had just changed their last name to Sayle so people would know the difference. And this Harvey Nichols saw Lucy and wanted her and I say she must have wanted him too because like I told you, Lue, she was mean and didn't do nothing she didn't want to do and nobody could force her because she was Mammy Ca'line's child and everybody round there respected Mammy Ca'line so much. And her daughter Lucy had this baby boy by this Connecticut Yankee named Harvey Nichols. They named the baby Gene Sayle. He was my Daddy, Lue. Your own grandfather and Mammy Ca'line's grandson. But oh, Lue, he was born with a withered arm.

"Yes, Lord, he was born with a withered arm and when he was still just a baby Lucy waited by the crossroad one night for Harvey Nichols to come to her and when he rode up on a white horse, she cocked up a rifle she had stole and shot him off his horse and killed him, Lue. And she didn't run away, she didn't run away, she waited right there by the body with the rifle in her hand till the horse coming back empty-saddled to the stable brought a mob to see what had become of Harvey Nichols. And when they got to the crossroad they found Lucy standing there with the rifle in her hand. And they didn't lynch her, Lue, cause she was Mammy Ca'line's child, and from Dahomey women. That's what I believe. Mammy Ca'line got one of the lawyer Sale family to defend her daughter, cause they was all lawyers and preachers in that family. They had a legal trial and Lucy was found guilty. And hanged. Mammy Ca'line took the baby boy Genie and raised him and never let him forget who he was. I used to ask her sometime, Mammy, was you scared back then bout Granma Lucy? And she would look right at me and say 'I'm scared for you, mister, that's all.' She always called me mister. She said I was Mister Sayle. And Lue, I always was."

And Lucy was hanged. Was hanged, the lady whose name they gave me like a gift had her neck pulled up by a rope until the neck broke and I can see Mammy Ca'line standing straight as a soldier in green Virginia apart from the crowd of silent Black folk and white folk watching them and not the wooden frame swinging her child. And their shame making distance between them and her a real thing. And I know she made no sound but her mind closed around the picture like a frame and I know that her child made no sound and I turn in my chair and arch my back and make this sound for my two mothers and all Dahomey women.

Later I would ask my father for proof. Where are the records, Daddy? I would ask. The time may not be right and it may just be a family legend or something. Somebody somewhere knows, he would say. And I would be dissatisfied and fuss with Fred about fact and proof and history until he told me one day not to worry, that even the lies are true. In history, even the lies are true.

And there would be days when we young Sayles would be trying to dance and sing in the house and Sammy would miss a step and not be able to keep up the music and he would look over in the corner of the room and holler "Damn Harvey Nichols." And we would laugh.

Anna Lee Walters
from *The Warriors*

Momma reported to me that the funeral was well attended by the Pawnee people. Uncle Ralph and I had said our farewells years earlier. Momma told me that someone there had spoken well of Uncle Ralph before they put him in the ground. It was said that "Ralphie came from a fine family, an old line of warriors."

Ten years later, Sister and I visited briefly at Momma's and Dad's home. We had been separated by hundreds of miles for all that time. As we sat under Momma's flowering mimosa trees, I made a confession to Sister. I said, "Sometimes I wish that Uncle Ralph were here. I'm a grown woman but I still miss him after all these years."

Sister nodded her head in agreement. I continued. "He knew so many things. He knew why the sun pours its liquid all over us and why it must do just that. He knew why babes and insects crawl. He knew that we must live beautifully or not live at all."

Sister's eyes were thoughtful, but she waited to speak while I went on. "To live beautifully from day to day is a battle all the way. The things that he knew are so beautiful. And to feel and know that kind of beauty is the reason that we should live at all. Uncle Ralph said so. But now, there is no one who knows what that beauty is or any of the other things that he knew."

Sister pushed back smoky gray wisps of her dark hair. "You do," she pronounced. "And I do, too."

"Why do you suppose he left us like that?" I asked.

"It couldn't be helped," Sister said. "There was a battle on."

"I wanted to be one of his warriors," I said with an embarrassed half-smile.

She leaned over and patted my hand. "You are," she said. Then she stood and placed one hand on her bosom and one hand on my arm. "We'll carry on," she said.

I touched her hand resting on my arm. I said, "Sister, tell me again. What is the battle for?"

She looked down toward the fence where a hobo was coming through. We waved at him.

"Beauty," she said to me. "Our battle is for beauty. It's what Uncle Ralph fought for, too. He often said that everyone else just wanted to go to the Moon. But remember, Sister, you and I done been there. Don't forget, after all, we're children of the stars."

Marian Yee
Wintermelons

Why are you standing there, Mother,
alone in the garden?
What is there behind the shy palms
of leaves that glow like white
wings in the moonlight? Come to bed—
these are only your melons.

Every summer you've planted wintermelons,
fussing there as if you were their mother,
smoothing the stems into their beds.
I've thought of you in your garden
when I was alone in distant places
and had only the wind to hold between my palms.

Once you held out your calloused palms
and talked of working among the rows of melons

grown at home in China. Here, where all is foreign
do you remember your own mother
as she bent to whisper charms over her garden?
You've kept those whispers—I've heard you listening.

Those words are in movement,
though today you sift bonemeal between your palms
and spread lime around your garden:
your words bring forth the melons.
Yet we haven't spoken much for years.
When I told you that I loved a foreign

man, you said that I was foreign
too. The first time I went to bed
with him, I wondered what you would say,
whether you knew the touch of palms
upon your breasts. Have you known
all along of this hidden garden?

Though I've left behind your garden
to discover things still new
to me, I always return to your melons
shaped in moonlight, round, imbedded
in their net of vines. Let me rest my palm
here a little longer. Tomorrow I am leaving, Mother.

Karen Dale Wolman
from *Telling Mom*

"Ma, the reason I called—"

"Your cousin Joanna will be calling you soon. She wants you to be one of the bridesmaids."

. . . I listen to her with half an ear, wondering exactly how I'm going to tell her: Ma, I'm in love with Renee, Ma, I'm gay, Ma, can I bring my girlfriend home for Sunday dinner?

None of them seem right, so I stall.

"The wedding's not for eight months, but there's a lot of work to be done. You have to try on dresses, go for fittings. Do you want to bring a date with you?"

I go for the opening. "You remember Renee who I keep talking about, Ma?" Renee sticks her head out of the bedroom and gives me a thumbs up and a bright smile. I fall in love all over again every time I see that smile.

"The writer, you mean? The one who does magazine articles?"

"Yes. That's her." I am surprised she remembers, surprised that she had listened so closely when I talked about Renee.

"We're living together now. Renee moved in with me." I hold my breath, waiting for the fireworks.

"I never did like the idea of you living alone in the city. Your rent is so high, maybe now you'll be able to save some money."

I never imagined that she wouldn't understand. Mom has always been very astute, very quick to grasp what hasn't been said.

I try again. "We're sharing the bedroom." Still no reaction. "Mom, she's very important to me."

"Good, good. Is she a nice girl? I never did like your

friend Wendy. She seemed like trouble right from the beginning.

Wendy hasn't been mentioned in years. Does Mom know that she was my first girlfriend in high school?

"Renee's not like Wendy, Mom. You'll like her." Renee is still standing in the doorway, questioning me with her eyebrows. I shrug. I'm not sure if Mom understands.

Before I know it, Mom's back to talking about the family. I can't let her do this. I'll never get the nerve to tell her again.

"I haven't finished telling you about Renee yet." I take a deep breath and oxygen blasts the words across the wires. "Ma, I love Renee."

"That's good. She sounds like a nice girl. You'll have to bring her to dinner one night."

I hold the phone between my shoulder and my chin as I shrug at my mother's incomprehension.

"Does she like brisket or should I make chicken? So many people won't eat red meat these days I never know what to cook for company."

"Ma, it doesn't matter what you cook. It's not important."

"You don't want your mother to make a good impression on your friend?"

Why this time do the subtleties of my words escape her? When I try purposely to be vague she cuts right to the point, but this time, when I need for her to know, she refuses to understand.

"Does she like salad?"

"Mom, stop talking about food. Can't you understand what I'm trying to tell you? Renee is my girlfriend. We're lovers. I'm gay."

She doesn't even pause for air. "So," the words come across the wire, bridging the miles and the years, "is she Jewish?"

"Ma," I say, before hanging up, "make the brisket."

Kate Douglas Wiggins and
Nora Archibald Smith, editors
from *Pinafore Palace*

I had a little pony,
    His name was Dapple-gray,
I lent him to a lady,
    To ride a mile away;
She whipped him, she lashed him,
    She rode him through the mire;
I would not lend my pony now
    For all the lady's hire.

———————————

Six little mice sat down to spin,
Pussy passed by, and she peeped in.
"What are you at, my little men?"
"Making coats for gentlemen."
"Shall I come in and bite off your threads?"
"No, no, Miss Pussy, you'll snip off our heads."
"Oh, no, I'll not, I'll help you to spin."
"That may be so, but you don't come in!"

———————————

Bobby Shaftoe's gone to sea,
Silver buckles on his knee;
He'll come back and marry me,
    Pretty Bobby Shaftoe.

Bobby Shaftoe's fat and fair,
Combing down his yellow hair;
He's my love for evermair,
    Pretty Bobby Shaftoe.

I'll tell you a story
About Mary Morey,
    And now my story's begun.
I'll tell you another
About her brother,
    And now my story's done.

    Solomon Grundy,
    Born on a Monday,
Christened on Tuesday,
Married on Wednesday,
Took ill on Thursday,
Worse on Friday,
Died on Saturday.
Buried on Sunday,
    This is the end
    Of Solomon Grundy!

Three children sliding on the ice
    Upon a summer's day,

As it fell out they all fell in,
  The rest they ran away.

Now had these children been at home,
  Or sliding on dry ground,
Ten thousand pounds to one penny
  They had not all been drowned.

Ye parents all, that children have,
  And ye that eke have none,
If you would keep them from the grave,
  Pray make them stay at home.

———————

The man in the wilderness asked me,
How many strawberries grew in the sea?
I answered him as I thought good,
As many as red herrings grew in the wood.

———————

If all the world were apple-pie,
  And all the sea were ink,
And all the trees were bread and cheese,
  What would we have for drink?

———————

I had a little nut tree, nothing would it bear
But a silver nutmeg, and a golden pear.

The King of Spain's daughter came to visit me,
And all was because of my little nut tree.
I skipped over water, I danced over sea,
And all the birds of the air, they couldn't catch me.

If you sneeze on Monday, you sneeze for danger;
Sneeze on a Tuesday, kiss a stranger;
Sneeze on a Wednesday, sneeze for a letter;
Sneeze on a Thursday, something better;
Sneeze on a Friday, sneeze for sorrow;
Sneeze on a Saturday, joy tomorrow.

When the wind is in the east,
'Tis good for neither man nor beast;
When the wind is in the north,
The skillful fisher goes not forth;
When the wind is in the south,
It blows the bait in the fishes' mouth;
When the wind is in the west,
Then 'tis at the very best.

Girls and boys, come out to play,
The moon doth shine as bright as day;
Leave your supper and leave your sleep,
And come with your playfellows into the street.

Come with a whoop, come with a call,
Come with a good will or not at all.
Up the ladder and down the wall,
A halfpenny roll will serve us all.
You find milk, and I'll find flour,
And we'll have a pudding in half an hour.

Hundreds of stars in the pretty sky,
  Hundreds of shells on the shore together,
Hundreds of birds that go singing by,
  Hundreds of birds in the sunny weather,

Hundreds of dewdrops to greet the dawn,
  Hundreds of bees in the purple clover,
Hundreds of butterflies on the lawn,
  But only one mother the wide world over.

Christina Rossetti
Who Has Seen the Wind?

Who has seen the wind?
   Neither I nor you:
But when the leaves hang trembling,
   The wind is passing through.

Who has seen the wind?
   Neither you nor I:
But when the trees bow down their heads,
   The wind is passing by.

Abbie Farwell Brown
Learning to Play

Upon a tall piano stool
   I have to sit and play
A stupid finger exercise
   For half an hour a day.

They call it "playing," but to me
   It's not a bit of fun.
I *play* when I am out of doors,
   Where I can jump and run.

But Mother says the little birds
   Who sing so nicely now,
Had first to learn, and practice too,
   All sitting on a bough.

And maybe if I practice hard,
  Like them, I too, some day,
Shall make the pretty music sound;
  Then I shall call it "play."

Eliza Lee Follen
The New Moon

Dear mother, how pretty
  The moon looks tonight!
She was never so cunning before;
  Her little two horns
  Are so sharp and so bright,
I hope she'll not grow any more.

If I were up there
  With you and my friends,
I'd rock on it nicely, you see;
  I'd sit in the middle
  And hold by both ends;
O, what a bright candle 'twould be!

I would call to the stars
  To keep out of the way,
Lest we should rock over their toes,
  And there I would rock
  Till the dawn of the day,
And see where the pretty moon goes.

And there we would stay
  In the beautiful skies,

And through the bright clouds we would roam;
    We would see the sun set
    And see the sun rise,
And on the next rainbow come home.

Dinah Maria Mulock Craik
Philip, My King

Look at me with thy large brown eyes,
    Philip, my king!
Round whom the enshadowing purple lies
Of babyhood's royal dignities.
Lay on my neck thy tiny hand
  With love's invisible sceptre laden;
I am thine Esther to command
  Till thou shalt find a queen-handmaiden,
    Philip, my king.

On the day when thou goest a-wooing,
    Philip, my king!
When some beautiful lips 'gin suing,
And some gentle heart's bars undoing
Thou dost enter, love-crown'd, and there
  Sittest love-glorified. Rule kindly,
Tenderly, over thy kingdom fair,
  For we that love, ah! we love so blindly,
    Philip, my king.

Up from thy sweet mouth—up to thy brow,
    Philip, my king!
The spirit that here lies sleeping now
May rise like a giant and make men bow

As to one heaven-chosen among his peers.
  My Saul, than thy brethren taller and fairer,
Let me behold thee in future years!
  Yet thy head needeth a circlet rarer,
            Philip, my king.

—A wreath not of gold, but palm. One day,
            Philip, my king!
Thou too must tread, as we trod, a way
Thorny and cruel and cold and grey:
Rebels within thee, and foes without,
  Will snatch at thy crown. But march on, glorious,
Martyr, yet monarch! till angels shout,
  As thou sit'st at the feet of God victorious,
            "Philip, the king!"

Mirra Lokhvitskaya
My Sky

The sky and all the delights of the sky I see
In my child's sweet face—and I cannot tear my eyes
  away . . .
Innocent angel, by chance fallen to the earth,
How much happiness you've brought! Child, how dear you
  are to me!

The wind gusts and your curls flicker with gold,
They glisten 'round your dear tiny head like a halo,
You're just like a little cloud, drenched by the light of dawn,
Pure like the forest lily-of-the-valley—May's charming
  bloom!

With a gentle caress your deep blue eyes
Look into my soul and seem like the color of the sky,
Darkening for an instant before a spring storm . . .
I contemplate the sky in your gaze, child!

Where is that land of which our fairy tales murmur?
I'd carry you in my arms to that wondrous realm,
Silently, barefoot on sharp stones would I walk,
If only to spare you—the thorns of earth's path!

God! When You sent me a child, You opened the sky for
    me!
My mind was cleansed of vain, petty desires!
Into my breast You breathed new, mysterious powers!
In my burning heart You kindled—the flame of immortal
    love!

Jane Cannary Hickok
from *Calamity Jane's Letters to Her Daughter*

May 30

O Janey I did hate to come back here. Why couldnt I have
stayed with you & Daddy Jim? Why didnt he ask me to
stay? I was so in hope that he would but darling your mother
is a misfit in a home like you have—or what can be wrong?
I had such a lovely time there. Why cant I ever be anybody
worthwhile. I likely will end up in the poor house in my
old age. I am so discouraged. One consolation I shall always
know you are alright & I thank God for your Daddy Jim.
I gave him $10000 to use for your education. There will be

more in that old gambling tent for me when Luck again comes my way. I met Abbott on the street. He asked me for the price of a meal. I gave him my last 50 cents. My pocket book looked so empty where only such a short while ago there could have been counted thousands that I tossed it out in the street. Abbott promised me a job in Deadwood so I'm hitting the trail to that place soon. I'll never forget that party & will always think of you when I got my first glimpse of you that day when your Daddy Jim called you in to meet me & when you asked me why I cried & I told you that you reminded me of a little girl I once knew & I told you of how she sailed away on a big ship & never came back to me & you said "my Daddy Jim & I sail on big ships to across the ocean lots of times. Once Mammy Ross & I went with him to Singapore, that's in China you know & we gave the beggar children American gold, poor little starved things. Their clothes were all rags & I could see their ribs sticking out & their hands were like little bird claws & their faces looked just like a starved kitten Daddy Jims sailors found below in the steerage. I couldnt eat my dinner that night. They made me feel sick for their eyes were poked out."

Then your Daddy Jim left us alone, remember Janey & you told me about the women on your Daddys ship & you mocked them makin eyes at him. O, you were so comical then & when I asked you where your mother was & You said "My mother is dead. She died a long time ago. She was Mother Helen O'Neil" & I said "O, I see" & then it was that I held you close Janey & it seemed for one moment I was back again with you in those terrible heart breaking days in Yellow Stone Valley faceing life without your own Father a future black & tragic for you darling. Then your Daddy Jim came. I know God sent him to me. & there I was in Omaha & watched the train carrying you away & then that letter from Helen O'Neil telling me you had gone out of my life forever for they had gone to England. I thought that was the end & that I would never see you again & there I was in your house in Virginia with you in my arms. You were such a little lady, darling, & I have never seen a little girl with so many pretty dresses. O I shall always remember when I looked back after I got in the cab & saw your Daddy Jim take you by the hand & you both waved goodby til the horses turned the corner shutting you from my sight. It will be years so many of them before I will ever see you again. Be good to Mammy Ross. She is so nice to you. That is what I wanted to tell you but didnt. There will never be for you the awful lonliness of empty years ahead Janey never as long as you have Mammy Ross & your Daddy Jim. How I wish I could say I had seen those countries where he has taken you. I hope you will think of me sometimes & of the things I told you so you would remember the woman your Daddy Jim called Jane & of the man I told you about we called Wild Bill Hickok, & you said "what a funny name" & when I showed you his picture you said "he isnt handsome like my Daddy Jim." There is nothing in this world quite so wonderful as the faith a child has in one they love. When you said your prayer that night to me you added "God bless Jane Hickok & that man who was shot in the back wherever he is. Bless him because Jane loved him." I wondered how you knew that I loved him.

Good Night little girl & may God keep you from all harm.

Part III

DREAMER

9
INTIMATE VISIONS

Introduction

The monologues in this section are intensely personal, mostly expressing the isolation that comes in dreams and in moments of deep despair, and which has at times been very fashionable among literary women. With Sappho and Pierre Louys we move to dreams of engagement. These involve the dreamer, and so the listener, in fancies and sensations but are characterized nonetheless by their intimacy. It is particularly important in preparing any of these pieces that they not be allowed to become too private. A close confidante, a mirror, or even a friendly pet can serve as the necessary audience.

Queen Elizabeth's *I Grieve and Dare Not Show My Discontent* is deceptive in its apparent simplicity. Possibly written in response to the departure of some favorite from court, this complaint has the added dimension of having been written by a queen not known for her "soft" and "melting" qualities, whose protestations of "I . . . dare not" ring curiously false. She assumes a role, plays a part, and anyone seeking to play *her* part must find and incorporate the fundamental sense of isolation that comes with power over others.

Writing under the pen-name "Orinda," Katherine Philips was England's most renowned female poet of the seventeenth century, and indeed for a couple of hundred years thereafter. One later critic praised her *Ode Against Pleasure* by stating: "That must have been a noble spirit which in such a licentious and gaudy era as the reign of Charles II could conceive and embody [these verses]," mentioning further that she was "as exemplary in the discharge of her domestic duties as she was celebrated for her practical abilities."

Christina Rossetti's *Passing and Glassing* is a kind of sombre "mirror, mirror, on the wall" that reflects ageing, loneliness, and resignation, even futility; and *Echo* is a call to one long dead to reunite with her in her dreams, a macabre sentiment beautifully executed. Further conversations with the dead inform the work of Emily Brontë, here represented by the poem *Remembrance*, an apology for forgetting, and an excerpt from *Wuthering Heights* that vividly depicts a nightmarish tug of war, through a broken casement window, with the ghost of the twenty-years-gone waif, Catherine Linton. Anna Kingsford's precarious expedition along her dream sea cliff harbors practical advice concerning her daughter's education . . . she is invited, then instructed, to let go. And her "underground laboratory" dream is an outburst of personal revulsion against vivisection that can easily function today as a powerful protest against animal testing and the luxury fur trade. It should be especially noted that while much of this material deals with dreams and other nonphysical manifestations, there should be nothing the least bit vague in the presentation of any of it. Actors are cautioned to keep their work specific, for it is the intense clarity of the vision that will create the illusion of unreality.

For the reclusive Emily Dickinson, observations on faith and eternity were a common pastime and this trio of verses spans much of her literary life. The first addresses the prospect of heaven in a light and modest fashion. The second is a somewhat grisly catalogue of the commonplace accoutrements of death. And the last sends an intricate, disjointed message across some great distance, catching living and dead with the delicate thread of words.

A prime model of the isolated woman, Hawthorne's Hester Prynne, branded with the scarlet "A" for her adultery and shunned by common folk, nevertheless obsessively imagines a bond to others and their secret shame. And the heroine of Charlotte Perkins Gilman's *The Yellow Wallpaper* becomes haunted by patterns on her wall: ". . . each breadth stands alone, the bloated curves and flourishes— a kind of 'debased Romanesque' with *delirium tremens*— go waddling up and down in isolated columns of fatuity." She not only believes that the pattern moves, she becomes convinced that there is a woman inside trying to escape; and then, of course, in true schizophrenic fashion, she becomes that woman. The piece is completely 'bizarre, but can make a fascinating presentation if a commitment is made either to complete stillness—suggesting that the narrative is being told at a later time or was, perhaps, completely imagined—or to the creeping activity described in the story, in which case the movement must remain constant throughout the telling.

Equally fascinating is Margaret Atwood's convoluted tour of the Royal Ontario Museum, with all of history becoming a projection of her private world. *The Park* is one of Gareth Owen's *Nineteen Fragments* of a young, near-suicidal woman's psyche. In this case, the call for "music," "harmony," and "peace" transcends the specific situation and strikes a desperately common chord for many.

Out of the darkness of dreams can come light and clarity, as is the case with Sappho's little prayer, her rationalization. A native of Mytilene on the Greek island of Lesbos around 600 B.C., she led a women's literary coterie dedicated to Aphrodite. Among the ancients, she enjoyed the title of "The Poetess"—placing her in the same rank as Homer, who was known as "The Poet"—and was admired even by Plato, who referred to her as the tenth Muse. Her extant poems, mostly quite short, are characterized for the most part by an alarming candor, an active engagement of the senses, and a purity of vision uncluttered by cumbersome literary devices.

In 1894 French poet and classicist Pierre Louÿs published his *Chansons de Bilitis*, inspired by Sappho and attributed to Bilitis, an invented persona about whom he even wrote a biographical sketch. The seven brief prose poems I have chosen encompass a life, at once ancient, alien, and familiar as any dream. Affirmations of all life, they are refreshingly sensuous and devout, full of striking images and unusual metaphors.

Queen Elizabeth I
I Grieve and Dare Not Show My Discontent

I grieve and dare not show my discontent;
　I love, and yet am forced to seem to hate;
I do, yet dare not say I ever meant;
　I seem stark mute, but inwardly do prate:
I am, and not; I freeze, and yet am burn'd,
Since from myself, my other self I turn'd.

My care is like my shadow in the sun,
　Follows me flying, flies when I pursue it;
Stands and lies by me, does what I have done;
　This too familiar care does make me rue it:
No means I find to rid him from my breast,
Till by the end of things it be supprest.

Some gentler passions slide into my mind,
　For I am soft and made of melting snow;

Or be more cruel, Love, and so be kind,
  Let me float or sink, be high or low:
Or let me live with some more sweet content,
Or die, and so forget what love e'er meant.

Orinda (Katherine Fowler Philips)
Ode Against Pleasure

There's no such thing as pleasure here,
  'Tis all a perfect cheat,
Which does but shine and disappear,
  Whose charm is but deceit:
The empty bribe of yielding souls,
Which first betrays, and then controls.

'Tis true, it looks at distance fair,
  But if we do approach,
The fruit of Sodom will impair,
  And perish at a touch;
It being than in fancy less,
And we expect more than possess.

For by our pleasures we are cloy'd
  And so desire is done;
Or else, like rivers, they make wide
  The channels where they run;
And either way true bliss destroys,
Making us narrow, or our joys.

We covet pleasure easily,
  But ne'er true bliss possess;

For many things must make it be,
  But one may make it less.
Nay, were our state as we would choose it,
'Twould be consum'd by fear to lose it.

What art thou, then, thou winged air,
  More weak and swift than fame?
Whose next successor is despair,
  And its attendant shame.
Th' experienc'd prince then reason had
Who said of Pleasure,—"It is mad."

Christina Rossetti
Passing and Glassing

All things that pass
　Are woman's looking-glass;
They show her how her bloom must fade,
And she herself be laid
With wither'd roses in the shade;
　With wither'd roses and the fallen peach,
　Unlovely, out of reach
　　Of summer joy that was.

All things that pass
　Are woman's tiring-glass;
The faded lavender is sweet,
Sweet the dead violet
Cull'd and laid by and car'd for yet;
　The dried-up violets and dried lavender
　Still sweet, may comfort her,
　　Nor need she cry Alas!

All things that pass
　Are wisdom's looking-glass;
Being full of hope and fear, and still
Brimful of good or ill,
According to our work and will;
　For there is nothing new beneath the sun;
　Our doings have been done,
　　And that which shall be was.

Echo

Come to me in the silence of the night;
    Come in the speaking silence of a dream;
Come with soft rounded cheeks and eyes as bright
    As sunlight on a stream;
        Come back in tears,
O memory, hope, love of finished years.

O dream how sweet, too sweet, too bitter sweet,
    Whose wakening should have been in Paradise,
Where souls brimfull of love abide and meet;
    Where thirsting longing eyes
        Watch the slow door
That opening, letting in, lets out no more.

Yet come to me in dreams, that I may live
    My very life again though cold in death:
Come back to me in dreams, that I may give
    Pulse for pulse, breath for breath:
        Speak low, lean low,
As long ago, my love, how long ago.

Emily Brontë
Remembrance

Cold in the earth, and the deep snow piled above thee!
Far, far removed, cold in the dreary grave!
Have I forgot, my Only Love, to love thee,
Severed at last by Time's all-wearing wave?

Now, when alone, do my thoughts no longer hover
Over the mountains on Angora's shore;
Resting their wings where heath and fern-leaves cover
That noble heart for ever, ever more?

Cold in the earth, and fifteen wild Decembers
From those brown hills have melted into spring—
Faithful indeed is the spirit that remembers
After such years of change and suffering!

Sweet Love of youth, forgive if I forget thee
While the World's tide is bearing me along:
Sterner desires and darker hopes beset me,
Hopes which obscure but cannot do thee wrong.

No other Sun has lightened up my heaven;
No other Star has ever shone for me:
All my life's bliss from thy dear life was given—
All my life's bliss is in the grave with thee.

But when the days of golden dreams had perished
And even Despair was powerless to destroy,
Then did I learn how existence could be cherished,
Strengthened and fed without the aid of joy;

Then did I check the tears of useless passion,
Weaned my young soul from yearning after thine;

Sternly denied its burning wish to hasten
Down to that tomb already more than mine!

And even yet, I dare not let it languish,
Dare not indulge in Memory's rapturous pain;
Once drinking deep of that divinest anguish,
How could I seek the empty world again?

from *Wuthering Heights*

I remember I was lying in the oak closet, and I heard
distinctly the gusty wind, and the driving of the snow; I
heard, also, the fir-bough repeat its teasing sound, and
ascribed it to the right cause: but it annoyed me so much,
that I resolved to silence it, if possible; and, I thought, I
rose and endeavoured to unhasp the casement. The hook
was soldered into the staple: a circumstance observed by
me when awake, but forgotten. "I must stop it, nevertheless!" I muttered, knocking my knuckles through the glass,
and stretching an arm out to seize the importunate branch;
instead of which, my fingers closed on the fingers of a little,
ice-cold hand! The intense horror of nightmare came over
me: I tried to draw back my arm, but the hand clung to it,
and a most melancholy voice sobbed, "Let me in—let me
in!" "Who are you?" I asked, struggling, meanwhile, to
disengage myself. "Catherine Linton," it replied shiver-
ingly . . . "I'm come home: I'd lost my way on the moor!"
As it spoke, I discerned, obscurely, a child's face looking
through the window. Terror made me cruel; and, finding
it useless to attempt shaking the creature off, I pulled its
wrist on to the broken pane, and rubbed it to and fro till
the blood ran down and soaked the bedclothes: still it

wailed, "Let me in!" and maintained its tenacious grip, almost maddening me with fear. "How can I!" I said at length. "Let *me* go, if you want me to let you in!" The fingers relaxed, I snatched mine through the hole, hurriedly piled the books up in a pyramid against it, and stopped my ears to exclude the lamentable prayer. I seemed to keep them closed above a quarter of an hour; yet, the instant I listened again, there was the doleful cry moaning on! "Begone!" I shouted, "I'll never let you in, not if you beg for twenty years." "It is twenty years," mourned the voice: "twenty years. I've been a waif for twenty years!" Thereat began a feeble scratching outside, and the pile of books moved as if thrust forward. I tried to jump; but could not stir a limb; and so yelled aloud, in a frenzy of fright.

Anna Kingsford
The Child on the Cliff

Having fallen asleep last night while in a state of great perplexity about the care and education of my daughter, I dreamt as follows.

I was walking with the child along the border of a high cliff, at the foot of which was the sea. The path was exceedingly narrow, and on the inner side was flanked by a line of rocks and stones. The outer side was so close to the edge of the cliff that she was compelled to walk either before or behind me, or else on the stones. And, as it was unsafe to let go her hand, it was on the stones that she had to walk, much to her distress. I was in male attire, and carried a staff in my hand. She wore skirts and had no staff; and every moment she stumbled or her dress caught and was torn by some jutting crag or bramble. In this way our progress was being continually interrupted and rendered almost impossible, when suddenly we came upon a sharp declivity leading to a steep path which wound down the side of the precipice to the beach below. Looking down, I saw on the shore beneath the cliff a collection of fishermen's huts, and groups of men and women on the shingle, mending nets, hauling up boats, and sorting fish of various kinds. In the midst of the little village stood a great crucifix of lead, so cast in a mould as to allow me from the elevated position I occupied behind it, to see that though in front it looked solid, it was in reality hollow. As I was noting this, a voice of some one close at hand suddenly addressed me; and on turning my head I found standing before me a man in the garb of a fisherman, who evidently had just scaled the steep path leading from the beach. He stretched out his hand to take the child, saying he had come to fetch her, for that in the path I was following there was room only for one. "Let her come to us," he added; "she will do very well as a fisherman's daughter." Being reluctant to part with her, and not perceiving then the significance of his garb and vocation, I objected that the calling was a dirty and unsavoury one, and would soil her hands and dress. Whereupon the man became severe, and seemed to insist with a kind of authority upon my acceptance of his proposition. The child, too, was taken with him, and was moreover anxious to leave the rough and dangerous path; and she accordingly went to him of her own will and, placing her hand in his, left me without any sign of regret, and I went on my way alone.

The Laboratory Underground

I dreamed that I found myself underground in a vault artificially lighted. Tables were ranged along the walls of the vault, and upon these tables were bound down the living bodies of half-dissected and mutilated animals. Scientific experts were busy at work on their victims with scalpel, hot iron and forceps. But, as I looked at the creatures lying bound before them, they no longer appeared to be mere rabbits, or hounds, for in each I saw a human shape, the shape of a man, with limbs and lineament resembling those of their torturers, hidden within the outward form. And when they led into the place an old worn-out horse, crippled with age and long toil in the service of man, and bound him down, and lacerated his flesh with their knives, I saw the human form within him stir and writhe as though it were an unborn babe moving in its mother's womb. And I cried aloud—"Wretches! you are tormenting an unborn man!" But they heard not, nor could they see what I saw. Then they brought in a white rabbit, and thrust its eyes through with heated irons. And as I gazed, the rabbit seemed to me like a tiny infant, with human face, and hands which stretched themselves towards me in appeal, and lips which sought to cry for help in human accents. And I could bear no more, but broke forth into a bitter rain of tears, exclaiming—"O blind! blind! not to see that you torture a child, the youngest of your own flesh and blood!"

And with that I woke, sobbing vehemently.

Emily Dickinson
Going to Heaven!

Going to Heaven!
I don't know when—
Pray do not ask me how!
Indeed I'm too astonished
To think of answering you!
Going to Heaven!
How dim it sounds!
And yet it will be done
As sure as flocks go home at night
Unto the Shepherd's arm!

Perhaps you're going too!
Who knows?
If you should get there first
Save just a little space for me
Close to the two I lost—
The smallest "Robe" will fit me
And just a bit of "Crown"—
For you know we do not mind our dress
When we are going home—

I'm glad I don't believe it
For it would stop my breath—
And I'd like to look a little more
At such a curious Earth!
I'm glad they did believe it
Whom I have never found
Since the mighty Autumn afternoon
I left them in the ground.

There's Been a Death

There's been a Death, in the Opposite House,
As lately as Today—
I know it, by the numb look
Such Houses have—always—

The Neighbors rustle in and out—
The Doctor—drives away—
A Window opens like a Pod—
Abrupt—mechanically—

Somebody flings a Mattress out—
The Children hurry by—
They wonder if it died—on that—
I used to—when a Boy—

The Minister—goes stiffly in—
As if the House were His—
And He owned all the Mourners—now—
And little Boys—besides—

And then the Milliner—and the Man
Of the Appalling Trade—
To take the measure of the House—

There'll be that Dark Parade—

Of Tassels—and of Coaches—soon—
It's easy as a Sign—
The Intuition of the News—
In just a Country Town—

I Cannot Live with You

I cannot live with You—
It would be Life—
And Life is over there—
Behind the Shelf

The Sexton keeps the Key to—
Putting up
Our Life—His Porcelain—
Like a Cup—

Discarded of the Housewife—
Quaint—or Broke—
A newer Sevres pleases—
Old Ones crack—

I could not die—with You—
For One must wait
To shut the Other's Gaze down—
You—could not—

And I—Could I stand by
And see You—freeze—
Without my Right of Frost—
Death's privilege?

Nor could I rise—with You—
Because Your Face
Would put out Jesus'—
That New Grace

Glow plain—and foreign
On my homesick Eye—
Except that You than He
Shone closer by—

They'd judge Us—How—
For You—served Heaven—You know,
Or sought to—
I could not—

Because You saturated Sight—
And I had no more Eyes
For sordid excellence
As Paradise

And were You lost, I would be—
Though My Name
Rang loudest
On the Heavenly fame—

And were You—saved—
And I—condemned to be
Where You were not—
That self—were Hell to me—

So We must meet apart—
You there—I—here
With just the Door ajar
That Oceans are—and Prayer—
And that White Sustenance—
Despair—

Nathaniel Hawthorne
from *The Scarlet Letter*

From first to last Hester Prynne had always this dreadful agony in feeling a human eye upon the token; the spot never grew callous; it seemed, on the contrary, to grow more sensitive with daily torture.

But sometimes, once in many days, or perchance in many months, she felt an eye—a human eye—upon the ignominious brand, that seemed to give a momentary relief, as if half of her agony were shared. The next instant, back it all rushed again, with still a deeper throb of pain; for, in that brief interval, she had sinned anew. Had Hester sinned alone?

Her imagination was somewhat affected, and, had she been of a softer moral and intellectual fibre, would have been still more so, by the strange and solitary anguish of her life. Walking to and fro, with those lonely footsteps, in the little world with which she was outwardly connected, it now and then appeared to Hester,—if altogether fancy, it was nevertheless too potent to be resisted, she felt or fancied, then,—that the scarlet letter had endowed her with a new sense. She shuddered to believe, yet could not help believing, that it gave her a sympathetic knowledge of the hidden sin in other hearts. She was terror-stricken by the revelations that were thus made. What were they? Could they be other than the insidious whispers of the bad angel, who would fain have persuaded the struggling woman, as yet only half his victim, that the outward guise of purity was but a lie, and that, if truth were everywhere to be shown, a scarlet letter would blaze forth on many a bosom besides Hester Prynne's? Or, must she receive those intimations—so obscure, yet so distinct—as truth? In all her miserable experience, there was nothing else so awful and so loathsome as this sense. It perplexed, as well as shocked her, by the irreverent inopportuneness of the occasions that brought it into vivid action. Sometimes the red infamy upon her breast would give a sympathetic throb, as she passed near a venerable minister or magistrate, the model of piety and justice, to whom that age of antique reverence looked up, as to a mortal man in fellowship with angels. "What evil thing is at hand?" would Hester say to herself. Lifting her reluctant eyes, there would be nothing human within the scope of view, save the form of this earthly saint! Again, a mystic sisterhood would contumaciously assert itself, as she met the sanctified frown of some matron, who, according to the rumour of all tongues, had kept cold snow within her bosom throughout life. That unsunned snow in the matron's bosom, and the burning shame on Hester Prynne's,—what had the two in common? Or, once more, the electric thrill would give her warning,— "Behold, Hester, here is a companion!"—and, looking up, she would detect the eyes of a young maiden glancing at the scarlet letter, shyly and aside, and quickly averted, with a faint, chill crimson in her cheeks; as if her purity were somewhat sullied by that momentary glance. O Fiend, whose talisman was that fatal symbol, wouldst thou leave nothing, whether in youth or age, for this poor sinner to revere?—such loss of faith is ever one of the saddest results of sin. Be it accepted as a proof that all was not corrupt in this poor victim of her own frailty, and man's hard law, that Hester Prynne yet struggled to believe that no fellow-mortal was guilty like herself.

Charlotte Perkins Gilman
from *The Yellow Wallpaper*

We shall sleep downstairs tonight, and take the boat home tomorrow.

I quite enjoy the room, now it is bare again.

How those children did tear about here!

This bedstead is fairly gnawed!

But I must get to work.

I have locked the door and thrown the key down into the front path.

I don't want to go out, and I don't want to have anybody come in, till John comes.

I want to astonish him.

I've got a rope up here that even Jennie did not find. If that woman does get out, and tries to get away, I can tie her!

But I forgot I could not reach far without anything to stand on!

This bed will *not* move!

I tried to lift and push it until I was lame, and then I got so angry I bit off a little piece at one corner—but it hurt my teeth.

Then I peeled off all the paper I could reach standing on the floor. It sticks horribly and the pattern just enjoys it! All those strangled heads and bulbous eyes and waddling fungus growths just shriek with derision!

I am getting angry enough to do something desperate. To jump out of the window would be admirable exercise, but the bars are too strong even to try.

Besides, I wouldn't do it. Of course not. I know well enough that a step like that is improper and might be misconstrued.

I don't like to *look* out of the windows even—there are

so many of those creeping women, and they creep so fast.

I wonder if they all come out of that wallpaper, as I did?

But I am securely fastened now by my well-hidden rope—you don't get *me* out in the road there!

I suppose I shall have to to get back behind the pattern when it comes night, and that is hard!

It is so pleasant to be out in this great room and creep around as I please!

I don't want to go outside. I won't, even if Jennie asks me to.

For outside you have to creep on the ground, and everything is green instead of yellow.

But here I can creep smoothly on the floor, and my shoulder just fits in that long smooch around the wall, so I cannot lose my way.

Why, there's John at the door!

It is no use, young man, you can't open it!

How he does call and pound!

Now he's crying for an axe.

It would be a shame to break down that beautiful door!

"John, dear!" said I in the gentlest voice, "the key is down by the front steps, under a plantain leaf!"

That silenced him for a few moments.

Then he said—very quietly indeed, "Open the door, my darling!"

"I can't," said I. "The key is down by the front door, under a plantain leaf!"

And then I said it again, several times, very gently and slowly, and said it so often that he had to go and see, and he got it, of course, and came in. He stopped short by the door.

"What is the matter?" he cried. "For God's sake, what are you doing?"

I kept on creeping just the same, but I looked at him over my shoulder.

"I've got out at last," said I, "in spite of you and Jennie!

And I've pulled off most of the paper, so you can't put me
back!"

Now why should that man have fainted? But he did, and
right across my path by the wall, so that I had to creep
over him every time!

Margaret Atwood
A Night in the Royal Ontario Museum

Who locked me

into this crazed man-made
stone brain
        where the weathered
totempole jabs a blunt
finger at the byzantine
mosaic dome

Under that ornate
golden cranium I wander
among fragments of gods, tarnished
coins, embalmed gestures
chronologically arranged,
looking for the EXIT sign

but in spite of the diagrams
at every corner, labelled
in red: YOU ARE HERE
the labyrinth holds me,

turning me around
the cafeteria, the washrooms,

a spiral through marble
Greece and Rome, the bronze
horses of China

then past the carved masks, wood and fur
to where 5 plaster Indians
in a glass case
squat near a dusty fire

and further, confronting me
with a skeleton child, preserved
in the desert air, curled
beside a clay pot and a few beads.

I say I am far
enough,   stop here   please
no more

but the perverse museum, corridor
by corridor, an idiot
voice jogged by a pushed
button, repeats its memories

and I am dragged to the mind's
deadend, the roar of the bone-
yard, I am lost
among the mastodons
and beyond: a fossil
shell, then

samples of rocks
and minerals, even the thundering
tusks dwindling to pin-
points in the stellar
fluorescent-lighted
wastes of geology

Gareth Owen
The Park

The park where the children play
Creates itself each day
For her eyes; defines itself
In a way which she cannot.
Dishevelled bushes
And a worn green
Are charged with sardonic malevolence.
There is much crying in her
But all is separate.
Her heel is worn on the right side
And her stockings wrinkle.

It is uncomfortable in this place,
There is no comfort here—
I think they call it the world—
It is too much in my mind,
I wish to be taken away.
Will the dark angel come today,
Will he keep the appointment?
But there is naught but staring.
    I am crying out for music,
For harmony to draw a bow
Across the strings of me.
Cry out the music.
Let me stretch myself upon you,
Wind me about in a child's song
Called peace.

Sappho
No

Oneiris, god of dreams, son of blackest night, you who lingers longest as morning's light lifts the last of sleep from my eyes . . .

Soothing god, you've shown me the strain, the discord that comes of separating burning wish from action . . .

I think I shall not flout your truth, your visions; and, sustained by the Blessed Ones, I shall not spurn the thing for which I moan.

When I was little, I was never so silly as to turn my back on a toy my mother held out to me . . .

So, may the Blessed Ones arrange occasion, quickly, to place me in the way of what I crave . . . I pray with expectation, as one who often honors them in poetry and song.

Pierre Louÿs
from *Les Chansons de Bilitis*

III. Maternal Advice

My mother bathes me in darkness, she dresses me in bright sunlight and arranges my hair in lamplight; but if I walk out into the moonlight she tightens my belt with a double knot.

She says to me: "Play with virgins, dance with little children; do not look out of the window; run from the promises of young men and fear the counsel of widows.

"One evening, someone will take you, as all are taken, amidst a great procession of ringing dulcimers and amorous flutes.

"That evening, when you go away, Bilito, you will leave me three gourds of gall: one for the morning, one for midday, and the third, the most bitter, the third for the days of festival."

VII. The Passer-by

As I was seated in the evening before the door of the house, a young man passed by. He looked at me, I turned away my head. He spoke to me, I did not answer.

He wanted to approach me. I took a sickle from the wall and I would have slit his cheek if he had advanced one step.

Then, retreating a little, he started to smile and blew a breath toward me across his hand, saying: "Receive this kiss," and I cried out! And I wept! So much so that my mother came running.

Alarmed, believing that I had been stung by a scorpion . . . I wept: "He kissed me." My mother also kissed me and embraced me and carried me away in her arms.

XXIX. The Pan-pipe

For the day of Hyacinthus he gave me a syrinx made of carefully cut reeds joined with white wax as sweet to my lips as honey.

He taught me to play, seated on his knees; but I trembled a little. He played after me; so softly that I could scarcely hear him.

We had nothing to say to each other, so near were we one to the other; but our languid songs replied to each other and, by turns, our lips joined on the flute.

It is late. There! the green frogs are singing, heralding the night. My mother will never believe that I have stayed so long looking for my lost belt.

XCI. Funeral Song

Sing a funeral song, muses of Mytilene, sing! The earth is sombre like a mourning-cloak and the yellow trees shiver like cut tresses.

Heraios! O sad, sweet month! the leaves fall gently like snow, the sun penetrates more and more into the clearing forest. . . . I no longer hear anything but silence.

See, they have carried to the tomb Pittakos, heavy with years. Many are dead that I knew. And she who lives is to me as if she were no more.

This is the tenth autumn I have watched die upon this plain. It is time for me also to disappear. Weep with me, muses of Mytilene, weep upon my footprints!

XCII. Hymn to Astarte

Mother inexhaustible, incorruptible, creatrix, first-born, self-begotten, self-conceived, your issue alone, taking joy in yourself, Astarte!

O perpetually fecund, O virgin and nourisher of all, chaste and lascivious, pure and possessive, ineffable, nocturnal, sweet, breather of fire, foam of the sea!

You who grant secret mercies, you who unite, you who love, you who seize the multiplying species of savage beasts with furious desire, and join sexes in the forests!

O Astarte, irresistible, hear me, take me, possess me, O moon, and, thirteen times each year, wrest from my bowels the libation of my blood!

XCIII. *Hymn to the Night*

Black masses of trees as immovable as mountains. Stars filling up an immense sky. A warm breeze like human breath caresses my eyes and my cheeks.

O Night, who beget Gods! how sweet you are upon my lips! how warm you are in my hair! how you enter into me this night, and how heavy I am grown with all of your springtime.

The flowers that shall bloom shall all be born of me. The wind that blows is my breath. The perfume that penetrates is my desire. All stars are in my eyes.

Your voice . . . is it the roar of the sea? Is it the silence of the plain? Your voice; I do not understand it, but it knocks me head over heels, and my tears wash both my hands.

The Tomb of Bilitis: First Epitaph

In the country where fountains arise from the sea, and where river beds are made from leaves of rick, I, Bilitis, was born.

My mother was Phoenician; my father, Damophylos, was Hellene. My mother taught me the songs of Byblos, sad as the first dawn.

I have adored Astarte at Cypros. I have known Psappha at Lesbos. I have sung as I have loved. If I have lived well, Passer-by, tell your daughter so.

And do not sacrifice the black goat for me; but in sweet libation, milk her over my tomb.

10
EPICS AND GOTHICS

Introduction

Here is Sappho again, in an uncharacteristic Homeric vein, parodying the epic mode so different from her own usual miniature masterpieces. The story of Hector's homecoming, accompanied by his bride Andromache, has every epic element: color, romance, scale, and even, by implication, tragedy. Her listeners would have known that this celebratory interlude would be followed soon enough by the fall of Troy.

Marie de France, a twelfth-century French poet at the court of Henry II and Eleanor of Aquitaine, made significant contributions to Arthurian legend in the form of *"lais"* which, while relatively unconnected with Britain's King Arthur, were based on a Breton tradition of "lays" or songs depicting the often supernatural exploits of great heroes and ladies. The Victorian translation of *"Lanval"* is appropriately archaic and quite in keeping with the two poems that follow: Charlotte Elliot's testimonial to the caring endurance of womankind, represented here by Sigyn, wife to the Norse deity Loki, the personification of fire, chained to a rock under a venomous serpent for his evil ways; and Mrs. Darmesteter's *A Ballad of Orleans*, a highly energetic and musical glorification of Joan of Arc's military prowess. Both of these set pieces demand a grand style of presentation, full-voiced and physically extended, even operatic if necessary.

Lady Wilde, Oscar Wilde's mother, was known for her researches into Irish legend, and her stories are best told with a suggestion that you, the teller, know more about such matters than you are letting on. Mary Byron churns

254

one such legend into a sweeping fairies' gallop, told from the point of view of their human victim; and in her *The Tryst of the Night*, she conjures a vast, haunting presence that loses none of its power or passion for its phrasing being a trifle cliché. But it is *Goblin Market*, Christina Rossetti's masterwork of the macabre, that truly frightens with its unsettling suggestion of evil as commonplace, even familiar, immediately present in the everyday world of garden and glen. Her verse rushes headlong, like the feverish wasting caused by the Goblin fruit, then seems to slow as morning comes and Lizzie is restored by virtue of her sister's tender ministrations. The epilogue, a moral for the children about the value of sisterhood, is a hackneyed homily altogether reassuring and welcome after the terrors of the night. Contemporary Iraqi poet Nazik al-Mala'ikah strikes a similar chord in *The Viper*, with her sense of being perpetually hunted by a barely seen, yet intimately known and ever-present enemy. These monologues can be tremendously affecting, but only if they are played with utmost seriousness, and only if the story is told without interference from the teller.

A horrific dream scene common to many gothic romances is played out in Ann Radcliffe's *The Romance of the Forest*, written in 1791, one of the earliest examples of the genre. Replete with an abandoned abbey, galleries, passages, and an inhabited coffin, the piece should be treated as a journey to be shared by speaker and audience. But it is for the innocence and appeal of their heroines that gothics have always been most notable, and Emily in Radcliffe's *The Mysteries of Udolpho* is typical in her "melancholy awe," as she passively allows herself to be led through the "solemn duskiness of evening" to the castle, "awful in obscurity." A good deal perkier is Charlotte Brontë's Jane Eyre, gratefully and excitedly confessing her misfortunes to Mr. Rivers and his family.

The three intervening ghost stories that follow offer not only distinctive and pleasing heroines, but different types of narrative as well. Elizabeth Gaskell's Hester in *The Old Nurse's Story* is a mature woman, fiercely protective of her charge's safety, and the story, first published at Christmas 1852, has an appropriately wintry chill to it. The opportunity for Hester to tell the little girl's story as well as her own makes this selection particularly fun. Cissy's tale in Lanoe Falconer's *Cecilia De Noël* also features a second speaking character, a ghost who is redeemed by the heroine's compassion. To support the intimacy and immediacy of this story, imagine a cozy fire and, beside it, a couple of dear friends for your audience. By contrast Mary E. Braddon's 1862 story, *The Cold Embrace,* is written in the third person and features innovative use of present-tense narrative. There is a rapid-fire newsreel feeling to this work, a sense of moving quickly through time achieved by juxtaposing images, now panoramic, now close up and intensely personal. Suggestive of some of Bertolt Brecht's narrative "distancing," the result is engaging rather than alienating, drawing the audience all the more fully into sympathy with the abandoned heroine.

Finally there is Mina, the lady who challenges Count Dracula himself. Her first journal entry is included for its vivid sense of foreboding and the threatening storm, the second for the more familiar naiveté Mina exhibits in the face of impending horror.

A curiosity somewhat in line with the romance and imagination of the gothic tradition is Robert W. Chambers's *The Rogue's Moon,* a 1928 adventure novel for young ladies, which centers around the piratical escapades of Mary Read, a real historical figure, seen through the wide eyes of seventeen-year-old Nancy Topsfield. I have included their first encounter, in which the astonished Nancy takes in Mary's outrageous and clearly dashing outfit and demeanor.

More curious still is *Too Far,* a punster's paradise by pulp-fiction master Fredric Brown. The utter contempt with which he treats his womanizing "hero" Wilkinson and the exuberance of the heroine transport the story to the realm of effective women's material. While the piece is written as a straightforward third-person narrative, the storyteller's whimsical presence is so strong that I suggest that the speaker assume the point of view of the doe-weremaid herself.

Sappho
The Homecoming of Hector and Andromache

The Herald Idaeus, powerful, swift-footed, arrives and announces the wonderful news—legendary tidings from the depths of Asia:

"Across the shining, salty sea by ship, from sacred Thebe and Plakia's plains, Hector comes, his comrades with him, bringing a delicate, dark-eyed girl—splendid Andromache. And a trove of golden bracelets, purple robes, spangled trinkets, ivory, and cups of silver, are borne on the winds over the sea."

So speaks the Herald, and Hector's beloved father rises nimbly as the news spreads to friends throughout the great city. Then . . . the people of Troy move as one. Men harness horses to fine chariots; and the wives and pretty-ankled girls—all but Priam's daughters—climb inside, surrounded by the youth of the city . . . then a Mighty People move mightily forward, charioteers and musically jingling horses, surging toward the harbor to greet the bride and groom.

Hector and Andromache ascend their car like gods, and the magnificent cavalcade, an entire city on the move, regains the gates of Troy to the accompaniment of honey-tongued flutes, lyres, castanets, and O, the crystal holy singing of young girls, sweet echoes reaching high Olympian heavens, the gods themselves laughing for very joy. There is joyous laughter in the streets below as well, as cups and bowls of wine are shared and from each shrine snake smoky tendrils of rich cassia, myrrh, and frankincense. Older women shout their joy. And men roar out a glorious hymn to the harper Apollo, the far-shooting god. All sing aloud for the godlike couple, Hector and Andromache.

———————

Marie de France
from *The Lay of Sir Launfal*

The Maiden herself showed such as I will tell you. Passing slim was the lady, sweet of bodice and slender of girdle. Her throat was whiter than snow on branch, and her eyes were like flowers in the pallor of her face. She had a witching mouth, a dainty nose, and an open brow. Her eyebrows were brown, and her golden hair parted in two soft waves upon her head. She was clad in a shift of spotless linen, and above her snowy kirtle was set a mantle of royal purple, clasped upon her breast. She carried a hooded falcon upon her glove, and a greyhound followed closely after. As the Maiden rode at a slow pace through the streets of the city, there was none, neither great nor small, youth nor sergeant, but ran forth from this house, that he might content his heart with so great beauty. Every man that saw her with his eyes, marvelled at a fairness beyond that of any earthly woman. Little he cared for any mortal maiden, after he had seen this sight. The friends of Sir Launfal hastened to the knight, to tell him of his lady's succour, if so it were according to God's will.

"Sir comrade, truly is not this your friend? This lady is neither black nor golden, mean nor tall. She is only the most lovely thing in all the world."

When Launfal heard this, he sighed, for by their words he knew again his friend. He raised his head, and as the blood rushed to his face, speech flowed from his lips.

"By my faith," cried he, "yes, she is indeed my friend. It is a small matter now whether men slay me, or set me free; for I am made whole of my hurt just by looking on her face."

The Maiden entered in the palace—where none so fair had come before—and stood before the King, in the presence of his household. She loosed the clasp of her mantle, so that men might the more easily perceive the grace of her person. The courteous King advanced to meet her, and all the Court got them on their feet, and pained themselves in her service. When the lords had gazed upon her for a space, and praised the sum of her beauty, the lady spake to Arthur in this fashion, for she was anxious to begone.

"Sire, I have loved one of thy vassals—the knight who stands in bonds, Sir Launfal. He was always misprized in thy Court, and his every action turned to blame. What he said, that thou knowest; for over hasty was his tongue before the Queen. But he never craved her in love, however loud his boasting. I cannot choose that he should come to hurt or harm by me. In the hope of freeing Launfal from his bonds, I have obeyed thy summons. Let now thy barons look boldly upon my face, and deal justly in this quarrel between the Queen and me."

The King commanded that this should be done, and looking upon her eyes, not one of the judges but was persuaded that her favour exceeded that of the Queen.

Since then Launfal had not spoken in malice against his lady, the lords of the household gave him again his sword. When the trial had come thus to an end the Maiden took her leave of the King, and made her ready to depart. Gladly would Arthur have had her lodge with him for a little, and many a lord would have rejoiced in her service, but she might not tarry. Now without the hall stood a great stone of dull marble, where it was the wont of lords, departing from the Court, to climb into the saddle, and Launfal by the stone. The Maiden came forth from the doors of the palace, and mounting on the stone, seated herself on the palfrey, behind her friend. Then they rode across the plain together, and were no more seen.

The Bretons tell that the knight was ravished by his lady to an island, very dim and very fair, known as Avalon. But none has had speech with Launfal and his faery love since then, and for my part I can tell you no more of the matter.

Lady Charlotte Elliot
The Wife of Loki

Cursed by the gods and crowned with shame,
    Fell father of a direful brood,
Whose crimes have filled the heaven with flame
    And drenched the earth with blood;

Loki, the guileful Loki, stands
    Within a rocky mountain-gorge;
Chains gird his body, feet, and hands,
    Wrought in no mortal forge.

Coiled on the rock, a mighty snake
    Above him, day and night, is hung,
With dull malignant eyes awake,
    And poison-dropping tongue.

Drop follows drop in ceaseless flow,
    Each falling where the other fell,
To lay upon his blistered brow
    The liquid fire of hell.

But lo, beside the howling wretch
    A woman stands, devoid of dread,
And one pale arm is seen to stretch
    Above his tortured head!

All through the day is lifted up,
    And all the weary night-time through,
One patient hand that holds a cup
    To catch the poison-dew.

Sometimes the venom overfills
    The cup, and she must pour it forth;

With Loki's curses then the hills
    Are rent from south to north.

But she in answer only sighs,
    And lays her lips upon his face,
And, with love's anguish in her eyes,
    Resumes her constant place.

Mrs. Darmesteter
(A. Mary F. Robinson)
A Ballad of Orleans, 1429

The fray began at the middle-gate,
    Between the night and the day;
Before the matin bell was rung
    The foe was far away.
There was no knight in the land of France
    Could gar that foe to flee,
Till up there rose a young maiden,
    And drove them to the sea.

    Sixty forts around Orleans town,
        And sixty forts of stone!
    Sixty forts at our gates last night—
        To-day there is not one!

Talbot, Suffolk, and Pole are fled
    Beyond the Loire, in fear—
Many a captain who would not drink,
    Hath drunken deeply there—
Many a captain is fallen and drowned,

And many a knight is dead,
And many die in the misty dawn
　While forts are burning red.

The blood ran off our spears all night
　As the rain runs off the roofs—
God rest their souls that fell i' the fight
　Among our horses' hoofs!
They came to rob us of our own
　With sword and spear and lance,
They fell and clutched the stubborn earth,
　And bit the dust of France!

We fought across the moonless dark
　Against their unseen hands—
A knight came out of Paradise
　And fought among our bands.
Fight on, O maiden knight of God,
　Fight on and do not tire—
For lo! the misty break o' the day
　Sees all their forts on fire!

Sixty forts around Orleans town,
　And sixty forts of stone!
Sixty forts at our gates last night—
　To-day there is not one!

Esperanza (Lady Wilde)
A Wicked Spell

When a girl wishes to gain the love of a man and to make him marry her, a dreadful spell called "Drimial Agus Thorial" is used. At dead of night, she and an accomplice go to a churchyard, exhume a newly-buried corpse, and take a strip of the skin from the head to the heel. This is wound round the girl as a belt with a solemn invocation to the devil for his help.

After she has worn it for a day and a night she watches her opportunity and ties it round the sleeping man whose love she desires; during which process the name of God must not be mentioned.

When he awakes the man is bound by the spell; and is forced to marry the cruel and evil harpy. It is said the children of such marriages bear a black mark round the wrist and are known and shunned by the people, who call them "sons of the devil."

A Woman's Curse

There was a woman of the Island of Innis-Sark who was determined to take revenge on a man because he called her by an evil name. So she went to the Saint's Well and, kneeling down, she took some of the water and poured it on the ground in the name of the devil, saying, "So may my enemy be poured out like water, and lie helpless on the earth!" Then she went round the well backwards on her knees, and at each station she cast a stone in the name of the devil and said, "So may the curse fall on him, and the power of the devil crush him!" After this she returned home.

Now the next morning there was a stiff breeze, and some of the men were afraid to go out fishing; but others said they would try their luck, and amongst them was the man on whom the curse rested. But they had not gone far from land when the boat was capsized by a heavy squall. The fishermen, however, saved themselves by swimming to shore; all except the man on whom the curse rested, and he sank like lead to the bottom, and the waves covered him, and he was drowned.

When the woman heard of the fate that had befallen her enemy, she ran to the beach and clapped her hands with joy. And as she stood there laughing with strange and horrid mirth, the corpse of the man she had cursed slowly rose up from the sea and came drifting towards her till it lay almost at her very feet. On this she stooped down to feast her eyes on the sight of the dead man, when suddenly a storm of wind screamed past her and hurled her from the point of rock where she stood. And when the people ran in all haste to help, no trace of her body could be seen. The woman and the corpse of the man she had cursed disappeared together under the waves and were never seen again from that time forth.

Mary C. G. Byron
The Fairy Thrall

On gossamer nights when the moon is low,
   And stars in the mist are hiding,
Over the hill where the foxglove's grow
    You may see the fairies riding.
     Kling! Klang! Kling!
     Their stirrups and their bridles ring,
   And their horns are loud and their bugles blow,
   When the moon is low.

They sweep through the night like a whistling wind,
   They pass and have left no traces;
But one of them lingers far behind
    The flight of the fairy faces.
     She makes no moan,
     She sorrows in the dark alone,
   She wails for the love of human kind,
   Like a whistling wind.

"Ah! why did I roam where the elfins ride,
   Their glimmering steps to follow?
They bore me far from my loved one's side,
    To wander o'er hill and hollow.
     Kling! Klang! Kling!
     Their stirrups and bridles ring,
   But my heart is cold in the cold night-tide,
   Where the elfins ride."

The Tryst of the Night

Out of the uttermost ridge of dusk, where the dark and the
   day are mingled,
  The voice of the Night rose cold and calm—it called
   through the shadow-swept air;
Through all the valleys and lone hillsides, it pierced, it
   thrilled, it tingled—
  It summoned me forth to the wild sea-shore, to meet
   with its mystery there.

Out of the deep ineffable blue, with palpitant swift repeating
  Of gleam and glitter and opaline glow, that broke in
   ripples of light—
In burning glory it came and went,—I heard, I saw it
   beating,
  Pulse by pulse, from star to star,—the passionate heart
   of the Night!

Out of the thud of the rustling sea—the panting, yearning,
   throbbing
  Waves that stole on the startled shore, with coo and
   mutter of spray—
The wail of the Night came fitful-faint,—I heard her stifled
   sobbing:
  The cold salt drops fell slowly, slowly, gray into gulfs of
   gray.

There through the darkness the great world reeled, and
   the great tides roared, assembling—
  Murmuring hidden things that are past, and secret things
   that shall be;

There at the limits of life we met, and touched with a
    rapturous trembling—
  One with each other, I and the Night, and the skies, and
    the stars, and sea.

Christina Rossetti
from *Goblin Market*

She cried, "Laura," up the garden,
"Did you miss me?
Come and kiss me.
Never mind my bruises,
Hug me, kiss me, suck my juices
Squeezed from goblin fruits for you,
Goblin pulp and goblin dew.
Eat me, drink me, love me;
Laura, make much of me;
For your sake I have braved the glen
And had to do with goblin merchant men."
    Laura started from her chair,
Flung her arms up in the air,
Clutched her hair:
"Lizzie, Lizzie, have you tasted
For my sake the fruit forbidden?
Must your light like mine be hidden,
Your young life like mine be wasted,
Undone in mine undoing,
And ruined in my ruin,
Thirsty, cankered, goblin-ridden?"—
She clung about her sister,
Kissed and kissed and kissed her:
Tears once again

Refreshed her shrunken eyes,
Dropping like rain
After long sultry drouth;
Shaking with anguish fear, and pain,
She kissed and kissed her with a hungry mouth.
  Her lips began to scorch,
That juice was wormwood to her tongue,
She loathed the feast:
Writhing as one possessed she leaped and sung,
Rent all her robe, and wrung
Her hands in lamentable haste,
And beat her breast.
Her locks streamed like the torch
Borne by a racer at full speed,
Or like the mane of horses in their flight,
Or like an eagle when she stems the light
Straight toward the sun,
Or like a caged thing freed,
Or like a flying hag when armies run.
  Swift fire spread through her veins, knocked at her heart,
Met the fire smouldering there
And overbore its lesser flame;
She gorged on bitterness without a name:
Ah! fool, to choose such part
Of soul-consuming care!
Sense failed in the mortal strife:
Like the watch-tower of a town
Which an earthquake shatters down,
Like a lightning-stricken mast,
Like a wind-uprooted tree
Spun about,
Like a foam-topped waterspout
Cast down headlong in the sea,
She fell at last;
Pleasure past and anguish past,

Is it death or is it life?
   Life out of death.
That night long Lizzie watched by her,
Counted her pulse's flagging stir,
Felt for her breath,
Held water to her lips, and cooled her face
With tears and fanning leaves:
But when the first birds chirped about their eaves,
And early reapers plodded to the place
Of golden sheaves,
And dew-wet grass
Bowed in the morning winds so brisk to pass,
And new buds with new day
Opened of cup-like lilies on the stream,
Laura awoke as from a dream,
Laughed in the innocent old way,
Hugged Lizzie but not twice or thrice;
Her gleaming locks showed not one thread of grey
Her breath was sweet as May
And light danced in her eyes.

   Days, weeks, months, years
Afterwards, when both were wives
With children of their own;
Their mother-hearts beset with fears,
Their lives bound up in tender lives;
Laura would call the little ones
And tell them of her early prime,
Those pleasant days long gone
Of not-returning time:
Would talk about the haunted glen,
The wicked, quaint fruit-merchant men,
Their fruits like honey to the throat
But poison in the blood;
(Men sell not such in any town):
Would tell them how her sister stood

In deadly peril to do her good,
And win the fiery antidote:
Then joining hands to little hands
Would bid them cling together,
"For there is no friend like a sister
In calm or stormy weather;
To cheer one on the tedious way,
To fetch one if one goes astray,
To lift one if one totters down,
To strengthen whilst one stands."

Nazik al-Mala'ikah
from *The Viper*

I will travel behind the sky
Past the frontiers of hope,
And suddenly one evening
I will hear the sound.
"Go ahead! Go ahead!
This is a lost road
Beyond the boundaries of place.
Here you will not be troubled by the viper's murmur
For this is a remote labyrinth,
Perhaps fashioned by an ancient hand
For a strange-natured prince.
Then the prince died and the trail was left
To the twitching hands of total loss."
I hear the sound all over the fields
And I go on.
Perhaps I shall wake here
From the blackness of my constant shameless nightmare.
Perhaps my enemy will lose his way.

Oh, how beautiful it is to walk
Without those deadly steps behind me,
Their frightening echoes faint and dying
Along my tortuous, twisting way.
He will never come.
No, he won't come.
He won't come.

But I hear . . . yes, a laugh full of hatred.
He has come.
Why should I go on?
I will say goodbye to my brief dream of freedom,
And yet, carrying its cold form with me,
I find I must go on.

So I will go on,
And my merciless, hidden enemy
Will follow me along each new road,
Past every evening,
And in the sorrowful black nights
He will be there.
I see him now on the distant horizon,
Looking at me
By the light of the moon,
With my unknown future,
My distant yesterdays.

Where, where can I escape
From my relentless enemy?
He is like destiny,
Eternal, hidden, everlasting,
Eternal,
Everlasting.

Ann Radcliffe
from *The Romance of the Forest*

She thought she was in a large old chamber belonging to the abbey, more ancient and desolate, though in part furnished, than any she had yet seen. It was strongly barricadoed, yet no person appeared. While she stood musing and surveying the apartment, she heard a low voice call her, and looking towards the place from whence it came, she perceived by the dim light of a lamp, a figure stretched on a bed that lay on the floor. The voice called again, and, approaching the bed, she distinctly saw the features of a man who appeared to be dying. A ghastly paleness overspread his countenance, yet there was an expression of mildness and dignity in it, which strongly interested her.

While she looked on him, his features changed, and seemed convulsed in the agonies of death. The spectacle shocked her, and she started back, but he suddenly stretched forth his hand, and seizing hers, grasped it with violence; she struggled in terror to disengage herself, and again looking on his face, saw a man, who appeared to be about thirty, with the same features, but, in full health, and of a most benign countenance. He smiled tenderly upon her, and moved his lips as if to speak, when the floor of the chamber suddenly opened, and he sunk from her view. The effort she made to save herself from falling, awoke her.

She thought she was bewildered in some winding passages of the abbey; that it was almost dark, and that she wandered about a considerable time, without being able to find a door . . . she saw a man enter the passage, habited in a long black cloak, like those usually worn by attendants at funerals, and bearing a torch. He called her to follow him, and led her through a long passage to the foot of a staircase. Here she feared to proceed, and was running back, when the man suddenly turned to pursue her, and with the terror, which this occasioned, she awoke.

Shocked by those visions, and more so by their seeming connection, which now struck her, she endeavoured to continue awake, lest their terrific images should again haunt her mind: after some time, however, her harassed spirits again sunk into slumber, though not to repose.

She now thought herself in a large old gallery, and saw at one end of it a chamber-door standing a little open, and a light within: she went towards it, and perceived the man she had before seen, standing at the door, and beckoning her towards him. With the inconsistency so common in dreams, she no longer endeavoured to avoid him, but advancing, followed him into a suite of very ancient apartments, hung with black, and lighted up as if for a funeral. Still he led her on, till she found herself in the same chamber she remembered to have seen in her former dreams; a coffin, covered with a pall, stood at the farther end of the room: some lights, and several persons surrounded it, who appeared to be in great distress.

Suddenly she thought these persons were all gone, and that she was left alone; that she went up to the coffin, and while she gazed upon it, she heard a voice speak as if from within, but saw nobody. The man she had before seen, soon after stood by the coffin, and lifting the pall, she saw beneath it a dead person, whom she thought to be the dying chevalier she had seen in her former dream: his features were sunk in death, but they were yet serene. While she looked at him, a stream of blood gushed from his side, and descending to the floor, the whole chamber was overflowed; at the same time more words were uttered in the voice she heard before; but the horror of the scene so entirely overcame her, that she started and awoke.

from *The Mysteries of Udolpho*

Towards the close of the day the road wound into a deep valley. Mountains, whose shaggy steeps appeared to be inaccessible, almost surrounded it. To the east a vista opened and exhibited the Apennines in their darkest horrors; and the long perspective of retiring summits rising over each other, their ridges clothed with pines, exhibited a stronger image of grandeur than any that Emily had yet seen. The sun had just sunk below the top of the mountains she was descending, whose long shadows stretched athwart the valley; but his sloping rays, shooting through an opening of the cliffs, touched with a yellow gleam the summits of the forest that hung upon the opposite steeps and streamed in full splendor upon the towers and battlements of a castle that spread its extensive ramparts along the brow of a precipice above. The splendor of these illuminated objects was heightened by the contrasted shade which involved the valley below.

"There," said Montoni, speaking for the first time in several hours, "is Udolpho."

Emily gazed with melancholy awe upon the castle, which she understood to be Montoni's, for, though it was now lighted up by the setting sun, the gothic greatness of its features and its moldering walls of dark grey stone rendered it a gloomy and sublime object. As she gazed, the light died away on its walls leaving a melancholy purple tint which spread deeper and deeper as the thin vapor crept up the mountain, while the battlements above were still tipped with splendor. From those, too, the rays soon faded and the whole edifice was invested with the solemn duskiness of evening. Silent, lonely, and sublime, it seemed to stand the sovereign of the scene and to frown defiance on all who dared to invade its solitary reign. As the twilight deepened, its features became more awful in obscurity; and Emily continued to gaze till its clustering towers were alone seen rising over the tops of the woods beneath whose thick shade the carriages soon after began to ascend.

Elizabeth Gaskell
from *The Old Nurse's Story*

Well, I went back to the west drawing-room, and I told Mrs. Stark we could not find Miss Rosamond anywhere, and asked for leave to look all about the furniture there, for I thought now that she might have fallen asleep in some warm hidden corner; but no! we looked, Miss Furnivall got up and looked, trembling all over, and she was nowhere there; then we set off again, every one in the house, and looked in all the places we had searched before, but we could not find her. Miss Furnivall shivered and shook so much that Mrs. Stark took her back into the warm drawing-room; but not before they had made me promise to bring her to them when she was found. Well-a-day! I began to think she never would be found, when I bethought me to look out into the great front court, all covered with snow. I was upstairs when I looked out; but it was such a clear moonlight, I could see, quite plain, two little footprints, which might be traced from the hall door, and round the corner of the east wing. I don't know how I got down, but

I tugged open the great, stiff hall door; and, throwing the skirt of my gown over my head for a cloak, I ran out. I turned the east corner, and there a black shadow fell on the snow; but when I came again into the moonlight, there were the little footmarks going up—up to the Fells. It was bitter cold; so cold that the air almost took the skin off my face as I ran, but I ran on, crying to think how my poor little darling must be perished, and frightened. I was within sight of the holly-trees when I saw a shepherd coming down the hill, bearing something in his arms wrapped in his maud. He shouted to me, and asked me if I had lost a bairn; and, when I could not speak for crying, he bore towards me, and I saw my wee bairnie lying still, and white, and stiff, in his arms, as if she had been dead. He told me he had been up the Fells to gather in his sheep, before the deep cold of night came on, and that under the holly-trees (black marks on the hillside, where no other bush was for miles around) he had found my little lady—my lamb—my queen—my darling—stiff and cold, in the terrible sleep which is frost-begotten. Oh! the joy, and the tears of having her in my arms once again! for I would not let him carry her; but took her, maud and all, into my own arms, and held her near my own warm neck and heart, and felt the life stealing slowly back again into her little gentle limbs. But she was still insensible when we reached the hall, and I had no breath for speech. We went in by the kitchen door.

"Bring the warming-pan," said I; and I carried her upstairs and began undressing her by the nursery fire, which Bessy had kept up. I called my little lammie all the sweet and playful names I could think of—even while my eyes were blinded by my tears; and at last, oh! at length she opened her large blue eyes. Then I put her into her warm bed, and sent Dorothy down to tell Miss Furnivall that all was well; and I made up my mind to sit by my darling's bedside the live-long night. She fell away into a soft sleep as soon as her pretty head had touched the pillow, and I watched her until morning light; when she wakened up bright and clear—or so I thought at first—and, my dears, so I think now.

She said that she had fancied that she should like to go to Dorothy, for that both the old ladies were asleep, and it was very dull in the drawing-room; and that, as she was going through the west lobby, she saw the snow through the high window falling—falling—soft and steady; but she wanted to see it lying pretty and white on the ground; so she made her way into the great hall; and then, going to the window, she saw it bright and soft upon the drive; but while she stood there, she saw a little girl, not so old as she was, "but so pretty," said my darling, "and this little girl beckoned to me to come out; and oh, she was so pretty and so sweet, I could not choose but to go." And then this other little girl had taken her by the hand, and side by side the two had gone around the east corner.

"Don't tell me!" said I, very stern, "I tracked you by your footmarks through the snow; there were only yours to be seen: and if you had had a little girl to go hand-in-hand with you up the hill, don't you think the footprints would have gone along yours?"

"I can't help it, dear, dear Hester," she said, crying, "if they did not; I never looked at her feet, but she held my hand fast and tight in her little one, and it was very, very cold. She took me up the Fell-path, up to the holly-trees; and there I saw a lady weeping and crying; but when she saw me, she hushed her weeping, and smiled very proud and grand, and took me on her knee, and began to lull me to sleep; and that's all, Hester—but that is true."

Lanoe Falconer
Cecilia's Gospel

"George, do you remember the day that grandmother died, when they all broke down and cried a little at dinner, all except Uncle Marmaduke? He sat up looking so white and stern at the end of the table. And I, foolish little child, thought he was not so grieved as the others—that he did not love his mother so much. But next day, quite by chance, I heard him, all alone, sobbing over her coffin. I remember standing outside the door and listening, and each sob went through my heart with a little stab, and I knew for the first time what sorrow was. But even his sobs were not so pitiful as the moans of that poor spirit. While I listened I learnt that in another world there may be worse for us to bear than even here—sorrow more hopeless, more lonely. For the strange thing was, the moaning seemed to come from so far far away; not only from somewhere millions and millions of miles away, but—this is the strangest of all—as if it came to me from time long since past, ages and ages ago. I know this sounds like nonsense, but indeed I am trying to put into words the weary long distance that seemed to stretch between us, like one I never should be able to cross. At last it spoke to me in a whisper which I could only just hear; at least it was more like a whisper than anything else I can think of, and it seemed to come like the moaning from far far away. It thanked me so meekly for looking at it and speaking to it. It told me that by sins committed against others when it was on earth it had broken the bond between itself and all other creatures. While it was what we call alive, it did not feel this, for the senses confuse us and hide many things from the good, and so still more from the wicked; but when it died and lost the body by which it seemed to be kept near to other beings, it found itself imprisoned in the most dreadful loneliness—loneliness which no one in this world can even imagine. Even the pain of solitary confinement, so it told me, which drives men mad, is only like a shadow or type of this loneliness of spirits. Others there might be, but it knew nothing of them—nothing besides this great empty darkness everywhere except the place it had once lived in, and the people who were moving about it; and even those it could only perceive dimly as if looking through a mist, and always so unutterably away from them all. I am not giving its own words, you know, George, because I cannot remember them. I am not certain it did speak to me; the thoughts seemed to pass in some strange way into my mind; I cannot explain how, for the still far-away voice did not really speak. Sometimes, it told me, the loneliness became agony, and it longed for a word or a sign from some other being, just as Dives longed for the drop of cold water; and at such times it was able to make the living people see it. But that, alas! was useless, for it only alarmed them so much that the bravest and most benevolent rushed away in terror or would not let it come near them. But still it went on showing itself to one after another, always hoping that some one would take pity on it and speak to it, for it knew of none save those in this world and in this place. And I said: 'Why did you not turn for help to God?'

"Then it gave a terrible answer: it said, 'What is God?'

"And when I heard these words there came over me a wild kind of pity, such I used to feel when I saw my little child struggling for breath when he was ill, and I held out my arms to this poor lonely thing, but it shrank back, crying:

" 'Speak to me, but do not touch me, brave human creature. I am all death, and if you come too near me the Death in me may kill the life in you.'

"But I said: 'No Death can kill the life in me, even though it kill my body. Dear fellow-spirit, I cannot tell you what

I know; but let me take you in my arms; rest for an instant on my heart, and perhaps I may make you feel what I feel all around us.'

"And as I spoke I threw my arms around the shadowy form and strained it to my breast. And I felt as if I were pressing to me only air, but air colder than any ice, so that my heart seemed to stop beating, and I could hardly breathe. But I still clasped it closer and closer, and as I grew colder it seemed to grow less chill.

"And at last it spoke, and the whisper was not far away, but near. It said: 'It is enough; now I know what God is!'

"After that I remember nothing more, till I woke up and found myself lying on the floor beside the bed. It was morning, and the spirit was not there; but I have a strong feeling that I have been able to help it, and that it will trouble you no more.

"Surely it is late! I must go at once. I promised to have tea with the children."

Mary E. Braddon
from *The Cold Embrace*

The first year of their betrothal is passed, and she is alone, for he has gone to Italy, on a commission for some rich man, to copy Raphaels, Titians, Guidos, in a gallery at Florence. He has gone to win fame, perhaps; but it is not the less bitter—he is gone!

Of course her father misses his young nephew, who has been as a son to him; and he thinks his daughter's sadness no more than a cousin should feel for a cousin's absence.

In the meantime, the weeks and months pass. The lover writes—often at first, then seldom—at last, not at all.

How many excuses she invents for him! How many times she goes to the distant little post-office, to which he is to address his letters! How many times she hopes, only to be disappointed! How many times she despairs, only to hope again!

But real despair comes at last, and will not be put off any more. The rich suitor appears on the scene, and her father is determined. She is to marry at once. The wedding-day is fixed—the fifteenth of June.

The date seems burnt into her brain.

The date, written in fire, dances for ever before her eyes.

The date, shrieked by the Furies, sounds continually in her ears.

But there is time yet—it is the middle of May—there is time for a letter to reach him at Florence; there is time for him to come to Brunswick, to take her away and marry her, in spite of her father—in spite of the whole world.

But the days and weeks fly by, and he does not write—he does not come. This is indeed despair which usurps her heart, and will not be put away.

It is the fourteenth of June. For the last time she goes

to the little post-office; for the last time she asks the old question, and they give her for the last time the dreary answer, "No, no letter."

For the last time—for tomorrow is the day appointed for her bridal. Her father will hear no entreaties; her rich suitor will not listen to her prayers. They will not be put off a day—an hour; tonight alone is hers—this night, which she may employ as she will.

She takes another path than that which leads home; she hurries through some by-streets of the city, out on to a lonely bridge, where he and she had stood so often in the sunset, watching the rose-coloured light glow, fade, and die upon the river.

Charlotte Brontë
from *Jane Eyre*

"Mr. Rivers," I said, turning to him, and looking at him, as he looked at me, openly and without diffidence, "you and your sisters have done me a great service—the greatest man can do his fellow-being; you have rescued me, by your noble hospitality, from death. This benefit conferred gives you an unlimited claim on my gratitude; and a claim to a certain extent, on my confidence. I will tell you as much of the history of the wanderer you have harboured, as I can tell without compromising my own peace of mind—my own security, moral and physical, and that of others.

"I am an orphan; the daughter of a clergyman. My parents died before I could know them. I was brought up a dependent; educated in a charitable institution. I will even tell you the name of the establishment, where I passed six years as a pupil, and two as a teacher—Lowood Orphan

Asylum: you will have heard of it, Mr. Rivers?—the Reverend Robert Brocklehurst is the treasurer.

"I left Lowood nearly a year since to become a private governess. I obtained a good situation, and was happy. This place I was obliged to leave four days before I came here. The reason of my departure I cannot and ought not to explain: it would be useless—dangerous; and would sound incredible. No blame attached to me: I am as free from culpability as any one of you three. Miserable I am, and must be for a time; for the catastrophe which drove me from the house I had found a paradise was of a strange and direful nature. I observed but two points in planning my departure—speed, secrecy: to secure these, I had to leave behind me everything I possessed except a small parcel; which, in my hurry and trouble of mind, I forgot to take out of the coach that brought me to Whitcross. To this neighborhood, then, I came, quite destitute. I slept two nights in the open air, and wandered about two days without crossing a threshold: but twice in that space of time did I taste food; and it was when brought by hunger, exhaustion, and despair, almost to the last gasp, that you, Mr. Rivers, forbade me to perish of want at your door, and took me under the shelter of your roof. I know all your sisters have done for me since—for I have not been insensible during my seeming torpor—and I owe to their spontaneous, genuine, genial compassion, as large a debt as to your evangelical charity."

Bram Stoker
Mina Murray's Journal

6 August:—Another three days, and no news. This suspense is getting dreadful. If I only knew where to write to or where to go to, I should feel easier; but no one has heard a word of Jonathan since that last letter. I must only pray to God for patience. Lucy is more excitable than ever, but is otherwise well. Last night was very threatening, and the fishermen say that we are in for a storm. I must try to watch it and learn the weather signs. To-day is a grey day, and the sun as I write is hidden in thick clouds, high over Kettleness. Everything is grey—except the green grass, which seems like emerald amongst it; grey earthy rock; grey clouds, tinged with the sunburst at the far edge, hang over the grey sea, into which the sand-points stretch like grey fingers. The sea is tumbling in over the shallows and the sandy flats with a roar, muffled in the sea-mists drifting inland. The horizon is lost in a grey mist. All is vastness; the clouds are piled up like giant rocks, and there is a "brool" over the sea that sounds like some presage of doom. Dark figures are on the beach here and there, sometimes half shrouded in the mist, and seem "men like trees walking." The fishing-boats are racing for home, and rise and dip in the ground swell as they sweep into the harbour, bending to the scuppers. Here comes old Mr. Swales. He is making straight for me, and I can see, by the way he lifts his hat, that he wants to talk. . . .

---

17 August:—No diary for two whole days. I have not had the heart to write. Some sort of shadowy pall seems to be

coming over our happiness. No news from Jonathan, and
Lucy seems to be growing weaker, whilst her mother's
hours are numbering to a close. I do not understand Lucy's
fading away as she is doing. She eats well and sleeps well,
and enjoys the fresh air; but all the time the roses in her
cheeks are fading, and she gets weaker and more languid
day by day; at night I hear her gasping as if for air. I keep
the key of our door always fastened to my wrist at night,
but she gets up and walks around the room, and sits at the
open window. Last night I found her leaning out when I
woke up, and when I tried to wake her I could not; she
was in a faint. When I managed to restore her she was as
weak as water, and cried silently between long, painful
struggles for breath. When I asked her how she came to
be at the window she shook her head and turned away. I
trust her feeling ill may not be from that unlucky prick of
the safety-pin. I looked at her throat just now as she lay
asleep, and the tiny wounds seem not to have healed. They
are still open, and, if anything, larger than before, and the
edges of them are faintly white. They are like little white
dots with red centres. Unless they heal within a day or
two, I shall insist on the doctor seeing about them.

Robert W. Chambers
Mary Read

Out into the deep bluish-purple current of the inlet I swam,
and there sported and floated—how long I did not realize,
until, suddenly remembering the ship, I swam to shallow.

There, rising and wading toward the sandy shore, I had
nearly reached the beach when, to my amazement and
fright, I saw a figure, suddenly dark against the sky, rise
up above the dune and come over it and straight down to
the shore.

The figure was that of a young woman, though clothed
in a strange and wanton fashion. For she wore a scarlet silk
vest, open to her belt, and very wide breeches of scarlet
silk that fell only above her naked knees; and, around her
hair—which was brown, and blew loosely about her face—
was bound a gold and red figured handkerchief of Barbary
tinsel stuff.

I stared at her in fear and astonishment—at her naked,
sunburned body and her legs in sagging boots of soft gray
leather, at her belt of shot silk which bristled with pistols
and daggers, at the short, heavy, guardless sword which
she carried in its silver filigree and crimson velvet sheath.

It was not until she had arrived nearly at the water's
edge that she lifted her brilliant dark eyes and saw me.
And plainly was as astounded as I.

Then, of a sudden, she began to laugh; and called out
to me in a pleasing and merry voice:

"Well, then, what are you, little one? A sea-sprite?"

I knew not what to answer, and stood there ankle-deep
in water until, smiling still, she bade me come ashore and
fear nothing.

"For," says she, "you may take me for a female pirate,
and you may be right, but I am a very gentle one to children

and would do a harm to no living creature only if driven to it."

So I waded timidly ashore. . . .

Fredric Brown
Too Far

R. Austin Wilkinson was a bon vivant, man about Manhattan, and chaser of women. He was also an incorrigible punster on every possible occasion. In speaking of his favorite activity, for example, he would remark that he was a wolf, as it were, but that didn't make him a werewolf.

Excruciating as this statement may have been to some of his friends, it was almost true. Wilkinson was not a werewolf; he was a werebuck.

A night or two nights every week he would stroll into Central Park, turn himself into a buck and take great delight in running and playing.

True, there was always danger of his being seen but (since he punned even in his thoughts) he was willing to gambol on that.

Oddly, it had never occurred to him to combine the pleasures of being a wolf, as it were, with the pleasures of being a buck.

Until one night. Why, he asked himself that night, couldn't a lucky buck make a little doe? Once thought of, the idea was irresistible. He galloped to the wall of the Central Park Zoo and trotted along it until his sensitive buck nose told him he'd found the right place to climb the fence. He changed into a man for the task of climbing and then, alone in a pen with a beautiful doe, he changed himself into a buck.

She was sleeping. He nudged her gently and whispered a suggestion. Her eyes opened wide and startled. "No, no, a dozen times no!"

"Only a dozen times?" he asked, and then leered. *"My deer,"* he whispered, *"think of the fawn you'll have!"*

Which went too far. He might have got away with it had his deer really been only a doe, but she was a weremaid—a doe who could change into a girl—and she was a witch as well. She quickly changed into a girl and ran for the fence. When he changed into a man and started after her she threw a spell over her shoulder, a spell that turned him back to a buck and froze him that way.

Do you ever visit the Central Park Zoo? Look for the buck with the sad eyes; he's Wilkinson.

He is sad despite the fact that the doe-weremaid, who is now the toast of New York ballet (she is graceful as a deer, the critics say) visits him occasionally by night and resumes her proper form.

But when he begs for release from the spell she only smiles sweetly and tells him no, that she is of a very saving disposition and wants to keep the first buck she ever made.

11
REVELATIONS AND TRANSFORMATIONS

Introduction

I begin this last section with a group of tributes to the creative powers of women in arts other than the domestic. First, Philo-Philippa, an anonymous Irishwoman responsible for this eulogy attached to the 1667 edition of Katherine Philips's works, celebrates "Orinda"—Philips's nom de plume—for her validation of all women's creative abilities. She was apparently inspired by Philips's translation of Corneille's tragedy, *The Death of Pompey*, which did cause something of a stir among literary and theatrical circles and which played in Dublin in February 1663. The poem, here excerpted, is remarkable for its extreme feminism.

Anne Killigrew's meditation on her own painting begins as a pleasant enough descriptive excursion, but turns, in its final lines, into another powerful vindication of women as poets. There is a purposely strong metric rhythm in the short iambic tetrameter lines that lulls the senses, setting up the listener for the punch line. As if more vindication were needed, Phillis Wheatley, a twenty-year-old native West African and slave to a Boston family, turns winter into summer in her 1773 *On Imagination*, a poem more than worthy of Alexander Pope. And Alice Meynell, using the image of a river fed by the springs of others' efforts, finds the source of her gifts as a poet, indeed, her own immortality, in the collective continuum. There has seldom been a fuller acknowledgment of both conscious influences and unknown antecedents than this poem, rife with the understanding that no artist functions alone or for himself exclusively.

Mary Shelley, in this portion of the introduction to her masterwork, *Frankenstein*, relates dream state to creative breakthrough, while exploring the relationship of terror to revelation.

Artistic inspiration is perhaps fundamentally not so different from religious visions and spiritual revelations. Elizabeth Melville's 1603 tour of hell, while altogether reminiscent of Dante's *Inferno,* is made exceptional by the vivid comforting presence of Christ and by the curiously open ending—"It is to come that I believ'd was past"—which links the nightmare to her everyday waking world. In 1830, Rebecca Cox Jackson experienced a powerful religious conversion, to be followed one year later by the gift of literacy, a sudden unexplained ability to read and to personally document her own visions. She became possibly America's most noted Black revivalist preacher, healer, and prophet. Her reveries are both vast and particular, shifting easily from the panorama of sky and earth to the prospect of a single white flower. The obvious way in which to handle her work is in a public, large-scale, evangelical manner, but a quieter, more subdued approach can also be surprisingly effective.

Dream experiences and sudden flashes of creative energy can change the way in which we perceive the world forever. Not just ideas and concepts, but the revelatory moments themselves, can be communicated through the actor, the intermediary. By putting herself in the author's place, into that very specific frame of reference, the actor can inhabit that particular world, experience it, and bring the audience into it as well, without artificially "becoming" a character.

Reminiscent of the grand tradition of Russian fairy tales, Lidiya Zinovyeva-Annibal's *The Wolves* offers liberating lessons about selflessness and transcending the physical body. In her "Levels and levels" diary entry, Anaïs Nin shares Zinovyeva-Annibal's appreciation of the intercon-

nectedness of people and things. But even if she is close
philosophically, her jazzy world of bars, dance halls, elevators, and planetariums bears no physical resemblance to
Russia's "monasteries and wild forests." Nin's feverish
stream-of-consciousness takes in everything around her to
a point approaching sensory overload, and the actor must
follow suit, visualizing all of those details, or the monologue
will sound false, mere idle chatter.

Israeli poet Dahlia Ravikovitch, in *Tirzah and the Wide
World*, also yearns to be part of all, and she finds in the
pull of what is most distant and foreign—"I'll grin among
strangers"—a freedom from the smallness and pettiness of
the everyday. Similarly, Iranian Furugh Farrukhzad samples the perspective of absolute power by imagining herself
as God, and then relinquishes that power to rest in another,
darker pleasure. In an altogether different kind of power
dream, Pet, Patricia Geary's unstoppable heroine, experiences the ultimate physical workout.

Malinche, or Malintzin (known in Spanish as Marina),
rose from obscurity as a slave girl to become mistress to
Hernando Cortés, interpreter for Chief Montezuma, and a
central figure in the Spanish conquest of Mexico. In the
1930s, Haniel Long, author of this version of her story
suggested that her importance might increase, as an em-
blem of "the life-idea that men and women as comrades
and friends are to carry on the work of generation, which
is nothing less than the entire business of transformation
and evolution, and thus inexpressibly more important than
begetting. She even symbolizes the truth that though
paired love and begetting fail, the individual can still work
for the germination of tomorrow." The two brief selections
I have included find Malinche, steeped in Aztec tradition,
joyfully anticipating the arrival of the Spaniards, whom she
sees as a manifestation of the deity Quetzalcoatl.

For Marion Zimmer Bradley, it is Morgaine, half-sister

to King Arthur and priestess of the Goddess, who serves as a model for a new age of women's awareness and power. The selection from *The Mists of Avalon* is a first-person narrative uncommon to her work which combines the detailed behavior of ritual with the skewed sense of time one experiences in dreams. I recommend walking the indicated pattern, or even setting down actual stones.

Fantasy, even when classified as science fiction, has for decades been the special province of some of the most gifted writers of this age, who have generated a multitude of alternative worlds which serve as backdrops for woman as leader, warrior, sage, and Goddess. The genre has always been suggestive to me of powers that women have, but choose to hide for safety or for reasons of social convenience. Those powers are hinted at in heroine Tenar's conversation with the witch Moss in *Tehanu*, Ursula K. LeGuin's epilogue to her classic *Earthsea* trilogy.

Zenna Henderson's *Pilgrimage* is her first collection of stories about The People, an extended family of earthbound extraterrestrial castaways, human in form and emotionally vulnerable, but possessed of perceptions and powers—among them telekinesis—far beyond those of normal folk. This selection is typical in the use of a fantastic premise to explore a very human moment by means of a wholly new perspective. Not so usual is the mix of images: the noisy overheated dance hall, the crisp freshness of the autumn night, the dizzying flight of leaves and lovers, and the evanescent music, all merging to the observer's very individual point of view.

The Book of the Night is a linguistic tour de force, a magnificent tale that merges all history in one timeless, critical moment when nothing is impossible. The first selection is the least personal, a chronicle in the medieval tradition that opens the novel and unleashes a word storm at once electrifying, exhilarating, and thoroughly dizzying.

In the second, Rhoda Lerman's heroine, Celeste, known as CuRoi to the monks among whom she lives as a boy with an unbalanced father, dons a robe of his making and courts exaltation and terror as an unwitting Icarus. The third excerpt is a sort of parable about the girl and her destiny and a spool of golden thread. Try any or all of these and get high on the words.

I have chosen four poems from *Tamsen Donner: A Woman's Journey* in order to convey something of the range of perception that informs this remarkable work. Ruth Whitman wrote her journal of an anonymous New Englander crossing 1840s America with her family, only to recognize in her protagonist a real person, Tamsen Donner, who, after being stranded in snow for six months, refused rescue in order to remain with her dying husband. Her story as Whitman composed it in 1977 indeed "invents the body of a land." Each experience, from the Fourth of July toast to the ultimate sacrifice, is perfectly and sparely communicated, and the last poem, "If my boundary stops here . . . ," achieves true transcendence. A powerful sense of place balances the introspective intimacy in these poems, and that should help keep the actor outwardly focused and involved. Attention should certainly be paid to Whitman's deliberate punctuation. Compare, for example, her list of household articles and necessaries, "pots tin plates silver service quilts salt meat rice sugar dried fruit coffee tea," with the catalogue of "unnecessary" books that are to be abandoned, "Shakespeare, Emerson, Gray's Botany . . . ," and see the going of these well-loved volumes, old friends, slowed by the commas.

I close this collection with one of Emily Dickinson's last poems, a minute affirmation of the wholeness of the universe.

Philo-Philippa
From *To the Excellent Orinda*

Let the male Poets their male *Phoebus* chuse,
Thee I invoke, *Orinda,* for my Muse;
He could but force a Branch, *Daphne* her Tree
Most freely offers to her Sex and thee,
And says to Verse, so unconstrain'd as yours,
Her Laurel freely comes, your fame secures:
And men no longer shall with ravish'd Bays
Crown their forc'd Poems by as forc'd a praise.
    Thou glory of our Sex, envy of men,
Who are both pleas'd and vex'd with thy bright Pen:
Its lustre doth intice their eyes to gaze,
But mens sore eyes cannot endure its rays;
It dazzles and surprises so with light,
To find a noon where they expected night:
A Woman Translate *Pompey*! which the fam'd
Corneille with such art and labour fram'd! . . .
Phoebus to *Cynthia* must his beams resigne,
The rule of Day, and Wit's now Feminine.
    That Sex, which heretofore was not allow'd
To understand more than a beast, or crowd;
Of which Problems were made, whether or no
Women had Souls; but to be damn'd, if so;
Whose highest Contemplation could not pass,
In men's esteem, no higher than the Glass;
And all the painful labours of their Brain,
Was only how to Dress and Entertain:
Or, if they ventur'd to speak sense, the wise
Made that, and speaking Oxe, like Prodigies.
From these thy more than masculine Pen hath rear'd
Our Sex; first to be prais'd, next to be fear'd.
And by the same Pen forc'd, men now confess,

To keep their greatness, was to make us less . . .
    Shall it be our reproach, that we are weak,
And cannot fight, nor as the School-men speak?
Even men themselves are neither strong nor wise,
If Limbs and Parts they do not exercise,
    Train'd up to arms, we *Amazons* have been,
And *Spartan* Virgins strong as *Spartan* Men:
Breed Women but as Men, and they are these;
Whilst *Sybarit* Men are Women by their ease . . .
Nature to Females freely doth impart
That, which the Males usurp, a stout, bold heart.
Thus Hunters female Beasts fear to assail:
And female Hawks more mettal'd than the male:
Men ought not then Courage and Wit ingross,
Whilst the Fox lives, the Lyon, or the Horse.
Much less ought men both to themselves confine,
Whilst Women, such as you, *Orinda*, shine . . .
A gliding Sea of Chrystal doth best show
How smooth, clear, full and rich your Verse doth flow:
Your words are chosen, cull'd, not by chance writ,
To make the sence as Anagrams do hit.
Your rich becoming words on the sence wait,
As Maids of Honour on a Queen of State.
'Tis not White Satin makes a Verse more white,
Or soft; Iron is both, write you on it.
Your Poems come forth cast, no File you need,
At one brave Heat both shap'd and polished.
    But why all these Encomiums of you,
Who either doubts, or will not take as due?
Renown how little you regard, or need,
Who like the Bee, on your own sweets doth feed?
    There are, who like weak Fowl with shouts fall down,
Doz'd with an Army's Acclamation:
Not able to indure applause, they fall,
Giddy with praise, their praises Funeral.

But you, *Orinda*, are so unconcern'd,
As if when you, another we commend.
Thus, as the Sun, you in your Course shine on,
Unmov'd with all our admiration:
    Flying above the praise you shun, we see
    Wit is still higher by humility.

Anne Killigrew
On a Picture Painted by Her Self, Representing Two Nimphs of Diana's, One in a Posture to Hunt, the Other Batheing.

We are *Diana's* Virgin-Train,
Descended of no Mortal Strain;
Our Bows and Arrows are our Goods,
Our Pallaces, the lofty Woods,
The Hills and Dales, at early Morn,
Resound and Eccho with our Horn;
We chase the Hinde and Fallow-Deer,
The Wolf and Boar both dread our Spear;
In Swiftness we out-strip the Wind,
An Eye and Thought we leave behind;
We *Fawns* and Shaggy *Satyrs* awe;
To *Sylvan Pow'rs* we give the Law:
Whatever does provoke our Hate,
Our Javelins strike, as sure as *Fate;*
We Bathe in Springs, to cleanse the Soil,
Contracted by our eager Toil;
In which we shine like glittering Beams,
Or Christal in the Christal Streams;

Though *Venus* we transcend in Form,
No wanton Flames our Bosomes warm!
If you ask where such Wights do dwell,
In what Bless't Clime, that so excel?
The Poets onely that can tell.

Phillis Wheatley
On Imagination

Thy various works, imperial queen, we see,
How bright their forms! how deck'd with pomp by thee!
Thy wond'rous acts in beauteous order stand,
And all attest how potent is thine hand.
 From *Helicon's* refulgent heights attend
Ye sacred choir, and my attempts befriend:
To tell her glories with a faithful tongue,
Ye blooming graces, triumph in my song.
 Now here, now there, the roving *Fancy* flies,
Till some lov'd object strikes her wand'ring eyes
Whose silken fetters all the senses bind,
And soft captivity involves the mind.
 Imagination! who can sing thy force?
Or who describe the swiftness of thy course?
Soaring through air to find the bright abode?
Th' empyreal palace of the thund'ring God,
We on thy pinions can surpass the wind,
And leave the rolling universe behind:
From star to star the mental optics rove,
Measure the skies, and range the realms above.
There in one view we grasp the mighty whole,
Or with new worlds amaze th' unbounded soul.
 Though *Winter* frowns to *Fancy's* raptur'd eyes

The fields may flourish, and gay scenes arise;
The frozen deeps may break their iron bands,
And bid their waters murmur o'er the sands.
Fair *Flora* may resume her fragrant reign,
And with her flow'ry riches deck the plain;
Sylvanus may diffuse his honors round,
And all the forest may with leaves be crown'd:
Show'rs may descend, and dews their gems disclose,
And nectar sparkle on the blooming rose.
   Such is thy pow'r, nor are thine orders vain,
O thou the leader of the mental train:
In full perfection all thy works are wrought,
And thine the sceptre o'er the realms of thought.
Before thy throne the subject-passions bow,
Of subject-passions sov'reign ruler thou:
At thy command joy rushes on the heart,
And through the glowing veins the spirits dart.
Fancy might now her silken pinions try
To rise from earth, and sweep th' expanse on high;
From *Tithon's* bed now might *Aurora* rise,
Her cheeks all glowing with celestial dyes,
While a pure stream of light o'erflows the skies.
The monarch of the day I might behold,
And all the mountains tipt with radiant gold,
But I reluctant leave the pleasing views,
Which *Fancy* dresses to delight the *Muse;*
Winter austere forbids me to aspire,
And northern tempests damp the rising fire;
They chill the tides of *Fancy's* flowing sea,
Cease then, my song, cease the unequal lay.

Alice Meynell
The Modern Poet: A Song of Derivations

I come from nothing; but from where
Come the undying thoughts I bear?
  Down, through long links of death and birth,
  From the past poets of the earth.
My immortality is there.

I am like the blossom of an hour.
But long, long vanish'd sun and shower
  Awoke my breast i' the young world's air.
  I track the past back everywhere
Through seed and flower and seed and flower.

Or I am like a stream that flows
Full of the cold springs that arose
  In morning lands, in distant hills;
  And down the plain my channel fills
With melting of forgotten snows.

Voices I have not heard possessed
My own fresh songs; my thoughts are blessed
  With relics of the far unknown;
  And mix'd with memories not my own
The sweet streams throng into my breast.

Before this life began to be,
The happy songs that wake in me
  Woke long ago, and far apart
  Heavily on this little heart
Presses this immortality.

Mary Shelley
from the 1831 introduction
to *Frankenstein*

When I placed my head on my pillow, I did not sleep, nor could I be said to think. My imagination, unbidden, possessed and guided me, gifting the successive images that arose in my mind with a vividness far beyond the usual bounds of reverie. I saw—with shut eyes, but acute mental vision,—I saw the pale student of unhallowed arts kneeling beside the thing he had put together. I saw the hideous phantasm of a man stretched out, and then, on the working of some powerful engine, show signs of life, and stir with an uneasy, half vital motion. Frightful must it be; for supremely frightful would be the effect of any human endeavour to mock the stupendous mechanism of the Creator of the world. His success would terrify the artist; he would rush away from his odious handiwork, horror-stricken. He would hope that, left to itself, the slight spark of life which he had communicated would fade; that this thing, which had received such imperfect animation, would subside into dead matter; and he might sleep in the belief that the silence of the grave would quench for ever the transient existence of the hideous corpse which he had looked upon as the cradle of life. He sleeps; but he is awakened; he opens his eyes; behold the horrid thing stands at his bedside, opening his curtains, and looking on him with yellow, watery, but speculative eyes.

I opened mine in terror. The idea so possessed my mind, that a thrill of fear ran through me, and I wished to exchange the ghastly image of my fancy for the realities around. . . .

Swift as light and as cheering was the idea that broke in upon me. "I have found it! What terrified me will terrify others; and I need only describe the spectre which had haunted my midnight pillow." On the morrow I announced that I had *thought of a story*.

Elizabeth Melville
from *Ane Godlie Dreame*

I looked down, and saw a pit most black,
Most full of smoke, and flaming fire most fell;
That ugly sight made me to fly aback,
I fear'd to hear so many shout and yell:
I him besought that he the truth would tell—
Is this, said I, the Papists' purging place,
Where they affirm that silly souls do dwell,
To purge their sin, before they rest in peace?

This pit is Hell, where through thou now must go,
There is thy way that leads thee to the land:
Now play the man, thou need'st not tremble so,
For I shall help and hold thee by the hand.
Alas! said I, I have no force to stand,
For fear I faint to see that ugly sight;
How can I come among that baleful band?
Oh, help me now, I have no force nor might!

Oft have I heard that they that enter there
In this great gulf, shall never come again:
Courage, said he, have I not bought thee dear?
My precious blood it was not shed in vain.
I saw this place, my soul did taste this pain,
Or ere I went into my Father's gloire;

Through must thou go, but thou shalt not remain;
Thou need'st not fear, for I shall go before.

I am content to do thy whole command,
Said I again, and did him fast embrace:
Then lovingly he held me by the hand,
And in we went into that fearful place.
Hold fast thy grip, said he, in any case
Let me not slip, whatever thou shalt see;
Dread not the death, but stoutly forward press
For Death nor Hell shall never vanquish thee.

Into that Pit, when I did enter in,
I saw a sight which made my heart aghast;
Poor damned souls, tormented sore for sin,
In flaming fire were burning fierce and fast:
And ugly sprites, and as we thought them past,
My heart grew faint and I began to tire;
Ere I perceived, one seized me at last
And held me high above a flaming fire.

The fire was great, the heat did pierce me sore,
My faith was weak, my grip was wondrous small,
I trembled fast, my fear grew more and more,
My hands did shake that I him held withal.
At length they loos'd, then they began to fall,
I cried, O Lord! and caught him fast again;
Lord Jesus, come! and take me out of thrall:
Courage, said he, now thou art past the pain.

With this great fear, I staggered and woke,
Crying, O Lord! Lord Jesus come again!
But after this no kind of rest I took,
I press'd to sleep, but that was all in vain.
I would have dream'd of pleasure after pain,

Because I know I shall it find at last:
God grant my guide may still with me remain,
It is to come that I believ'd was past.

Rebecca Cox Jackson
from *Gifts of Power*

March 11, 1843:—In the morning I found myself under
great power of God. An Angel came in the room, and I
found my body under strange feeling. I thought I was dying.
I was seized with a trembling within and without my body,
and I was then carried away. The earth trembled and a
great storm came from the south. The house that I was in
began to shake, and the people all ran out. I stood still.
The house began to sail on dry ground. It went eastward
and southward, and then it brought me back to the same
place again safe. And then I was all alone, and my vision
ended, and I was very happy.

Sunday, 12th of March, after midnight, I laid down, fell
asleep and dreamt I was in a house in the north. I went
out at the east door and looked up into the air, saw wonderful strange colored clouds coming from the east. And I
then looked into a cloud and saw a company in it coming
north where I was. I then came into the house again, came
in the same door I went out at. This house had three doors,
one east, one north, one south. The windows, one north,
one west, one south. After I came in, it began to rain, as
if it were cotton, until the earth was covered.

I stood in the middle of the floor with my face toward
the west. There was a man with his children, in great distress about his wife and acrying, "It is the Day of Judg-

ment." He stood in the south door. He did not find his wife.

The house tilted three times toward the east. I stood still in secret prayer, for I spoke not a word during the whole scene. After the house tilted, it then stood firm and moved no more in the time of this raining of cotton, and the moving of these strange clouds, and the coming of this army of people.

All the houses, trees, and everything else disappeared. And then the rain changed from cotton to sweet-smelling flowers. There was one clap of thunder and a great noise in the heaven.—I should have mentioned that before all things disappeared, the people were in great distress, running to and fro seeking a place to go, but could find none. They were all lost in the storm.

This was a little white flower. They fell in bunches, the flower in between two beautiful green leaves. I stepped to the door, picked some up, tasted them. Their taste was sweet just like the smell. I then put some in my bosom, but I am not able to tell what they smelt like. The whole air was so perfumed with their odor, yea, with their heavenly smell.

Then there came a sound from heaven which had never been heard before. And in that storm came streams of light. And they came in the form of hoops, white as snow, bright as silver, passing through the shower of flowers. They went like the lightning. They were moved by female angels, and they were beyond the tongue of mortals to describe their heavenly appearance. I wondered where Mary was, for I saw her not. I then awoke, and went right to sleep again.

I was in the same house again and saw Mary. I told her I had a dream, and then I called her to the south window to show her where I saw the armies coming north. I then said, "Oh, Mary! Why, it ain't a dream! It is true! Here they are! Come see them!" She came to the window, but could not see them, though she tried hard.

And while I looked at these armies, under them I saw three mountains, one in the east, one in the south, one in the west—Yet they were all south, though they laid southeast, south, and southwest. They were about half a mile apart. And before these mountains lay a great many people in the earth, with their heads to the south. And while I was trying to show Mary all these things, the people by the west mountain got up and shook themselves. And I saw that their bed was dirt and their covers dry sods, and it fell all off, and in a moment, as it were, they were all in the west mountain. And it became a house for the poor. And I stood in their midst. And there was an Irish girl about ten years old, ateasing them. And they were unwilling to bear with her. I told them to bear it, for her time was short. So they heard me, and I comforted them with the words that was given to me for them. They were all colored people, and they heard me gladly. . . .

Then I woke and found the burden of my people heavy upon me. I had borne a burden of my people for twelve years, but now it was double, and I cried unto the Lord and prayed this prayer, "Oh, Lord God of Hosts, if Thou art going to make me useful to my people, either temporal or spiritual,—for temporally they are held by their white brethren in bondage, not as bound man and bound woman, but as bought beasts, and spiritually they are held by their ministers, by the world, the flesh, and the devil. And if these are not a people in bondage, where are there any on the earth?—Oh, my Father and my God, make me faithful in this thy work and give me wisdom that I may comply with Thy whole will."

Lidiya Zinovyeva-Annibal
from *The Wolves*

"Do you know what it means when two people live in the same person? . . . Even in you! It's always been so with me. One person coveted everything, was greedy and miserly, wanted everything for herself, and did not know how to give. She might yearn for a flower garden . . . like a huge carpet; or maybe a coffee with thick fresh cream; or for a little feather pillow under her head; or for Little Dove or Voloden'ka—your dead brother, and for his little grave; or for the old house where your father was born and raised, and where she'd been . . . happy . . . before he abandoned us . . . well, even for old Elenushka, so that she could always prepare white dresses for her . . . clean, comfortable . . . and for our ravine, for Ambramov Springs . . . even for the linden tree in front of the wing of the house! . . . It's all one and the same thing. All of this is selfishness; that first person clings to it all. Yet there's a second person, who is very free and knows only how to love, but is free of selfish desires. That person rarely spoke within me. I rarely knew how to listen to her, when I was well. But when I became bedridden like this forever, then I heard her. And the flower garden became dear to me, and Elena became dear, and Volodya's little grave with its tiny flowers or even simply with wild grass was dear, and your papa who is far away was also dear and blessed, and our old house, and you, my little children still living— everything became dear to me for its own sake, and not for my own gratification. My love was no longer filled with selfishness, but with a greater freedom. You see, there is nothing else which holds me here."

Mama began to laugh quietly, as if she were cooing.

"All this seems silly to you? No? Not yet. It's still the

pure truth. But now I'll begin the silly part. Only believe me still, if only for the last time, believe me. You know I can't even reach the railing of the balcony by myself. If I tried to get out of this chair, I'd start to sway right here, and fall. Nevertheless, not only can I get down to our ravine without the use of my legs, or to the hay harvest; I will wander throughout all of Russia, through the entire land, in the mountains and villages and cities, the monasteries and wild forests . . . I'll travel as a beggar, homeless, with no belongings nor any sort of ties, and I'll help people with a word of wisdom and my strong and free hands. Nothing will frighten me, neither cold, nor hunger, nor death. Every tree will be my father, and every old woman I meet—my mother, and every animal, innocent and obedient to nature—my brother, every blade of grass—my little sister . . . All of God's children on this earth will be my sons and daughters, and you, my beloved ones, will also be in my heart. Because man has endless space within his heart, and the fire of love is greater than necessary to inflame the entire world. But this fire of love does not consume; it is just like the fire which left the Burning Bush untouched, yet kept burning and never burned out . . . That's the second person, Verochka. She loves, but is free of selfishness. And my soul depends not on my legs to reach out, but on my love. That's why I say that, though I can't even reach the railing, I have traveled, and still travel, the whole world. You know, Verochka, I've become a completely different person since my illness. Verochka, I've reevaluated many things here, alone, but now I've told you everything all at once. It's not important that my illness is taking its course, and that my soul will again grow dark. Whoever has glimpsed just once, will enter his own new world. . . ."

Anaïs Nin
from *Diary, Volume 2*

I love the world so much, it moves me deeply, even the ordinary world, the daily world, even the bar table, the tinkling ice in the glasses, the waiter, the dog tied in the coat room. . . .

Levels and levels. It is as if I were in an elevator, shooting up and down, hundreds of floors, hundreds of lives. Up to heaven, terraces and planetariums, gardens, fountains, clouds, the sun. The wind whistles down the shafts. On the next to the last floor, dance halls and restaurants, and music. In the rooms, bars of shadows on the walls from the casement windows. A bower. A confessional. A couch to lie on. Something to lie on, to rest on, to cling to. Faith. Red lights! Down! Down! The telephone operator announces: a man who limps, a man whose hand is paralyzed, a man in love with his mother, a man who cannot write the book he wants to write, a woman deserted, a woman blocked by guilt, a woman crying with shame for her love of another woman, a girl trembling with fear of man. Free the slaves of incubi, of ghosts and anguish. Listen to their crying. A tough political partisan says: "I feel soft and iridescent." Another one says: "It is a weakness to listen to the complaints of the child in us." I say: "It will never cease lamenting until it is consoled, answered, understood. Only then will it lie still in us, like our fears. It will die in peace and leave us what the child leaves to the man—the sense of wonder." The telephone announces: "A cable for you, shall I send it up?" "Yes, yes." "Happy birthday, happy birthday, love." Red lights! Down! White lights! Going up! Playing at being God, but a god not tired of listening, all the while wondering how the other god can watch people suffer. Music, the solace. Through music we rise in swift noiseless elevators to the heavens, breaking through the roof. Red lights! Down! At the drug store I buy stamps, mail letters, ask for a coffee. Physically I am cracking. It is not the change of floors, the sudden rise and descents which make me dizzy, but the giving. Parts of my life, parts of my energy are passing into others. I feel what they feel. I identify with them. Their anguish tightens my throat. My tongue feels heavy. I wonder whether I can go on. I have no objectivity, no indifference. I pass into them to illumine, to reveal, but I cannot remain apart from them, be indifferent to their bad nights, or their hopes, or their cries, or even their happiness. I look out of my window as Rank looked out of his window. People are skating in the Park. The band is playing. It is Sunday. I could be walking through the streets of Paris, joyous, lively streets where people are in love with life and even with their tragedies. I could be walking along the human and beautiful Seine. I did not recognize my happiness then. I yearned for adventure. The children's laughter rises to the twenty-fifth floor, to the window at which I stand. Red lights! Down! All the way down I am thinking of the problem of emotional symmetry. People's need of retaliation, revenge, need to balance anger against anger, humiliation against humiliation, indifference against indifference.

Dahlia Ravikovitch
Tirzah and the Wide World

Take me to the distant northlands,
Take me to the Atlantic,
Put me down amid different people,
People I've never seen before,
There I'll eat wild berry cakes
And speed on a train in Scandinavia.

Take me to the Pacific Ocean,
Put me down amid the brown fish,
Amid the dolphins, sharks, and salmon,
Amid the pelicans dozing on masts,
I won't even bat an eye
When you take me to the Atlantic.

Take me to the crying rivers
And to the destitute shores,
Where kangaroo hunts kangaroo
And both are garbed in striped coats,
Bring me to the kangaroo
And set me down in the forest marsh.

Wait for me in the belly of the ship
And set me up an electric train,
I'll come quickly
To live among different peoples
I'll grin among the strangers
Like a salmon in the sea.
If you cannot give me an ocean
Give me mountains coated with snow.

Set me down among Christian sailors,
Bring me to the Norwegian coasts,

Bring me to the Australian desert
Most wretched desert in the world;
I'll teach the kangaroo
To read and write, religion and math.
Tell these strange people
I'll be with them soon.

Tell them I'll be
In the midst of the sea next year;
Tell them to ready their nets
And pull up for me
Ring after ring.

Furugh Farrukhzad
Divine Rebellion

If I were God, I would summon the angels one night
To let loose the disc of the sun in the furnace of darkness.
Out of anger I would tell the servant gardeners of the world
To separate the yellow leaf of the moon from the branches
          of night.

At midnight behind the curtains of my own great hall
My angry, rough hands would turn the world upside down.
My weary hands, after thousands of years of silence,
Would throw the mountains down into the open mouths of
          the sea.

I'd release the shackles from the feet of thousands of fe-
          verish stars;
I'd spread the blood of fire into the silent veins of the forests;

I'd rip the curtains of smoke so that, in the blowing wind,
The daughter of the fire would dance drunkenly in the
     embrace of the forest.

I'd blow into the enchanting flute a nocturnal wind
So that creatures would rise up from river beds like hungry
     snakes,
And weary from a life of slithering on a damp chest,
They would descend into the heart of the dark whirlpool
     of the night sky.

I'd quietly tell the winds
To set into motion the intoxicating boat of the red perfume
     of flowers across the strait of fevered night;
I'd open up the graves
So that thousands of wandering souls might once again hide
     themselves within the enclosure of bodies.

If I were God, I'd summon the angels one night
To boil the water of heaven in the furnace of hell,
And with burning torch in hand drive out
The flock of ascetics from the green pastures of heaven.

Weary of divine asceticism, in the middle of the night
     in Satan's bed
I'd seek refuge in the slopes of a fresh sin.
I'd choose at the price of the golden crown of divinity
The dark and painful pleasure of the embrace of a sin.

Patricia Geary
from *Strange Toys*

My knees are rigid, sturdily encased in elastic bandages. I goosewalk to the squat rack. My solar plexus is shielded by the massive power belt. My muscles are aligned, at the ready like enthusiastic soldiers.

No one else is in Roy's Gym.

I grasp the bar firmly and duck my head underneath, as I've done so often before. The bar and its heavy cargo of iron rest not across my deltoids but on the fleshy mound of the upper trapezius.

Merely holding the bar in place stresses my arms. Yet, this lift is designed primarily for the legs and secondarily for the back. *Arms, forgive me, I underworked you. But don't fail me now!*

My body pressed under the load of weight, I step away from the bar.

Pause.

Then my knees bend, slowly, slowly. Sinking! And there must be total control.

This is the bottom. I am squashed down, stasis, time has stopped. In this moment my body is as alive as a body can be.

Va-va-voom!

My quadriceps belong to Paul Bunyan! I am a mythological beast! I have seen the perfect clarity of Nothing, the Tibetan temple bells pinging out in the void—and survived!

"Come on, baby, way to go!"

As I stagger back to the squat rack, someone helps me hoist the bar back into place.

I have unofficially broken the world's record.

I have lifted a thousand pounds.

Haniel Long
from *Malinche*

I want my country to grow, to be fine enough for all who ever come to it.

I rise and begin dancing without knowing why.

It is not to be dreamt of that my countrymen can overcome the White God. But they will fight, and when they are conquered, they will have to give him girls and gold.

I am not good enough, but O newly-returned White God, I shall die if I am not among the presents given you.

What are you whom I love? To what warmth do I nestle?

Now I begin to know why I am dancing.

The sea is a dusk-deep lazuli.

We sail along the shore in big boats. Five Cintla girls are aboard with me, and they are unhappy. They are afraid to be in a strange world with such powerful men. I say to them:

"Is it a time to be happy or unhappy? Tell the sea what you are thinking. Hold up your right hand and talk to the sea. Everything will hear you and understand you, and good thoughts will go into your hearts.

"If Quetzalcoatl came as a scorpion, as a vulture, as a wild pig, should we not receive him? Yet these are handsome young men—he whom they call Alvarado is golden as the sun. Surely for a good purpose did the spirits cause our people to give us to these persons. Our country must be large and wide enough for the White God who returns to us."

Marion Zimmer Bradley
from *The Mists of Avalon*

Once in the far hills I found a ring of stones, not a great one like that which stood on the Tor at Avalon, nor the greater one which had once been Temple of the Sun on the great chalk plains; here the stones were no more than shoulder-high even on me (and I am not tall) and the circle no greater than the height of a tall man. A small slab of stone, the stains faded and overgrown with lichens, was half-buried in the grass at the center. I pulled it free of weed and lichen, and as I did whenever I could find food unseen in the kitchens, left for her people such things as I knew seldom came to them—a slab of barley bread, a bit of cheese, a lump of butter. And once when I went there I found at the very center of the stones a garland of the scented flowers which grew on the border of the fairy country; dried, they would never fade. When next I took Accolon out of doors when the moon was full, I wore them tied about my brow as we came together in that solemn joining which swept away the individual and made us only Goddess and God, affirming the endless life of the cosmos, the flow of power between male and female as between earth and sky. After that I went never unattended beyond my own garden. I knew better than to look for them directly, but they were there and I knew they would be there if I needed them. It was not for nothing that I had been given that old name, Morgaine of the Fairies . . . and now they acknowledged me as their priestess and their queen.

I came to the stone circle, walking by night, when the harvest moon sank low in the sky and the breath of the fourth winter grew cold on the eve of the Day of the Dead. There, wrapped in my cloak and shivering through the night, I kept the vigil, fasting; snow was drifting out of the sky when I rose and turned my steps homeward, but as I left the circle I turned my foot on a stone which had not been there when I came thither, and, bending my head, I saw the pattern of white stones arranged.

I bent, moving one stone to make the next in sequence of the magical numbers—the tides had shifted and now we were under the winter's stars. Then I went home, shivering, to tell a story of being benighted in the hills and sleeping in an empty shepherd's hut—Uriens had been frightened by the snow, and sent two men to seek me. Snow, lying deep on the mountainsides, kept me within doors much of the winter, but I knew when the storms would lift and risked the journey to the ring stones at Midwinter, knowing the stones would be clear . . . snow lay never within the great circles, I knew, and I guessed that it would be so here in the smaller circles, where magic was still done.

And there at the very center of the circle I saw a tiny bundle—a scrap of leather tied with sinew. My fingers were recapturing their old skill and did not fumble as I untied it and rolled the contents into my palm. They looked like a couple of dried seeds, but they were the tiny mushrooms which grew so rarely near Avalon. They were no use as food, and most folk thought them poison, for they would cause vomiting and purging and a bloody flux; but taken sparingly, fasting, they could open the gates to the Sight . . . this was a gift more precious than gold. They grew not in this country at all, and I could only guess how far the little folk had wandered in search of them. I left them what food I had brought, dried meats and fruits and a honeycomb, but not in repayment; the gift was priceless. I knew that I would lock myself within my chamber at Midwinter, and there seek again the Sight I had renounced. With the gates of vision thus opened I could seek and dare the very presence of the Goddess, begging to repronounce what I had forsworn. I had no fear that I would be cast forth again. It was she who sent me this gift that I might seek again her presence.

And I bent to the ground in thanksgiving, knowing that my prayers had been heard and my penance done.

Ursula K. LeGuin
from *Tehanu: The Last Book of Earthsea*

"What's wrong with men?" Tenar inquired cautiously.

As cautiously, lowering her voice, Moss replied, "I don't know, my dearie. I've thought on it. Often I've thought on it. The best I can say it is like this. A man's in his skin, see, like a nut in its shell." She held up her long, bent, wet fingers as if holding a walnut. "It's hard and strong, that shell, and it's all full of him. Full of grand man-meat, man-self. And that's all. That's all there is. It's him and nothing else, inside."

Tenar pondered awhile and finally asked, "But if he's a wizard—"

"Then it's all his power, inside. His power's himself, see. That's how it is with him. And that's all. When his power goes, he's gone. Empty." She cracked the unseen walnut and tossed the shells away. "Nothing."

"And a woman, then?"

"Oh, well, dearie, a woman's a different thing entirely. Who knows where a woman begins and ends? Listen, mistress, I have roots, I have roots deeper than this island. Deeper than the sea, older than the raising of the lands. I go back into the dark." Moss's eyes shone with a weird brightness in their red rims and her voice sang like an instrument. "I go back into the dark! Before the moon I was. No one knows, no one knows, no one can say what I am, what a woman is, a woman of power, a woman's power, deeper than the roots of trees, deeper than the roots of islands, older than the Making, older than the moon. Who dares ask questions of the dark? Who'll ask the dark its name?"

The old woman was rocking, chanting, lost in her incantation; but Tenar sat upright, and split a reed down the center with her thumbnail.

"I will," she said.

She split another reed.

"I lived long enough in the dark," she said.

Zenna Henderson
from *Pilgrimage*

She was gone. I glanced around the room. Nowhere the swirl of blue echoing the heavy brown-gold swing of her ponytail.

There was no reason for me to feel apprehensive. There were any number of places she might have gone and quite legitimately, but I suddenly felt an overwhelming need for fresh air and swung myself past the romping dancers and out into the gasping chill of the night. I huddled closer inside my jacket, wishing it were on right instead of merely flung around my shoulders. But the air tasted clean and fresh. I don't know what we'd been breathing in the dance hall, but it wasn't air. By the time I'd got the whatever-it-was out of my lungs and filled them with the freshness of the night I found myself halfway down the path over the edge of the railroad cut. There hadn't been a train over the single track since nineteen-aught-something, and just beyond it was a thicket of willows and cottonwoods and a few scraggly piñon trees. As I moved into the shadow of the trees I glanced up at the sky ablaze with a skrillion stars that dissolved into light near the lopsided moon and perforated the darker horizon with brilliance. I was startled out of my absorbtion by the sound of movement and music. I took an uncertain step into the dark. A few yards away I saw the flick of skirts and started to call out to Twyla. But instead I rounded the brush in front of me and saw what she was intent upon.

The Francher kid was dancing—dancing all alone in the quiet night. No, not alone, because a column of yellow leaves had swirled up from the ground around him and danced with him to a melody so exactly like their movement that I couldn't be sure there was music. Fascinated, I watched the drift and sway, the swirl and turn, the treetop-high rise and the hesitant drifting fall of the Francher kid and the autumn leaves. But somehow I couldn't see the kid as a separate Levied flannel-shirted entity. He and the leaves so blended together that the sudden sharp definition of a hand or a turning head was startling. The kid was just a larger leaf borne along with the smaller in the chilly winds of fall. On a final minor glissade of the music the Francher kid slid to the ground.

He stood for a moment, head bent, crumbling a crisp leaf in his fingers; then he turned swiftly defensive to the rustle of movement. Twyla stepped out into the clearing. For a moment they stood looking at each other without a word. Then Twyla's voice came so softly I could barely hear it.

"I would have danced with you."

"With me like this?" He gestured at his clothes.

"Sure. It doesn't matter."

"In front of everyone?"

"If you wanted to. I wouldn't mind."

"Not there," he said. "It's too tight and hard."

"Then here," she said, holding out her hands.

"The music—" But his hands were reaching for hers.

"Your music," she said.

"My mother's music," he corrected.

And the music began, a haunting lilting waltz-time melody. As lightly as the leaves that stirred at their feet the two circled the clearing.

I have the picture yet, but when I return to it my heart is emptied of adjectives because there are none for such enchantment. The music quickened and swelled, softly, richly full—the lost music that a mother bequeathed to her child.

Twyla was so completely engrossed in the magic of the moment that I'm sure she didn't even know when her feet no longer rustled in the fallen leaves. She couldn't have known when the treetops brushed their shoes—when the long turning of the tune brought them back, spiraling down into the clearing. Her scarlet petticoat caught on a branch as they passed, and left a bright shred to trail the wind, but even that did not distract her.

Before my heart completely broke with wonder the music faded softly away and left the two standing on the ragged grass. After a breathless pause Twyla's hand went softly, wonderingly, to Francher's cheek. The kid turned his face slowly and pressed his mouth to her palm. Then they turned and left each other, without a word.

Twyla passed so close to me that her skirts brushed mine. I let her cross the tracks back to the dance before I followed.

Rhoda Lerman
Dawn Is Far Away

August fifteenth. Dawn is far away and the night large and I small and my brothers are together and I alone on the strand in a cup of sand at the lip of the high and treacherous sea and the crescent blade of a new moon cuts at my throat. Meteors fly from the northeast. Something ice-eyed moves boldly above me through the bushes on the cliff. Stars fall and die and vastness is out there pulling at the sea waves and my faith. Injured that vastness. Moaning it is in the shower of stars, in pain, and I wish mightily for the light and the end of night. But I wait as the old Abbot commanded me in his second sight, a marvel, for the first treasure in the morning nets. My brothers wear saffron robes and climb on their knees to the peak of Dun Hi to praise the Lord of the Elements. Their songs, sweet and fervent, drift to me through the crash of the waves. That the crops blast, that the fields come rich with corn and barley, that the thighs of the mountain be berry-filled and the barn without monsters—for these things they pray. And I that I would be with them rather than in this sheephole at the end of the world.

The Abbot Isaac chews the flesh of his thumb and knows what will be. "Something in the nets, Chronicler. Something large and with great value." And so I am here and they are there.

The sea sifts through its bits of time and tosses up on our shores its waste of past things and future things, known things and unknown things, rolling, turning, mixing the harvest of articles and particles of time in its great-stemmed groves of sea flesh, of olive tangle and black wrack. Sea shells we find and bomb shells, donkey beads and crusted coins, Pop-sickle sticks from Father Time, puns from the Argonauts, argot from the Punic Wars, cargo from the nets of Naught, Naughts that are not, sea-belched they come. A whore's comb, a warrior's mantle from a battle yet unfought, shards of blue majolica and flower-traced crockery, amphorae, bullets, pelts of beasts, boxes of gold, nails, sand pails, shovels, and the dead. Always the dead.

We are only the scavengers of a vast existence beyond time. What we find is what the sea selects from all time and no time: one part to the monks, one part to the crofters, seven parts to the finder—which is why the Abbot has me here—and the tenth, the jubilee part, tossed back to the sea into the crack of the Dark Gods, into the knots of the nets of Naught.

The Vestments He Wove

The vestments he wove for the Church Fathers were precious silks of the sea and the sunset, with white lilies and silver eyes, golden keys, crosses, fish, goblets, and vast great-bird wings of sleeves. And that was perhaps why, one day when he was gone with the old Abbot, I took a finished robe and held it against my cheek and slipped into it and held it up over my ankles and raced flapping down the mountainside and over the millstream and beyond the High Cross of Moses and over a causeway of boulders and moss to the beach, where I flew, billowing, a great bird along the White Strand, scarlet and gold. The flocks of ordinary birds lifted in fear and wonder and the great ancestral herd of cows, standing in the water to their hocks eating seaweed, rolled their eyes and snorted at me as I flapped along. When my chest ached as if squeezed, I fell on the sand, an angelic creature, shimmering, my wings spread, and gasped for air and from the sky, glossy and black and cold and heavier than a quern stone, a dead gull, whistling, fell and cut its shape into the sand at my head. Terrified as I had never been before, I shook sand from the scarlet of my sin, wiped its hems on my own trousers, folded it in a small square, and ran home. My heart arrived before I did.

Weaving, my father had forgotten I'd gone nor known I'd returned. His shuttle looped through startling goods: claw, stick, bone, dunged wool. And he wove equal marvels into lists: "Ark, d'ark, argo, cargo, argonaut, argotique, gothic. So. Alevai, Halloween, mistletoe, mazeltov." He saw me and stopped immediately, hand and mouth, his face flushed, and he drew out my Dark Horse Copy Book. Had I looked somehow on his nakedness? I scratched steadfastly for him my A's and B's and ice cream cones and my name, Celeste.

A Spool of Golden Thread

Once I took a spool of golden thread from my father's loom and, holding it at one end, let it roll down the mountainside, connecting my place with the world, finding my way, searching for meaning as the thread wandered. But I ran after it for we were attached and I was controlling it and it twisted against a clump of nettle. I sat at that clump and waited as if I would then find my destiny, as if an angel were to visit on the spot, as if someone were to stretch out a great hand and lift me into a high place of answer where I belonged. But there was no place, just the clump of nettle and the ball of thread in my own hand, and my questions. I rolled the thread tightly as I climbed and laid it back with the other spools.

Ruth Whitman
July 4, 1846, at Fort Laramie

Dressed in our best clothes, which we have saved for this
occasion, we come together in a grove and open the bottle
of wine our old friends in Springfield gave us. They promised they would toast us today, facing towards the west, as
we drink to them, lifting our glasses to the east.

So do we make a link
between what we were
and what we have become:

we are inventing
the body of a land
binding together

two halves of a whole
as we touch each other
across a thousand miles

and I who started
a thousand miles before
feel in my flesh

the stretch of the land
as we give it birth
the long spill of it
unrolling before us

September 6, 1846, in the Desert

Go light go light I must walk lightly

as I moved from one life to another
more and more followed me:
gowns books furniture
paints notebooks

now the seven of us—even the little girls—
must have substance
to carry into the new country

we are transporting a houseful:
barrels of flour stuffed with porcelain
pots tin plates silver service quilts
salt meat rice sugar dried fruit
coffee tea
            the wagon sags
and the oxen falter
                    one wagon founders
what shall I let go? books:
                      the least
needed for survival: in the cold
desert night
          George lifts my heavy
crate of Shakespeare, Emerson, Gray's
Botany, spellers and readers for my school
and hides it in a hill of salt
while the children sleep parched
and the cows and oxen stand mourning:
I put aside my desk with the inlaid pearl
our great fourposter with the pineapple posts
my love my study

what else can I part with?
I will keep one sketchbook one journal
to see me to the end of the journey

go light
go light
I must walk lightly

━━━━━━━━━━━━━━━━━

March 15, 1847, by Alder Creek

I send my three little ones away with the second rescue
party. I dress them in layers of their best clothes and tell
them to be sure to say to everyone they meet that they are
children of George Donner. I take them to the other camp,
kiss them each, and beg them not to cry. I walk back alone
to our empty nest.

My children move in my mind
like miniatures
painted on ivory:
one light and willowy
one rosy dark
and the littlest
a frisky animal
that refuses to be tamed:
she reaches through the frame
and pulls at my skin
a baby sloth
clutching its mother's fur

I etch them in my brain
like diamond scratches on a windowpane:

arrest their images as though I were
a limner passing through, a peddler
of portraits

Where Is the West

If my boundary stops here
I have daughters to draw new maps on the world
they will draw the lines of my face
they will draw with my gestures my voice
they will speak my words thinking they have invented them

they will invent them
they will invent me
I will be planted again and again
I will wake in the eyes of their children's children
they will speak my words

Emily Dickinson
Go Thy Great Way!

Go thy great way!
The Stars thou meetst
Are even as Thyself—
For what are Stars but Asterisks
To point a human Life?

SELECT BIBLIOGRAPHY

Baxandall, Rosalyn, Linda Gordon, and Susan Reverby, eds. *America's Working Women, A Documentary History 1600 to the Present*. New York: Random House, 1976.

Brook, Stephen, ed. *The Oxford Book of Dreams*. Oxford & New York: Oxford University Press, 1983.

Copeland, Lewis and Lawrence W. Lamm, eds. *The World's Great Speeches*. New York: Dover Publications, 1942.

Cosman, Carol, Joan Keefe, and Kathleen Weaver, eds. *The Penguin Book of Women Poets*. New York: Viking Penguin, 1979.

Culley, Margo, ed. *A Day at a Time: The Diary Literature of American Women from 1764 to the Present*. New York: The Feminist Press, 1985.

Dalby, Richard, ed. *Victorian Ghost Stories by Eminent Women Writers*. New York: Carroll & Graf Publishers, Inc., 1989.

Evans, Elizabeth. *Weathering the Storm: Women of the American Revolution*. New York: Paragon House, 1975.

Fernea, Elizabeth Warnock and Basima Qattan Bezirgan, eds. *Middle Eastern Muslim Women Speak*. Austin: University of Texas Press, 1977.

Fisher, Jo. *Mothers of the Disappeared*. Boston: South End Press, 1989.

Greer, Germaine, Susan Hastings, Jeslyn Medoff, and Melinda Sansone, eds. *Kissing the Rod: An Anthology of Seventeenth-Century Women's Verse*. New York: Farrar Straus Giroux, 1989.

Hughes, Langston and Arna Bontemps, eds. *The Poetry of the American Negro 1746–1970*. New York: Doubleday, 1970.

Kahn, Kathy. *Hillbilly Women*. New York: Doubleday, 1972 & 1973.

Larson, Ann E. and Carole A. Carr, eds. *Silverleaf's Choice: An Anthology of Lesbian Humor*. Seattle: Silverleaf Press, 1990.

Lerner, Gerda, ed. *Black Women in White America: A Documentary History*. New York: Random House, 1972.

Lim, Shirley Geok-lin and Mayumi Tsutakawa, eds. *The Forbidden Stitch: An Asian American Women's Anthology*. Corvallis, Oregon: Calyx Books, 1989.

Moffat, Mary Jane and Charlotte Painter, eds. *Revelations: Diaries of Women*. New York: Random House, 1974.

Post, Elizabeth L., ed. *Emily Post's Etiquette: Twelfth Revised Edition*. New York: Funk and Wagnalls, 1969.

Randall, Margaret. *Sandino's Daughters: Testimonies of Nicaraguan Women in Struggle*. Vancouver & Toronto: New Star Books, 1981.

Saywell, Shelley. *Women in War: From World War II to El Salvador*. Markham, Ontario: Penguin Books Canada Ltd., 1985.

Schuster, M. Lincoln, ed. *The World's Great Letters: From Ancient Days to Our Own Time*. New York: Simon and Schuster, 1940.

Stratton, Joanna L. *Pioneer Women: Voices from the Kansas Frontier*. New York: Simon and Schuster, 1981.

Terkel, Studs. *The Great Divide: Second Thoughts on the American Dream*. New York: Pantheon Books, 1988.

Terkel, Studs. *The Good War*. New York: Pantheon Books, 1984.

Terkel, Studs. *Working: People Talk About What They Do All Day and How They Feel About What They Do*. New York: Pantheon Books, 1972 & 1974.

Walker, Nancy and Zita Dresner, eds. *Redressing the Balance: American Women's Literary Humor from Colonial Times to the 1980s*. Jackson & London: The University Press of Mississippi, 1988.